"A public speaking book unlike any other: a joy to read, personal, engaging, interesting, faith-directed, and practical. Schultze's experiences and stories often make this book read more like a novel than a textbook. It is the kind of book you will want to keep and use repeatedly—and give to friends who are afraid of speaking or who have never really learned how to speak well."

—**Martin Medhurst**, Baylor University

"Rarely are instructional books relevant and excellent. This is one such innovative rarity, with impeccable pedagogy and masterful writing."

—**Clifford Christians**, University of Illinois
at Urbana–Champaign (emeritus)

"This is the most interesting, thorough, and useful speaking text I have ever encountered! It is my dream. I can't wait to use it. It includes exactly what I need to teach others. Schultze beautifully integrates Christian principles and practices with comprehensive material on ethical and effective speaking. Everything I have wanted in a text for students in my public speaking courses is in this book."

—**Mary Albert Darling**, Spring Arbor University

"Since our human communication reflects God's communication to us, we should not hesitate to invite God's wisdom into our efforts. Schultze's *Essential Guide to Public Speaking* does just that, lending biblical insight and Christian sensitivity to the sphere of public speaking."

—**Paul A. Soukup, SJ**, Santa Clara University

"Master teacher Quentin Schultze's timely text on public speaking is more than a guidebook on learning how to communicate effectively in diverse settings. It is truly an essential guide for articulating one's faith with confidence and joy and living out one's life with humility and virtue. Readers will discover how loving one's audience may even chase out the fear of public speaking."

—**Terry Lindvall**, Virginia Wesleyan College

"The speech-making process no longer has to be a nail-biter, full of stress and anxiety. Schultze has created a Christ-oriented speaking guide that functions as a lifeline for those involved in the art and practice of public speaking. This wonderful book is theoretically grounded, organized for easy reference, and written in an engaging way that informs, inspires, and entertains. Speakers, both novice and advanced, will find helpful explanations and useful tips throughout the book's pages. Anyone seriously applying this information to their own speaking behaviors will see their skills grow."

—**Don Simmons**, Asbury University

"Dr. Schultze's subtitle captures the heart and soul of this wonderful book: serving audiences with faith, skill, and virtue. I have witnessed Schultze himself using the principles in his book. What a joy to learn from a true servant speaker. He has poured himself into this book to enable us to embody these qualities. I can't wait to see our campuses filled with servant speakers!"

—**Patricia R. Harris**, president, Kuyper College

"Pithy, principled, and practical, Schultze's second edition of *An Essential Guide to Public Speaking* serves as a thorough handbook for preparing and delivering speeches in the interest of faithful communication. You can tell that Quin has been there—in loving his audience, planning his talks, and serving with integrity and grace. Appropriate for professors, pastors, students, and people in the pew who hope to gain wisdom and credibility for speaking well."

—**Bill Strom**, Trinity Western University

"This commendable book integrates rhetoric, faith, and speaking skills. By far the best text for teaching public speaking at Christian universities."

—**John Pauley**, Eastern University

"*An Essential Guide to Public Speaking* is the necessary alternative to secular public speaking texts—compellingly replete with biblical insights and lessons from church history. Schultze powerfully serves his reading audience by building around the central premise, employed from the Savior, that the greatest speech performer will be the servant of all, including opponents and even the seemingly disinterested. Characteristics of effective service are centrally tied to the nine fruits of the Spirit, which is offered as a chief preparatory filter for 'servant speaking.' This is truly a biblically informed offering. I've loved what I've learned!"

—**Paul D. Patton**, Spring Arbor University

"*An Essential Guide to Public Speaking* integrates the importance of Christian faith and civic virtue. Dr. Schultze encourages readers to become servant communicators who love God and, therefore, bring their own voices into harmony with God's to love and serve others. With topics like 'prophetic voice' and 'advocating for others,' he goes beyond other public speaking primers and helps Christians develop their own virtuous voices. This is the perfect text for public speaking courses at Christian universities."

—**Brandon Knight**, William Carey University

"Dr. Schultze's new edition is even better than the excellent one I used for years. It is interesting, engaging, and even inspiring—all in a textbook that seamlessly integrates faith and skill. I yearn to get back in the classroom with this terrific book."

—**Lew VanderMeer**, senior pastor, New Community Church, Grand Rapids, Michigan

"*An Essential Guide to Public Speaking* is a 'God-send' for instructors teaching at Christian colleges and universities. Students will appreciate the warm, inviting voice of the author and the multiple contemporary examples he uses to illustrate his advice. They will also quickly realize that the guidance Schultze offers will help them to be more successful in class and with outside audiences. Instructors will appreciate the way Dr. Schultze uses rhetorical theory to undergird the guidance he gives and his emphasis on ethical considerations and speaker integrity. They may also find the organizational structure of the text a model for how they want to structure the progression of assignments in their syllabus."

—**Em Griffin**, Wheaton College (emeritus)

"Schultze has done it again! Written directly to students, as his 'audience neighbors,' this text imparts rich Augustinian and ancient rhetorical scholarship while providing practical advice on overcoming anxiety."

—**Elizabeth W. McLaughlin**, Bethel University, Indiana

An Essential
GUIDE
to PUBLIC
SPEAKING

SECOND EDITION

An Essential
GUIDE
to PUBLIC
SPEAKING

Serving Your Audience
with Faith, Skill, and Virtue

Foreword by Martin J. Medhurst

Quentin J. Schultze

Afterword by Clifford G. Christians

B
Baker Academic
a division of Baker Publishing Group
Grand Rapids, Michigan

© 2006, 2020 by Quentin J. Schultze

Published by Baker Academic
a division of Baker Publishing Group
PO Box 6287, Grand Rapids, MI 49516-6287
www.bakeracademic.com

Printed in the United States of America

Library of Congress Cataloging-in-Publication Data
Names: Schultze, Quentin J. (Quentin James), 1952– author.
Title: An essential guide to public speaking : serving your audience with faith, skill, and virtue / Quentin J. Schultze.
Description: Second Edition. | Grand Rapids : Baker Academic, a division of Baker Publishing Group, 2020.
Identifiers: LCCN 2019028746 | ISBN 9781540961884 (paperback)
Subjects: LCSH: Rhetoric—Religious aspects—Christianity. | Public Speaking—Religious aspects—Christianity.
Classification: LCC BR115.R55 S38 2020 | DDC 808.5/1—dc23
LC record available at https://lccn.loc.gov/2019028746

21 22 23 24 25 26   7 6 5 4 3

Contents

Expanded Table of Contents

Spotlight Topics

Foreword

MARTIN J. MEDHURST

Quentin Schultze has written a public speaking textbook unlike any other. For one thing, it is a joy to read—personal, engaging, interesting, and practical. Schultze's experiences and stories often make this book read more like a novel than a textbook. It is the kind of book you will want to keep and use repeatedly—and give to friends who are afraid of speaking or have never really learned how to speak well. For another thing, this book is thoroughly Christian in the best sense. It makes faith come alive in the process of planning and delivering speeches for all occasions.

Taking his inspiration from the ancient rhetorician and Christian bishop Saint Augustine, Schultze has produced a Christian meditation on what it means to be a "servant speaker." Like Augustine, he begins from explicitly Christian premises—that Jesus is the Son of God, that he gave his life on the cross for the redemption of humankind, that the Bible is the Word of God, and that truth resides in the Christian message of grace, redemption, and reconciliation. In short, everything that is necessary for a Christian approach to human communication is already present in the life and ministry of Jesus and the evangelistic messages of his followers over the past two thousand years. Throughout this book, Schultze integrates such personal faith and theology with the art of speaking.

Augustine was a professional teacher of rhetoric, and Schultze draws on his many insights in books such as *Confessions* and *On Christian Teaching*.

In so doing, he crafts an approach to public speaking featuring the speaker as a servant of others, especially the audiences a speaker chooses to address. The goal of such speaking is nothing less than human flourishing. One speaks for the good of the other, not so much to conquer or persuade or convince as to listen and love and be a vessel of grace to the hearer. Public speaking in practice thus becomes a way to love one's neighbor as one's self, to serve the other with faith, skill, and virtue. Every speech, as Schultze notes, "is an act of faith."

This explicitly Christian orientation is the bedrock on which the traditional topics of inventing speech content, organizing the speech, stylizing the discourse, memorizing key points, and delivering the speech in a way that is inviting and compelling are erected. Traditional topics are not simply covered; they are absorbed into this Christian worldview and thereby transformed from standard secular lore to transformational biblical principles.

There is much wisdom in this book as Schultze draws from more than forty years of university teaching and speaking to both Christian and non-Christian audiences. I have heard him speak many times. He practices what he preaches in this book. And by careful study and application of these principles, you too can become a servant speaker—one motivated by the love of God to go forth and serve others.

Acknowledgments

I would like to acknowledge some of the people who have helped make this book a reality.

Two special friends and champions of my work are Rick DeVos and Brad Van Arragon. I am very thankful for their support and encouragement.

Contributors to chapters and sections of this book include Heidi Petak, Kathleen Sindorf, Clifford G. Christians, Karl Payton, Andrew Harris, Martin J. Medhurst, and Richard C. Harris. Their names are associated with their contributions in the book. Most of them reviewed drafts of the entire manuscript as well. What a joy to work with them.

I am deeply grateful for the candor and insights of colleagues who critiqued versions of the manuscript. They include Gerald J. Mast, Diane Badzinski, Mark Fackler, David Hartwell, Randall Bytwerk, Kenneth Chase, Peter A. Kerr, Paul D. Patton, L. Ripley Smith, Mary Albert Darling, Em Griffin, Lisa Dunne, Don Simmons, Paul A. Creasman, Elizabeth McLaughlin, Brandon Knight, Lew Vandermeer, Timothy Muehlhoff, Kevin T. Jones, and Stephanie Bennett.

My students at Kuyper University helped ensure that the prose was relevant and lucid for my intended audience. My gratitude to Kristyn De-Nooyer, Samantha Jansma, Allison Dyke, Miriam McDonald, Moses D. E. Kayuni, Ricardo Alfaro Castro, Casey Cohoon, Hunter Herich, Philip Johnson, and Bizzy Hulsether.

Baker Publishing Group has served me well once again from acquisition to editing and publicity. I would especially like to thank Robert Hosack, Jeremy Wells, Julie Zahm, Ryan Davis, Kristopher Rolls, and Paula Gibson.

Introduction

Billionaire Warren Buffet says that learning public speaking skills can boost your value to employers by 50 percent.[1] He understates the benefits. Becoming an effective public speaker can change your life. It did mine.

Like most people, I feared public speaking. I had terrible anxiety and panic attacks. I would do just about anything to avoid giving presentations. The larger the audience, the worse my fear.

But God has a sense of humor. I became a teacher. Then a professor. A communication professor! Bit by bit, I learned how to overcome my fear and speak well. Speaking became fun. I still get anxious, but that helps me remember to prepare well.

Anyone can learn to be an effective speaker. All that is needed is a willingness to give it a try. If you are willing to learn, I am willing to teach you.

In this book I show you step by step how to go beyond fear to comfortable speaking, from comfortable speaking to effective speaking, and from being effective to being courageous.

As Buffet says, you will increase your value in the marketplace. More than that, you will increase your self-confidence for life. Learning public speaking is a lifelong benefit.

God is in the business of using people like you and me to make a difference in others' lives. As I explain in chapter 1, God calls people to speak up. All kinds of people. Not just great speakers. Often anxious and fearful ones.

I wrote this book for Christians who want to learn public speaking with faith, skill, and virtue. I learned public speaking by doing it myself, mentoring others, and teaching at Christian universities and seminaries. In this book I share decades of experience.

From a Christian perspective, public speaking is what I call "servant speaking." We can serve God, our audiences, and others every time we speak. Learning to do this well has become one of the most rewarding things in my life. It is a gratifying way to serve.

You can use this book on your own as a handbook, or you can use it to learn with others. I wrote it specifically for classroom settings, but I filled it with examples and illustrations so readers can learn on their own as well.

This book includes the following features:

- clear, reader-friendly prose with minimal idioms, only obvious metaphors, and no complicated grammar for second-language users
- concrete examples and illustrations from others' and my own public speaking (including humorous tales of things that went wrong as well as right)
- many examples and illustrations of speech topics of interest to students, including career, anxiety and depression, social media, and interpersonal relationships
- chapter-by-chapter spotlight topics on many aspects of planning, rehearsing, and delivering speeches
- "servant speaking tips" throughout the book that offer short-but-essential practical tips
- engaging discussion questions at the end of each chapter, which can also serve as reviews of key concepts and practices
- online materials to help educators use the book (most of these eSources are on the Baker Publishing Group website—http://bakeracademic .com/professors—with some on my personal website and YouTube channel)

I wrote this book to help you use the gift of speech to love others with faith, skill, and virtue. I thank God for calling me to this project and giving me the patience and courage to complete it.

Please let me know how I might serve you with instructor or other resources. I am always delighted to conduct live video discussions with university classes and other groups reading my books. My website (www .quentinschultze.com) includes my contact information.

ONE

Speak to Serve

Rick and Barb were Christians and decided to marry. Rick was a virgin; Barb was not. Before they wed, Barb discovered she was HIV positive. She wondered if Rick would end the relationship. Doctors said Barb had less than a year to live, but she and Rick married anyway. Barb lived on, for over twenty years and counting. So did their marriage. Along the way, Rick and Barb discovered that they could serve others by speaking publicly about living with HIV/AIDS and forming healthy marriages.[1]

They never imagined launching a speaking ministry. They were not trained public speakers, and their story was embarrassing. Nevertheless, they faithfully responded to God's call for them to serve others.

This chapter is an invitation to accept God's call to become a faithful public speaker—a servant speaker. *Servant speaking* is using God's gift of speech publicly to love our neighbors as ourselves.

Start with Neighbor Love

Speech is part of how we live as God's image bearers. We speak in order to grow friendships and marriages, to teach and to preach, to lead and to learn. Some of our speech is *public*—in front of groups or larger audiences.

When we begin public speaking, we tend to focus on skills. But what about our motives? Should we speak primarily to serve ourselves or others? How do we serve the Lord as public speakers?

Desire to Love Others with the Gift of Speech

God calls and equips each of us to use the gift of communication to serve our neighbors, who potentially include everyone in need. Our ability to speak is a present from God. We inherit the gift as God's creatures, made in his image.

What should we do with such an amazing gift? Give thanks for it, develop it, and even enjoy it—all in the service of others as well as ourselves. In short, we are called daily to love others with the gift of communication. Servant speaking is one way for us to respond faithfully to God's command that we love God and our neighbors as ourselves (Luke 10:27).

Sometimes we are asked to speak formally, perhaps at work, church, or a wedding. Other times we might feel we must speak up in order to right a wrong. In any case, our words should come from our loving hearts (Matt. 15:18). When we desire to love others, our words can specially bless them.

Seek Shared Understanding for Community

Communication is *sharing understanding*. Successful communication creates shared understanding. Whether we agree or disagree with one another, we still can seek to understand one another. We just need to keep trying. The alternative is *ex-communication*—breaking off our communication.

God's gift of communication is also the gift of community. Communication is how we build communities of understanding, hope, and love. Communication is one of the most powerful ways that we put our love of God and neighbor into action for community. When we break off communication, we dissolve community. When we deliver an effective speech, we form community with our audience.

Listen for Ways to Serve

If we listen to others and to the Holy Spirit's prompting, we discover many speech callings in our lives. In Scripture, *listening* is becoming intimate with reality—with the way things really are in our relationships, communities, and the wider world. When we listen to God and others, we become personally aware of particular neighbors' needs.

The greatest listener was Jesus Christ, who humbled himself by taking "the very nature of a servant" (Phil. 2:7–8). Jesus "did not come to be served, but to serve, and to give his life as a ransom for many" (Matt.

Our Responsibility to Listen to Speakers

Listening well to speakers is a responsibility as well as a skill. We are morally obligated to do our best to understand speakers, just as they are obligated to make themselves understandable. We need to give every speaker our full, undivided attention, take notes if it helps us, and avoid letting our own biases interfere with gaining an understanding of what the speaker is saying. We should evaluate a speaker's content only after we are sure we understand it. Sometimes we might even need to discuss a speech with someone else who attended before we assume that we understood the speaker.

20:28). He started speaking publicly as a boy in a synagogue. His public speaking continues today through Scripture.

As followers of Jesus, we humbly pay attention to others' needs. As we listen, we discover which of our neighbors we might serve by speaking—and what to say to best serve them. A servant speaker must be a good listener, and a good listener, with an open heart and mind, will feel called to serve others.

We do not normally speak just to promote our own interests, although sometimes we should speak up in order to protect our names, defend our faith, and even appropriately advance our careers in church or society. The principles of public speaking are excellent for job interviews.

Even as we practice public speaking in a classroom or online setting, we should do our best to serve others. As we think and practice "service," we are well on the road to becoming servant speakers.

We learn to find things to speak about when we listen to our own life experiences. Our lives include many parable-like experiences, which are stories waiting to be told. In fact, we tell personal tales all the time to friends, family, and coworkers. Such personal storytelling is a major part of our *interpersonal communication*—face-to-face or digital interaction between persons. Our own life experiences can be powerful examples and illustrations for speeches. For instance, we might personally have been a victim of verbal bullying or harassment. We might have been shunned by friends or coworkers. These could be stories worth sharing.

We might have been wonderfully blessed by people who walked alongside us when we lost a loved one. Our faith might have been deepened by a parent or grandparent, a particular minister, teacher, counselor, or physician. These too might be stories worth sharing.

> ### Jesus Calls Us to Love
>
> "Love the Lord your God with all your heart and with all your soul and with all your mind and with all your strength." . . . "Love your neighbor as yourself." There is no commandment greater than these.
>
> Mark 12:30–31

See Audiences as Neighbors

The biblical analogy for servant speaking is the story of the Good Samaritan, who stopped along the road to help the man who was robbed, beaten up, and left for dead after religious people passed by without assisting him. Jesus uses the parable to explain that fulfilling God's law is about loving God and loving neighbor as self. Our neighbors are all of those in need, including our audiences (Luke 10:25–37).

Speak Up for Neighbors beyond Audiences

In addition to serving our audience-neighbors directly, we can love our audiences by informing and persuading them to serve others. If we have the power and platform that others lack, we can speak up for them. In effect, we serve our audiences by becoming Jesus's ambassadors for the *voiceless*— those who do not have a means and audience to speak up for themselves.

What gets in the way of our speaking up for others? Primarily ego and fear. Even when we overcome the fear, we tend to think that we own our

> ### Be a Good Samaritan
>
> Ask God, "Please give me a heart like the Good Samaritan's to serve others with my voice and ears." Consider adding that simple, one-sentence request to your daily prayers for the next month. If you do, you will discover that you are gaining a more willing, servant-oriented heart to love others with the gift of communication.
>
> We speak as Good Samaritans in a world robbed of spiritual, psychological, moral, and social goodness. We speak up for people who have been beaten down by liars and manipulators. We speak to people who need encouragement and hope. We speak to those who seek knowledge, information, and skill. We speak to give others joy and delight. In short, we speak to love our neighbors as ourselves.

> ## U2's Bono on Rock Singers' Egos
>
> [The] only thing worse than a rock star is a rock star with a conscience. . . . But worse yet is a singer with a conscience, . . . [an] activist with a Lexus and a swimming pool shaped like his head. . . . A singer is someone with a hole in his heart almost the size of his ego. When you need twenty thousand people screaming your name in order to feel good about your day, you know you're a singer.
>
> Harvard University Commencement Address, 2001, https://www.americanrhetoric.com/speeches/bonoharvardcommencement.htm

ears and voices solely for our own self-interested use. Our egos keep us focused on ourselves.

Parents of a disabled son discovered that the Christian school system in their area did not adequately address the needs of such children. They researched the best ways of serving disabled children, shared their findings with other parents, and soon were speaking to school administrators and wider community audiences. They spoke up in love for "the least of these," advocating for God's young image bearers who were not able to speak up for themselves (Matt. 25:40). Their convicting message was that when disabled children are served well, the entire community benefits.[2]

Listen for God's Calls

God calls us to use our voices, when he desires, for his plans. We are his speech agents, no matter how fearful or unskilled we are.

God called Moses, a very reluctant and challenged speaker (perhaps a stutterer, with "faltering lips"), to address the Israelites and Pharaoh (Exod. 6:30), even giving him Aaron to help (Exod. 4:14–15). God called Jeremiah, whose excuse for not wanting to obey God was that he was too young (Jer. 1:6).

God called the apostle Paul, who admitted he was not a great speaker, to become the first major Christian evangelist (2 Cor. 11:6). Paul told the Corinthians, "I did not come with *eloquence* [smooth, effective speaking] or human wisdom as I proclaimed to you the testimony about God" (1 Cor. 2:1). Paul might have lacked speaking skills, but he made up for it in being a hard-working servant to particular audiences.

These biblical examples can give us hope in God's power to speak through us. I was an awful communicator for many years, gripped by a

Called from the Ku Klux Klan to Speak for Jesus

Richard Harris
Professor of Communication

One afternoon when I was four years old, I listened to my parents arguing with my grandmother about taking me to a speech therapist. She insisted that I should be speaking plainly by now. My parents kept telling her they understood what I was saying and saw no need for a speech therapist. My grandmother won. I was in speech therapy for seven years. After that, I could speak plainly. But during those seven years I was constantly bullied by kids making fun of the way I spoke. I was angry. I wanted to get even. I wanted to be the bully, not the bullied.

At sixteen, I joined the infamous Ku Klux Klan (KKK). Because of my ability to speak publicly, I rose to leadership quickly. By the time I was eighteen, I was the Grand Dragon of the Indiana KKK, giving speeches all around the nation. I used my gift of speech to spread evil, hatred, and violence.

Four years later, I met Jesus, who radically changed my heart. I quit the Klan. They let me out after putting a gun to my head with the warning, "You talk, you die." I kept quiet for fifteen years. But God's call was to use my speaking gifts to serve others with truth, love, and justice. I started speaking out against racism, the KKK, and other white supremacist groups. I committed my life to using my voice to build bridges of understanding and better communication between races. Answering God's call to use his gift responsibly has opened doors for me to speak to churches, to civic groups, to corporate gatherings, and even on Capitol Hill in Washington, DC.

As I serve my audiences with my new message, my new goal in life is to help people relate, communicate, and resonate across racial lines.

panicky fear of public speaking. Yet God kept calling me into situations where I could serve others with speech. Often I protested, "God, why me?" I eventually became a professor of communication and a frequent public speaker. I am still astonished. I worked hard, but the Holy Spirit accompanied me, revealed my neighbors' needs, convicted me, and gave me courage. This is what God does if we attentively listen for his calls and follow faithfully.

At a minimum, we can be prepared to answer everyone who asks us to explain the source of our hope by giving testimony to our faith (1 Pet. 3:15). This usually happens in interpersonal situations, but sometimes we will feel called to share our faith in small groups or with larger audiences.

We need to stay attentive to all opportunities for *impromptu speaking*—speaking when we have little or no time to prepare. I went to a board meeting at a Christian elementary school just planning to listen, but I ended up feeling called to speak comforting words of hope in the midst of a tense situation with angry parents and defensive school administrators. Thanks to the Holy Spirit's guidance, my words redirected the course of the meeting for good. If I had thought I would have had to stand up and speak, however, I probably would have stayed home.

IN THE SPOTLIGHT

Common Speech Situations

- praying during worship
- leading a tour
- coaching a team
- giving a eulogy
- teaching a lesson
- introducing a speaker
- offering a wedding toast
- giving a brief devotional

Speak Courageously

An acquaintance asked me to lead a prayer on the street for a group of residents concerned for the welfare of their missing neighbor. I was uncomfortable praying, partly because I did not know the missing person well. Once asked, however, I felt called to serve my neighborhood. The Holy Spirit seemed to be prompting me. I prayed for the police and relatives as well as nearby neighbors. I prayed for comfort and hope. I just tried to express what we all were thinking and feeling.

Months later, the neighbor was found murdered. I was stunned. Suddenly my shaky prayer seemed even more important. My impromptu prayer was not fancy, but it came from my heart on behalf of my neighborhood community. I was glad that I had the courage to accept the call to serve my literal neighbors.

Conclusion

Barb and Rick heard the call to become servant speakers, helping married couples grow in the Lord and teaching the church the truth about HIV/AIDS and its victims. They did not imagine Barb's discovery that she was HIV positive would have led to such a calling. God opened up opportunities in the midst of their difficulties.

God often uses our weaknesses to demonstrate his glory (2 Cor. 12:9). God does not require us to be perfect speakers. He wants us to learn how to speak the truth in love, with a servant's heart, just as the Good Samaritan reached out to a needy victim on the side of the road.

FOR DISCUSSION

1. When is public speaking a call to serve others? Is everyone called?
2. When did you feel like you should speak up but then decided not to? Why?
3. What difference would it actually make if we thought of our audiences as our biblical neighbors? How might we plan speeches differently?
4. Why not think about public speaking just as a way for speakers to influence audiences? Is that unbiblical?

TWO

·

Plan Neighbor-Serving Speeches

A student wanted to give a speech to classmates on how to tune up a bicycle. He asked me what I thought. "Great idea for an informative speech," I replied. "But a few questions: Do many students ride bikes? Will classmates be interested in the topic? Can you make it interesting and maybe even fun?" The student considered my questions. Then he said, "Yes, yes, and yes." He went for it, delivering a great speech. I will explain later how he did it.

This chapter summarizes a seven-step speech planning process that is expanded on in later chapters.

Step 1: Identify a Topic

The most important way to begin preparing a speech is to identify a topic that is related to our neighbors' needs and that we are or can get passionate about. For instance, we might teach our audience a skill or a good daily habit that we find interesting and helpful to ourselves. We might show our audience how to reduce interpersonal conflicts, how to find an internship, or how to protect privacy on social media.

Sometimes we will speak to our audience on behalf of other neighbors who will not be in our audience. For instance, we might aim to persuade classmates to teach English as a second language (ESL) to non-native speakers. We might encourage them to serve in a local tutoring program for disadvantaged children.

IN THE SPOTLIGHT

Finding a Neighbor-Serving Speech Topic

1. List all your major interests and passions—the things you really care about and perhaps know a lot about from your studies, travel, hobbies, work, family life, and more. Add any topics that you are really motivated to learn more about, especially those that involve personal wants, needs, interests, concerns, and pleasures.

2. Talk to people who represent your identifiable neighbors (people in need) so that you can verify your understanding of their needs.

3. Determine where 1 and 2 intersect—where your own passion and knowledge connect with your neighbors' needs.

4. If you cannot find any intersections between 1 and 2, address one of the needs of your neighbors that is not too complicated and that you can learn about without spending excessive time researching the topic.

Most of the time, the needs of our audience members and other neighbors will overlap. For example, we might speak to inform our audience about how to communicate with those suffering from clinical depression. The audience will likely include people with depression, which on university campuses is a major issue. I had a student who was so severely affected by depression that she could barely say anything in class. But she was so passionate about the topic that she outlined and delivered a moving speech on depression to help others understand what she was going through. She served every one of us in that audience because we either were suffering from depression ourselves or knew people who were.

Years ago I started collecting possible classroom speech topics as examples. Since I read a lot—both print and online—I run across possible topics almost daily. Here are a few from just the last couple of days:

- How to Curb Stress by Increasing Gratitude
- How to Deal with Facebook's Privacy Issues
- What Kinds of Toothpaste Actually Reduce Coffee Breath?
- How to Write a Funny Joke Yourself—like Seinfeld Has for Years
- How to Compose a Portfolio for a Job Search When You Are Not in the Arts
- Why Artificial Intelligence Is a Scam
- Why You Need to Learn How to Be a Follower before Even Thinking about Becoming a Leader
- What My Autistic Sibling Taught Me about Autism

Step 2: Define the Audience

There is no sense speaking to an unknown audience. We can serve only those we know something about. This is the very nature of servant speaking: knowing and serving audiences.

If we are going to speak to a class, for instance, what do we know about the students? What is on their minds? What is in their hearts? What worries them or gives them joy? What would they like to know how to do better? Here is an intriguing question: What do they not like about the school that they would like to see changed? Or what do they like about the school that they would like to see further developed? Imagine giving a persuasive speech on improving cafeteria fare or library hours.

There are many ways of defining audiences. The key is relating the audience to our possible speech topic. Usually this takes some basic research. If we are speaking in a university class, we can talk to some students. We can discover where they are from, their cultural backgrounds, and what they are thinking about.

Common topics that define audiences often have to do with careers— both identifying them and preparing for them. When I bring up career-related communication topics, students are immediately interested. They tend to define themselves in terms of their quest for a career.

Another general topic that can define audiences is relationships. Students want to know how to "do" relationships well—with God, others, and even themselves. An interesting speech topic is *intrapersonal communication*— communicating with self. We can call it reflection, thinking, meditating, and the like. It is a dying but essential art.

I heard a terrific speech on the topic of praying ceaselessly. The idea was to help the audience learn how to stay alert to personal communication by remembering that the Holy Spirit is always present, listening to and guiding our speech. We all know that we sometimes say or text things that we should not. We can define many audiences in terms of the need to learn how to keep from speaking hastily.

I give an effective speech on how my wife and I learned to do this by reminding each other of one word: "Ouch!" The speech is aimed especially at younger couples who want to prevent escalating arguments. When my wife or I say "Ouch!" we know it is time to cool off and listen.

Yet another way of defining an audience in terms of needs and interests is to focus on what we as human beings all have in common—the human condition. This can be a bit challenging, but the possible topics are stimulating and wide-ranging.

IN THE SPOTLIGHT

Defining Audiences by Common Human Experiences

- *Ethics*—how to do the right thing
- *Meaning*—how to discover value and purpose in life
- *Faith*—how to live and worship in fellowship with God
- *Fear*—how to deal with specific and general fears and phobias
- *Friendship*—how to build true, deep relationships for romantic love or just companionship
- *Conflict*—how to overcome disagreements, arguments, and resentments in relationships

The key to speaking on a broadly human subject is narrowing it down to specific topics for specific audiences. For instance, fear is human; overcoming the fear of public speaking is a specific topic for fearful speakers. Similarly, relational conflict is human; reducing premarital conflicts is a topic for an audience of couples.

Remember: speech topics and audiences go together.

Step 3: Research the Topic and Audience

Normally we need to know more about a speech topic than we already do from personal experience. And we need audience credibility. If we consult and cite experts in a speech, our audience is more likely to believe us—even if we could say the same things from personal experience. Also, we need to be informed so we do not just display our ignorance (Prov. 19:2). We might not know as much as we think we do. Finally, we need to know enough about our audience to confidently address that audience; sometimes this too requires research beyond our personal experience.

I researched stress among university students, hoping it would help me as a chapel speaker. I discovered that most students feel highly stressed, and many are being clinically diagnosed with depression and anxiety. As a result, I design many of my chapel addresses to inform and encourage such students.

Conduct Primary, Secondary, and Autobiographical Research

Primary research is discovering for ourselves what others do not yet know. We can conduct surveys, interviews, experiments, and focus groups. We can informally observe and talk with people.

Secondary research is searching for what people already know about a topic/audience—what others discovered and have written or spoken about.

For a topic such as student stress, we could interview campus counselors (primary research) and search scholarly journals (secondary research). I

Say One Thing Well

Andrew Harris
Professor of Communication

Shakespeare probably never sat down to compose and said, "I've got it! I shall write unsurpassed plays that will be performed for centuries!"

I imagine it was more like, "What if there was this Scottish guy, and some witches told him he was going to be king, and he believed them?"

Then Bill just wrote the best play that he could.

In order to accomplish something, we have to limit ourselves as God's creatures. This is especially true for servant speaking.

When we choose an informative speech topic, we need to avoid trying to solve the world's problems. That is God's business more than ours.

A topic like the drug epidemic, for instance, is huge and complicated. Perhaps we could address the issue just in our city, school, or church. We could look at what our own church or another group is doing through after-school programs for elementary students. We could talk about what the police are trying to do—and how citizens might help.

A speech that is narrower and deeper is better than one that is broad and shallow.

Moreover, when we truly care about a speech topic, we probably will give more speeches on it. The more speeches we give on the drug epidemic, for instance, the more others will ask us to speak to their groups as well. Before we know it, we might become a respected speaker, serving our community.

As servant speakers, we journey forward, one speech at a time, seeking progress rather than perfection—and always mindful of our calling to love our neighbors with the gift of speech.

We begin with one narrow topic—and speak well. Maybe that's how even a Shakespeare is made, by grace.

found articles written by both psychologists and education specialists. We could also speak with some stressed-out and relatively stress-free students; perhaps the latter group could give us practical suggestions for coping with stress. We could even do an informal survey of students, potentially using some resulting quotes and data in our speech.

Autobiographical research is examining our own experiences—a form of primary research. Some great speeches involve people talking about what they learned from overseas travel, business failures and successes, growing up in various cultures and family situations, deciding to leave a church and searching for a new one, learning how to succeed at job interviews, and volunteering at organizations to serve others and gain professional experience.

Narrow Down the Topic and Audience

The main problems we discover when researching our topic and audience are (1) our topic is far too broad and (2) our audience is not defined. We need to avoid speaking about "something in general" for "no one in particular." We might as well just stand on a downtown street corner and hope that someone stops to listen. It will not work.

Research can help us narrow down our topic in tune with audience interests. We are not going to write a two-hundred-page book. We are going to give a short speech. Research helps us refine the topic appropriately for the length of our speech as well as our particular audience. We can keep our speaking simple and direct.

Step 4: Establish a Speaking Purpose

We always need to establish a *speaking purpose*—what we seek to accomplish with our speech. Of course, our overall purpose is to love our neighbors. But how do we intend to do that?

Aim Primarily to Inform, Persuade, or Delight the Audience

An excellent way of clarifying our purpose is to use one of three ancient rhetorical purposes: to *inform* (teach/instruct), to *persuade* (move/influence), or to *delight* (entertain/please) audiences. Augustine of Hippo (354–430), one of the great Christian *rhetoricians* (public persuaders), said we should use these purposes even when preaching and teaching within the church.[1] "So when advocating something to be acted on," he advises, "the Christian orator should not only *teach* his listeners so as to impart instruction, and *delight* them so as to hold their attention, but also *move* them so as to conquer their minds."[2]

> **SERVANT SPEAKING TIP**
>
> Use an informative speech to increase audience knowledge. Use a persuasive speech to change audience beliefs and actions.

Consider the Most Fitting Speaking Purpose for the Situation

Often the speaking situation will determine our purpose—such as teaching a skill,

> ### Express a MAIN IDEA Specifically
>
> - An overly general MAIN IDEA: "This speech is about TV, parents, and children."
> - A specific MAIN IDEA: "Teach your children media discernment by building strong relationships and discussing media with them."

persuading friends to go somewhere specific for spring break, or delighting an audience with a wedding toast. We can combine all three purposes—informing, persuading, and delighting—in one speech, but only one of them should guide most of our speech research, writing, planning, and delivery.

Step 5: State a MAIN IDEA

We need a MAIN IDEA (sometimes called a thesis statement or a central idea) that meets our speaking purpose and summarizes our speech for our specific audience. Our *MAIN IDEA* is the one-sentence version of our speech—like an elevator pitch. If I were speaking on the topic of this book, I might use this persuasive MAIN IDEA: "Use God's gift of public speech to love your audience-neighbors as yourself."

Suppose we discover that the two best ways for university students to reduce stress are getting adequate sleep and exercising regularly. We also find that the most stress-reducing sleep occurs when students get up early at the same time daily. Research further tells us that exercising for forty minutes three times weekly reduces stress.

After talking with some students (part of our informal primary research), we conclude that convincing students to get up early every day would be too difficult. We believe that far more students would be open to a regular exercise program.

We decide on a persuasive purpose with this MAIN IDEA: "Exercise three times weekly for forty minutes to reduce your stress in school." We could make our MAIN IDEA even more direct and personal: "I would like to convince you to exercise three times weekly for forty minutes to reduce your stress in school." In other words, we aim to persuade our audience to adopt particular exercise habits.

 **IN THE SPOTLIGHT**

MAIN IDEA Requirements

- in tune with a speech purpose—to inform, persuade, or delight
- supported by your topical and audience research
- a message that will serve your audience-neighbors
- one sentence

For an informative instead of persuasive speech, we might use this MAIN IDEA: "Experts say that university students who exercise for forty minutes at least three times per week reduce their stress."

Everything we say in our speech should support our MAIN IDEA. Our MAIN IDEA directs our research, equips us to know what we are going to say, and keeps us from wandering off track as we write our outline.

Step 6: Write a Speech Outline

We can finally begin crafting our *speech outline*—a well-ordered list of the points that support our MAIN IDEA. Our outline summarizes the significant points in our speech and how we are going to begin and end our speech, along with how we will transition between parts of the speech.

Reviewing all our research materials and guided by our speaking purpose (informing, persuading, or delighting), we identify the information that best supports our MAIN IDEA. We also order the items most effectively.

When we start drafting our outline, we decide how best to serve our audience in light of our speaking purpose. We write our outline for our particular audience—with a message aimed directly at them: "This is how to tune up your bicycle."

Step 7: Adapt the Speech to the Audience

When we follow the process of servant speaking summarized above, we will already know pretty well how to adapt our speech to our audience. We will even be able to imagine ourselves as audience members—hearing the speech from their perspective and with their preexisting attitudes in mind.

For example, we might decide whether we wish to strike a more humorous or serious tone. We can decide which examples, illustrations, and sources to use. As long as everything we do supports our MAIN IDEA and speaking purpose for our particular audience, all our speech-crafting ideas are worth considering.

Suppose we have decided to persuade (the purpose) our college classmates (our audience-neighbors) to exercise three times weekly to reduce stress (our MAIN IDEA). How can we best adapt our message to our audience? Would students respond favorably to our persuasive speech on stress if we delivered it like a typical class lecture?

What Is Rhetoric?

Rhetoric is the ancient art of effective public speaking, especially persuasion. Aristotle (384–322 BC), the most influential ancient rhetorician, said that rhetoric is "the faculty of observing in any given case the available means of persuasion."*

Although his definition focuses on persuasion, we can use most of the principles to inform and delight audiences as well.

*Aristotle, *Rhetoric* 1.2, 1355b26f, trans. W. Rhys Roberts (Mineola, NY: Dover, 2004), 6.

Would they be more likely to exercise if we ourselves had tried exercising to reduce stress—and it worked for us? If so, perhaps we could develop our speech partly as a kind of personal testimony.

What about quoting experts from our research? Maybe this would help, especially if we think that students would listen to and trust particular kinds of experts. Perhaps we could use a few short video clips of experts. In short, how shall we make our neighbor-serving case rhetorically effective?

Suppose our research shows that students are most easily persuaded by humorous appeals—that they do not like preachy appeals. Based on our research, we conclude that a lecture-like speech about stress would probably fail. We also confirm what we know personally: students are very busy. We worry that our audience will not consider adding more activities to their schedules, including exercise.

We conclude that we can best accomplish our purpose by persuading students to multitask while exercising. We decide to refine our MAIN IDEA as follows: "I would like to encourage you to reduce your stress through multitasking while exercising three times weekly."

The Five Canons of Rhetoric

Ancient rhetoricians developed five canons (rules) for persuasive speeches that essentially cover all the steps in this chapter.

- *Invention*—researching
- *Arrangement*—outlining and organizing
- *Style*—adapting the message to audiences with fitting language
- *Memory*—committing all or parts of a speech to memory
- *Delivery*—delivering the speech to the audience

We develop a list of possible multitasking activities that could be done while exercising, including listening to recorded class lectures, praying, having phone conversations (maybe with relatives who have been asking us to call more frequently), and even dating (by going on dating walks). To add humor, we include staged photos of real students multitasking on campus. Finally, we organize our speech in terms of a list of specific multitasking practices.

Conclusion

The most important question to ask ourselves in preparing a speech is how we intend to serve particular audience-neighbors. We need to research, organize, write, adapt, and practice our speeches with the goal of serving our neighbors. Along the way, we need to determine exactly what we would say to our audience if we had time to deliver only one sentence: our well-researched, audience-focused, purpose-driven MAIN IDEA.

The student giving the bicycle speech asked one of his classmates to introduce him while he remained in the hallway. Then he rode his bike into the classroom, hopped off, looked at his classmates, and said, "I'm going to show you in six minutes how to tune up this bike. Along the way, I'm going to prove to you that knowing how to tune a bike will get you dates, burn off school stress, and make you more money than you can earn at any other job—about forty-five dollars an hour. Here we go. . . ."

Getting dates? He claimed that few cyclists will turn down an opportunity to have someone fix up their bikes. And forty-five dollars an hour? That is what he charges for a one-hour tune-up.

FOR DISCUSSION

1. How can we determine what our audience's needs really are?
2. What needs do we have personally that others probably have as well? Which of them might be worth addressing in a speech?
3. Choose a possible campus or work audience and identify a speech topic that would serve that audience and is anchored in a broadly human experience (e.g., ethics, faith, fear, or conflict).
4. Suggest a couple of broad topics and then discuss how you might narrow down the topics for a short speech.

THREE

Conquer Speaking Fears

A small-town pastor was invited to address a convention of toastmasters—people who meet regularly to practice public speaking. When he arrived ten minutes before the event, he discovered that the audience was actually postmasters who run local post offices. Totally unprepared, he panicked.

Many of us fear public speaking—even more than death. What would we have done in that situation? Later, I will explain how he won over the audience.

This chapter addresses the fear of public speaking from a Christian perspective. Our fears of speaking are as natural as Adam and Eve hiding in the garden. By openly addressing our fears, we can gain skills and self-confidence that improve our lives as well as our speaking. I know personally. I had horrible stage fright with panic attacks.

Admit Fear

When we admit our fears to others, the fears no longer affect us so deeply. We are able to live better in spite of them.

Holocaust survivor Elie Wiesel, author of *Night*, was probably the finest public speaker I ever heard. His speeches were so engaging, sincere, and convicting that audiences usually responded with lengthy standing ovations.

In spite of decades of successful public speaking worldwide, however, Wiesel still suffered from "an accursed companion who never lets go." He lamented, "I suffer pangs of hell. Butterflies in my stomach. The expression

The Importance of Speaking Up

I appeal to you: Be our [the Jews'] allies. Justify the faith we have in your future. Fight forgetfulness. Reject any attempt to cover up the past . . . and remember: a conscience that does not speak up when injustices are being committed is betraying itself. A mute conscience is a false conscience. Remember some lessons from your past and ours: Words can kill, just as they can heal.

Elie Wiesel, addressing West Germans in 1987,
From the Kingdom of Memory: Reminiscences
(New York: Schocken, 1990), 199.

is apt." As he would ascend a speaking podium, his body would be "seized by trembling" that threatened to paralyze his brain.[1]

Wiesel's panicky fear stayed at his side. "I am never sure of myself," he admitted. "Will I be able to communicate, to stimulate, to hold the listeners' attention, to logically articulate my ideas? And what if I forget the necessary quotation or the critical point? Once the last sentence has been uttered, I ache to escape."[2]

How did Wiesel deal with such deep fear? He acknowledged it. He even wrote publicly about it. And he kept moving forward, speaking in spite of his fears.

I suffer from a number of terrible phobias because of a rough childhood. Yet as I identified my fears with the help of a therapist, they no longer gripped me so horribly. Then I began talking with others, including my students, about my own fears. Year by year, my fears lost most of their power over me.

I am still anxious about public speaking. But like Wiesel, I move forward. I discovered that stage fright has its benefits.

Understand Nakedness

Speech apprehension—fear of public speaking, sometimes called "stage fright"—seems to be part of the human condition. Speaking before an audience is like inviting others to inspect us, including what we look and sound like. Public speaking feels like standing naked in a huge fish bowl, with spectators staring at us from all angles.

What causes such naked fear? Perhaps Scripture offers insight. After eating the forbidden fruit, Adam and Eve hid from God and clothed themselves. Suffering from broken fellowship with God, others, and even ourselves, we all try to hide our *human nakedness* (our guilt and shame).

When it comes to public speaking, for instance, we worry: Will we perform poorly? Will others gossip about our nervousness or slipups? Will our audience disagree with us? Worst of all, will others see us as we really are and then reject us? We might want to run and hide in order to protect our dignity and maintain our self-esteem.

Fear Like Moses

After God appeared in the burning bush and commanded Moses to tell the Egyptian leaders to liberate his people, Moses anxiously replied, "What if they do not believe me or listen to me?" (Exod. 4:1). God responded by giving Moses some signs to prove to the Egyptians that God was on his side.

Still anxious, Moses pleaded with God, "Pardon your servant, Lord. I have never been eloquent, neither in the past nor since you have spoken to your servant. I am slow of speech and tongue" (Exod. 4:10). Moses even told God that he needed the help of a smooth talker—as if God's authority and commands were insufficient. Before enlisting Aaron to assist him, God reminded Moses that the Lord himself gave human beings the gift of speech (Exod. 4:11).

Later, Moses became "powerful in speech" (Acts 7:22). Clearly, he was fearful before becoming somewhat successful—and maybe afterward as well. We all seem to have some of Moses in us.

Fear Like the Apostle Paul

Paul told the Corinthians that he came to them "in weakness with great fear and trembling" (1 Cor. 2:3). He admitted that he was not particularly eloquent or wise when he testified about God. Yet he was effective. There is some Paul in all of us.

None of us will ever be able to fully live up to our own and others' expectations for us. None of us can overcome all our shame and guilt. None of us will become perfect public speakers, faultless in the eyes of our audiences and ourselves. So what?

 IN THE SPOTLIGHT

Negative Consequences of Excessive Speech Apprehension

- fretting excessively while researching your speech topic
- procrastinating until it is too late to prepare well
- coming across as overly self-conscious when starting delivery
- worrying during delivery that you will forget what to say, lose your place, look foolish, panic, or even pass out

Rather than comparing yourself self-critically to other, seemingly better speakers, grow into a servant speaker at your own pace. Seek progress, not perfection.

All public speakers—including the most famous, respected, and influential Christians—know in their hearts that they are imperfect and might yet fail horribly. They feel better about some of their speeches than others. At some level, they still fear being foolish and inarticulate in front of an audience. They, like us, are in good company with Moses and Paul.

Embrace the Benefits—Motivation and Adrenaline

Speaking fears are helpful. If I do not have any fear going into a speaking situation, I know I will not do well. I should worry about failing! So many speakers have wasted my time that I do not want—ever—to waste others' time. We have an obligation as servant speakers to get fired up, even excited. We need some adrenaline. Fear helps create it.

The main thing with fear, beyond keeping it from controlling us, is using it to our advantage. It can motivate us to work early on our speeches and practice them. Procrastination is far worse than fear if we truly want to speak well. I start writing down ideas for a speech on the same day I agree to give it.

I think that people who never fear public speaking are not so much gifted as confused. They do not seem to understand how important their words are in the service of others. Consequently, many of them are boring speakers.

IN THE SPOTLIGHT

Benefits of Speech Apprehension

- adrenaline for energetic delivery
- motivation to prepare well
- encouragement to trust in God even as we work hard
- reminder to seek progress, not perfection—particularly to keep our speech simple and direct

Grow in Community

After working with others and on my own for decades, I have learned that speakers grow less fearful in community. Gaining self-confidence is not meant to be a solo act. One key to reducing speech apprehension is gradually practicing among people who love us. They already know us, so we feel less naked around them. Also, we will be less likely to worry about our looks—since friends already know our appearance—and focus more on serving our audience.

When I became a teacher, I struggled with speech apprehension, including panic attacks. I was fearful even as a professor of communication. I saw people with less education who were more confident and inspiring speakers. Worse yet, I recalled occasions when I had failed as a speaker, such as the time I let down my university classmates in a group presentation. I was the weak link, and their grades suffered because of my fear.

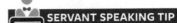

SERVANT SPEAKING TIP

Interview a teacher or pastor you admire about their own speech apprehension and how they addressed it. Share your apprehensiveness with them. After the interview, thank them, and later prayerfully thank God for them.

To come out of my fear-induced shell, I needed a beloved community. We all can grow as servant speakers when we practice in a community where we feel cared for, protected, and appreciated even in our brokenness. The community might be a group of friends, a class of co-learners, or a public group that meets to practice.

For me, this included three groups: my family, church, and friends. I began speaking up in conversations at appropriate times and settings. I

How I Began Overcoming Stage Fright

When I started speaking at churches, I began with small groups, preferably fewer than fifteen participants. I conversed rather than orated. Usually I placed chairs in a circle, including one for me. I kept my notes on index cards. I would make a point and then encourage discussion before moving on to the next one.

In effect, I combined speaking and discussion in an informal setting to reduce my apprehension, increase my self-confidence, and test my content with other followers of Jesus who wanted me to succeed.

I moved naturally from such informal conversation to public speaking. I practiced *gradual desensitization*—desensitizing myself to fears and phobias by slowly increasing my exposure to them.

The group-oriented presentations also helped me get a sense of how well I was serving my audiences. Feedback was nonthreatening. If someone disagreed with me, I simply thanked them and asked others what they thought. I did not argue. After all, I might be wrong; I had plenty to learn.

Within such community, I learned not to take others' disagreements personally. I discovered it could even be beneficial to receive negative feedback. The more I served these conversational groups, the more I realized that they were preparing me to speak more knowledgeably, effectively, and confidently to larger audiences. I grew to appreciate even their seemingly negative feedback.

SERVANT SPEAKING TIP

Consider joining a local speaking group such as Toastmasters or attending speaking-related Meetup (meetup.com) groups. Some employers will pay the fees for taking a Dale Carnegie class on the topic.

shared personal stories, including about my dismal childhood. I could do so because I knew that these people would not make fun of me or reject me; they wanted the best for me, no matter how much shame I felt about myself.

My apprehension slowly subsided, and I increasingly enjoyed serving audiences. When I failed, I figured out what went wrong and learned from my mistakes. I realized that audiences forget our mistakes and continue to appreciate us when we try to serve them. What we ourselves see as major mistakes are rarely perceived so negatively by audiences. We tend to be too hard on ourselves; we see our own nakedness more intimately than anyone other than God can.

The advantages of faith-based speaking practice include mutual prayer and a deeper community of unconditional love. We can be more transparent without fear of rejection. The Holy Spirit helps us trust others in community so we can learn together how to love and serve one another. Our beloved faith communities provide special opportunities to practice our servant speaking with others who fear public speaking.

Defy Panic

Sometimes while speaking, we suddenly get confused, worried, frustrated, or distracted. We then become overly self-conscious. Panic sets in. It is scary.

The first time I walked out on a stage where the lights were so bright that I could not see the audience, I panicked. My heart raced. I got dizzy. I feared I would pass out and drop to the floor. Such experiences taught me seven ways to defy panic.

IN THE SPOTLIGHT

Common Causes of Panic While Speaking

- losing our place
- getting distracted by audience noise or movement
- spotting someone in the audience who we wish was not there
- suffering technical problems such as a bad microphone or remote control
- feeling like we are failing

Prepare Well

Many panic sufferers tend not to prepare well for speeches because the preparation itself causes emotional discomfort. Procrastination eventually creates greater fear. If we are well prepared, we will be calmer when we deliver our speech.

Two general ways to prepare that usually work for anxious speakers are (1) exercising well about two hours before a speech and (2) practicing deep breathing in the days leading up to a speech and just before speaking.

Plan Responses to Triggers

Sometimes, particular things tend to trigger panic. If we know them in advance, we can plan how to deal with them. For instance, I always get panicky when standing in front of a new audience for the first time. To deal with my initial anxiety, I look over attendees' heads, not at their eyes. I also do some deep breathing if I feel a trigger coming on. Once I calm down after beginning a speech, I start looking directly at the audience.

Identify Panic Attacks Quickly

If we wait until the attack starts overwhelming us, it will be harder to address. When one begins to strike me, I say to myself, "Okay, here it comes. I know what you are—a panic attack! You can't fool me." I remind myself that I am not going crazy, but just experiencing temporary anxiety. Life will go on.

Do the Next Practical Thing Needed

Thinking about an emerging panic attack can make it worse. We can defy the oncoming attack by shifting our mind from the panicky feelings to what we need to do next in the speech. We essentially deny the attack a spot in our mind by replacing it with other practical actions.

No matter where I am in a speech, I can determine in a couple of seconds what I need to do next. Do I need to look at my outline or manuscript? Do I need to tell a story? Do I need to show the next PowerPoint slide? There is always something practical waiting to be done. As soon as I start doing whatever I practically need to do, the panic begins disappearing.

Improvise with Practical Techniques

When I first walked into a stage spotlight, the lights blinded my view of the room and audience. I worried that I could not see my outline on an index card. Panic set in.

I thought to myself: "I need to be practical, not emotional." I pretended that I was speaking to a small group of people sitting straight ahead of me, at eye level; I avoided looking up at the blinding lights or down at the lit floor.

While the audience was still applauding, I held up my note card within my palm to see if I could read it. I determined that I could see the card in the spotlight by turning slightly to the side. This was my practical response to an emotional panic.

Soon audience members started responding to my speech even though I could not see them—applause, laughter. After a while, I was enjoying speaking to an invisible audience.

When something new causes panic, we can improvise with whatever practical technique works to keep our speech going and our thoughts off the panic.

Take Time

What might seem to us like an eternity when we are speaking makes little difference to audiences. Panic attacks can come and go in ten seconds. By the time we finish defying the attack, audience members are still thinking about the last thing we said. To them, nothing is occurring other than our speech. Time is on our side. As long as our speech is interesting and audience-focused, listeners will continue thinking about what we last said while we pause to address our panic.

Focus on Gratitude

I conclude with this technique for defying panic in order to emphasize it. In a sense, focusing on gratitude is like the first step in servant speaking. But it is a kind of spiritual preparation, not a speech-focused one. It has more to do with our overall spiritual condition than just our speaking techniques.

When panicky feelings begin, we can focus on something for which we are truly grateful. As we do so we can look up, above the audience, so we are not distracted by others' faces. As we recall something for which we are grateful, we clear our minds of fear and doubt. This is just as true in life as in speaking. When we do it while speaking, it will bring a smile to our face, reflecting our grateful heart.

I picture someone for whom I am sincerely grateful, such as my wife, children, or grandchildren. I imagine myself doing something I love with one or more of them. I especially imagine doing something that makes me feel accepted, loved, and filled with joy. Usually this warms my heart, makes me smile, and deflates my panic. It takes about five seconds, and the audience never notices the short delay.

This technique can be the ultimate defense against panic if we are already living gratefully. Feelings of thankfulness come naturally when we practice them. The more worshipful our lives, the more natural and effective this is. The less inclined we are to criticize or blame others, the more genuinely grateful we will be.

SERVANT SPEAKING TIP

Rarely is it a good idea to tell the audience that we are panicky or even nervous. It takes away from our message and suggests that our audience should expect us to do poorly.

Apparently, gratitude and panic cannot emotionally coexist in us. I do not fully understand it, but I experience it as a speaker who was raised in fear and grew up with severe stage fright.

Now, while preparing speeches, I place at my side some photos of loved ones. They are always with me in spirit, cheering me on. Loving me for who I am, nakedness and all. They are God's soul-soothing ambassadors to me, a fearful but grateful servant speaker.

Conclusion

When the youth leader realized that he was totally unprepared to speak to postmasters, he panicked. He could not run and hide, like Adam and Eve in the garden. He had to speak. What could he do? First, my friend convinced himself that he had nothing to lose. He remembered that, when in doubt about what to say, we can speak about something we know first-hand and are passionate about. Something that will motivate us to speak from the heart.

He decided to speak about feelings we all share. He spoke about his own sense of loneliness, insignificance, and meaninglessness—even as a pastor, often working alone. He imagined, as he spoke, the postal workers feeling unappreciated for their work. He also talked about how he dealt with the problem—faith in God and love of family and friends.

Initially stunned by the last-minute audience change, and then shocked by the audience's enthusiastic response to his unprepared remarks, he discovered afresh the power of speaking honestly and directly to the real needs of an audience. He began in panic, with a potential speaking disaster, and ended up with a standing ovation.

The Spirit can and will see us through our fear and panic. We ought to prepare well, but the Holy Spirit can speak through us even when we feel inadequate.

FOR DISCUSSION

1. To what extent is speech apprehension part of the human condition? How much is it related to our sense of guilt and shame?
2. Which of the listed ways of defying panic might work the best for you? Why?
3. Which of the benefits of speech apprehension can you identify with? Can you think of any additional benefits?
4. Can you describe a time when you felt so secure with a group of beloved friends that you could speak publicly to them?

FOUR

Compose an Outline

W hen I was a graduate student, I attended a lecture by a prominent communication scholar. Within five minutes I was totally lost. At the end of the speech, there was silence. Finally, a distinguished professor spoke up. "Sir, when I read your brilliant work, I get it. But after just listening to you, I wonder if you lost it." A few attendees chuckled.

After shifting around at the lectern, the famous lecturer replied, "When I got up this morning, I thought I had it. But after hearing my own lecture, I'm wondering if I lost it during breakfast." We all laughed.

Unlike the lecturer, we need to make our MAIN IDEA clear and obvious. In fact, we need to base our entire speech on our MAIN IDEA—keep it simple and direct. We do that by writing a solid outline to speak from.

This chapter addresses the importance of writing a clear, well-organized speech outline based on common organizational patterns. It also considers how to plan the three major parts of a speech: the introduction, body, and conclusion.

Revere the Outline

No speech is better than the speaker's outline. In most cases, a *speech outline* is a short list of the points that support our MAIN IDEA—perhaps three to five points. The points should flow well and be written in complete sentences.

> **SERVANT SPEAKING TIP**
>
> As you write your outline, imagine yourself in the audience listening to a speech that consists of only your MAIN IDEA and your outline points. Does the speech make sense, point by point? Do all the points support your MAIN IDEA?
>
> The MAIN IDEA is a one-sentence speech summary—like an elevator pitch. The outline is a thirty-second speech summary during an elevator ride to the eightieth floor.

An outline is like a list of directions to a location, with scheduled turns and distances. Each "turn" is a transition to a new speech point. The "distances" are periods of time. By glancing at our outline "directions," we can see where we are in the speech, where we are going, and whether we are on time for our scheduled arrival at our speech's conclusion.

The prominent communication scholar apparently failed to write a MAIN IDEA or an outline. Listening to his lecture was like reading the book of Leviticus without the historical-biblical context. I kept thinking, "What's his point?"

He had a purpose: informing us about his research study. But without a MAIN IDEA, a supporting outline, and helpful transitions from point to point, he just confused us.

To the audience, poorly outlined speeches are disconnected statements. They baffle and frustrate listeners. Audiences feel like the speaker is ill-prepared and perhaps ill-informed.

Write an Appropriately Organized Outline

A solid outline covers all our major and minor points in complete sentences. Every one of the points must support our MAIN IDEA. Moreover, the outline should be appropriately organized for our speech purpose—to inform, persuade, or delight.

In some cases, the MAIN IDEA itself can summarize the points in the speech. This kind of preview works well with three or fewer outline points.

> **SERVANT SPEAKING TIP**
>
> Include your speech purpose (to inform, persuade, or delight) at the top of your outline along with your MAIN IDEA in order to keep your outlining consistent with your goal.

"I would like to convince you of three reasons why you should organize your speeches well."

Consider Different Organizational Approaches

The outline example above is organized topically, with three supporting points. There are

A Well-Organized Outline with Complete Sentences for a Ten-Minute Persuasive Speech

MAIN IDEA: As servant speakers, we should organize our speeches well so they are *easier to follow, more pleasing to listen to,* and *more convincing.*

Introduction of the Speech

Body of the Three-Part Speech

1. We should organize our speeches well to make them *easier to follow.* (3 mins.)
2. We should organize our speeches well to make them *more pleasing to listen to.* (3 mins.)
3. We should organize our speeches well to make them *more convincing.* (3 mins.)

Conclusion of the Speech

other ways of organizing our outline—and thereby organizing our thoughts for effective speaking. Generally speaking, our MAIN IDEA will suggest how we should organize our outline.

The most commonly used organizational approaches are topical, chronological, spatial, cause and effect, two-sided (or pro and con), and problem and solution. Most of them are covered more fully in the chapters on persuasive and informative speaking.

In my experience, as I start researching my speech topic, one of the organizational patterns naturally emerges. The questions I start asking about my topic lead me to think about ways of organizing my thoughts and eventually my outline.

In other words, we need to consider not just what we want to accomplish with our speech but also the kind of organizational pattern that naturally fits our topic and our main point.

Develop a Unified Introduction, Body, and Conclusion

When we deliver our speech, we need to (1) state our MAIN IDEA, (2) develop our MAIN IDEA, and (3) restate our MAIN IDEA. These three elements are called the *introduction, body,* and *conclusion* of a speech.

IN THE SPOTLIGHT

Ways of Organizing Speech Content

- *Topical.* We cover various aspects of our topic, often with the most important ones last and first, since those generally are better remembered.
- *Chronological.* We cover points in a time frame, such as first to last, beginning to end, or the steps for accomplishing a particular task (e.g., the sequence of events leading to a sports victory, or the steps required to write a résumé).
- *Spatial.* We cover our topic in terms of physical place (e.g., geographic regions, areas in a public park, or sections of the human ear).
- *Cause and effect.* We cover what is causing a particular phenomenon, or the effects of a phenomenon on something else (e.g., the causes of the increase in college tuition, or the effects of such tuition increases on current or future students).
- *Two-sided (or pro and con).* We cover the pros and cons of our topic (e.g., the pros and cons of earning a college education, or the pros and cons of leasing versus purchasing a vehicle).
- *Problem and solution.* We cover one or more solutions for a definable problem (e.g., how to get better sleep, solve a relational problem, or eat healthfully on a low budget).

Our outline covers primarily the body of our speech, but we can also add a summary of our introduction and conclusion along with any transition statements we will use between points in the speech.

As a rhetorical art, crafting speeches includes unifying the introduction, body, and conclusion. We should make our overarching point so clear during our speech that our listeners never get lost—unlike the audience of the prominent lecturer who offered plenty of data but no MAIN IDEA.

Begin a Speech—the Introduction

We need to engage our audience right away. Boring introductions lose audience attention.

Often, the best way of quickly engaging an audience is with a story that illustrates our MAIN IDEA. Many engaging stories are personal.

If we are speaking to persuade classmates to replace some social media usage with prayer time, for instance, we probably have already done it ourselves. When did we realize that our prayer life was suffering? How did we respond? What did we learn along the way? By asking ourselves such questions, we can compose a personal story illustration.

A second way to begin is with a significant but not commonly known fact or quotation. If we use a quotation, the person or the person's organization should be credible to the audience: "The American College Health Association recently found that 40 percent of students said they were so depressed that it was difficult for them to function, and 61 percent said that they felt overwhelming anxiety."[1]

The way we begin can also establish our *servant ethos*—that we are there not just to speak but to serve. Our *ethos* is how the audience views us, especially our character and motive. We want our audience to know that we are there to serve. The most natural way to establish this ethos is by stating the relevance or value of our topic for our audience: "So I would like to help you lower your stress by . . ."

We certainly want to gain our audience's attention, but not with silly jokes, off-topic tales, and most types of questions. Normally, beware of beginning a speech with two types of questions: (1) *rhetorical questions* that are really like obvious statements ("Are you tired of cafeteria food?"), and (2) *exclusive questions* that only some audience members would have asked themselves (e.g., "Have you ever asked yourself . . . ?"). Both can be effective, but we have to use them carefully.

In my experience, the only kind of opening question that consistently works well is an *inclusive question* that asks something that everyone in the specific audience truly wants answered and is the question that your speech answers. For a Christian audience: "Why does God permit evil?" or "How can we know God's will for us?" For an audience of nonresidential university students on tight budgets: "How can we eat nutritionally on ten dollars a day?" For an audience of people entering the job market: "What is the best way to prepare for a job interview?" In each case, the inclusive question reflects the needs of most of the audience and sets up our speech as the answer.

IN THE SPOTLIGHT

An Audience-Serving Introduction

- If appropriate, give thanks to your host for the invitation and to the audience for attending.
- Engage your audience with an interesting story, fact, or idea—never a gimmick designed just to catch attention.
- Clarify your purpose.
- State your MAIN IDEA in one clear sentence.
- Tell listeners why they should care about what you have to say; why they should listen rather than start texting or even leave.
- Preview briefly your outline points.
- Establish your servant ethos.
- Transition to the body of the speech, usually by restating your MAIN IDEA.

Develop the Main Section of a Speech—the Body

During the body of a speech, we state outline points, make claims, offer supporting evidence, provide illustrations and examples, and sometimes address likely audience objections—especially for persuasive speeches.

An Audience-Serving Conclusion

- Restate your MAIN IDEA.
- Summarize the main points of the speech.
- Refer back to your speech introduction, particularly if you used a story. You might even conclude the story if there is more to it than what you covered in the introduction.
- Call for an audience response, if appropriate, such as the action you would like the audience to take after a persuasive speech. Be specific. What exactly are you asking the audience to know, believe, or do?
- Finish strongly, with courage and conviction.
- Deliver your last sentence as a crescendo, the high point of your speech.

The chapters on informative and persuasive speeches cover body content more fully, such as using logic and emotion.

Finish the Speech—the Conclusion

If we began our speech with an illustration or example, we normally should refer back to it (like at the conclusion of this chapter, where I refer back to the disorganized lecturer). If not, we can refer to any other particularly important story or data we presented earlier. This helps create a sense of unity across the entire speech.

If we are speaking to inform, we can simply summarize our main points.

If we are speaking to persuade, we summarize our main points and then challenge the audience to believe or do exactly what we are seeking to accomplish. We specify what we would like the audience to do: "So I would like to challenge you for the next three days to spend ten minutes less with social media and ten minutes more in prayer."

Include Transition Statements

Audiences often get lost when we fail to signal when we are moving from one part of a speech to the next, or when we fail to remind the audience about earlier parts of our speech. In nearly all speeches, we need *transition statements*—sentences that link together the sections—both backward and forward. Transitions can signal where we have been in the speech (*summary transitions*) and especially where we are going (*preview transitions*).

The three essential places to use transitions are (1) between the introduction and the body, (2) between sections of the body, and (3) between the body and the conclusion.

I consider transitions so important that I include them in my speech outlines, word for word. Often I memorize them.

Transition Statement Explanations and Samples

Here are abbreviated sections of the speech described above (see "A Well-Organized Outline with Complete Sentences for a Ten-Minute Persuasive Speech"). Note how the transition statements help the audience identify and follow the two parts of the Main Idea: organizing speeches well to make them (1) easier to follow and (2) more pleasing to listen to.

Speech Introduction

"When my fiancé and I were in premarital counseling, we attended an amazing speech on how to create a great marriage. I'll never forget the speaker's two points: be respectful and encourage each other. The speech was so well organized around those two essential points that I learned not only how to build a solid marriage but also how to compose a great speech. In this speech I would like to convince you to serve your audiences by organizing your speeches well so they are both easier to follow and more pleasing to listen to—just like the good-marriage speech."

Transition to the first point in the speech:

"First, we should organize our speeches well to make them easier for listeners to follow."

(Note that this transition statement reflects the first of the two points in the speech. The speaker could then talk about how the marriage speech's organization made it easy to listen to even though the topic—respectfulness—might have been complicated.)

Transition to the second point in the speech:

"Second, in addition to organizing our speeches well to make them easier to follow, we should organize our speeches well so they are more pleasing to listen to."

(Note that this second transition statement mirrors the form of the first transition statement and directly conveys the second part of the speech. Note as well how it summarizes the first part of the speech about using organization to make speeches easier to follow.)

Transition statement at the beginning of the conclusion of the speech:

"In conclusion, I would like to urge you to serve your audiences by organizing your speeches well, thereby making them easier to follow and more pleasing to listen to."

(Note that this transition to the conclusion summarizes the two main parts of the speech and also indicates that the speech is concluding. Presumably, the speaker would then refer back to the opening example, as below.)

Speech Conclusion:

"In conclusion, I would like to urge you to serve your audiences by organizing your speeches well, thereby making them easier to follow and more pleasing to listen to. I will remember to be a respectful and encouraging spouse as my fiancé and I embark on our marital journey. That one speech was so well organized that I could easily take its message to heart. I encourage you to compose well-organized speeches to serve your audiences just as effectively."

Transition statements are notoriously difficult to write in a way that makes them sound natural rather than contrived. Sometimes the way we deliver them is important for how audiences will respond. If we suddenly switch to a more formal style when stating a transition, it will seem abrupt. As best we can, we should compose transitions that fit with our overall style for a speech and seem natural instead of forced.

To make our transitions more creative and memorable, we can employ some simple but effective techniques: numbered points, visual metaphors, and acronyms.

Numbered Outline Points

Probably the most frequently used way of capturing the points in a speech is numbering them (first, second, third, etc.). A three-part persuasive speech on losing weight could include the following sequential outline points as transitions:

The first way to shed a few pounds is to say no to sugary desserts.

A second way to lose weight is to check the calorie count on packaged food labels and stay within your set range.

A third way to reduce weight is to burn calories by being more active, such as taking daily walks or developing a regular exercise program.

Visual Metaphors

Another way of capturing speech points with effective transitions is to use one or more visual metaphors for outline points, preferably related directly to our speech topic. Such metaphors might include a painting, drawing, photograph, or artifact. In a four-point speech about environmental stewardship, a four-leaf clover might work, with each of the leaves representing one outline point. PowerPoint or posters could show each of the labeled leaves as we add them to the clover.

Acronyms

A third common way of building memorable, integrative transitions into a well-organized speech is to use acronym-based outline points: "SLIM down by *saying* no to desserts, *looking* up calorie counts on labels, *increasing* water intake, and *moving* around to burn calories." Acronyms can seem trite or forced, so we have to use them carefully.

Conclusion

The scholar who gave the disorganized lecture sounded like he was speaking impromptu, without an outline. He rattled off data. But he had no "it"—no MAIN IDEA and outline, just a lot of disconnected points.

Outlines help us organize our thoughts about our MAIN IDEAS. They serve us as speakers and our audiences as listeners. We need to start with a well-composed outline that engagingly introduces our MAIN IDEA and then maps, with transition markers, the route and time to our concluding destination.

FOR DISCUSSION

1. What would be an example of a speech topic about a current event that would best be organized spatially?

2. When, if ever, should a servant speaker use a rhetorical question at the beginning of a speech?

3. Consider this proposition: "A speaker should never explicitly state in an introduction his or her goal to serve the audience, because it is prideful (rather than humble) and builds excessive audience expectations." Do you agree or disagree? Why?

4. When does it make sense in the speech-writing process to share an outline with a friend for review? How would you select the person?

FIVE

Speak Extemporaneously

I heard a well-known sociologist give a superb lecture about the effects of social media on interpersonal relationships. He explained the benefits and drawbacks. What most impressed me was his delivery. He spoke for fifty minutes without notes. The audience was fully engaged.

He had learned *extemporaneous speaking*—speaking from an outline. He tracked his own thinking as he spoke, developing each point from his outline.

This chapter is an invitation to learn to speak extemporaneously. When we read a manuscript, it might seem to some listeners like we are not personally engaged with the subject and the audience. When we speak extemporaneously, we can be considerably more effective. In fact, extemporaneous speaking is the most effective way of delivering most speeches.

Pursue Extemporaneous Speaking

TED Talks are popular partly because the speakers are trained to engage audiences extemporaneously. The program prohibits reading from manuscripts. Of course, there are other stylistic requirements as well—such as using the first person and telling engaging stories—but extemporaneously speaking is critically important in TED Talks.

The cultural trend seems clear: Those who can speak authentically from the heart, without reading a manuscript, have a growing rhetorical advantage. Lecture-like speakers who read manuscripts are losing impact. In effect, audiences are saying, "Don't lecture me!" or "Don't preach at me!" Instead, "Speak to me!" "Tell me your story."

Understand Basic Extemporaneous Speaking

Extemporaneous speaking (often called "extemp") involves speaking from an outline rather than reading a full manuscript or reciting a memorized speech. As the sociologist did, we use a printed or digitally displayed outline to keep us on track. We add to our outline the source quotations that are too long or difficult to memorize and that we need to read word for word.

I write my short, final outline on a small index card and tape printed copies of quotations on the back for reading. Sometimes I just put my outline and quotations on my phone or tablet instead, but I prefer being able to discreetly review my small card, which I hold in my palm.

IN THE SPOTLIGHT

Common Criticisms of Speakers

- *Long-winded.* Speaker did not seem to know when to conclude.
- *Irrelevant.* Speaker did not relate content to real life with concrete examples.
- *Repetitive.* Speaker kept making the same points.
- *Boring.* Speaker was dull and lacked enthusiasm.
- *Disengaged.* Speaker just read a print manuscript or the text on a screen.
- *Superficial.* Speaker just presented commonly known material without researching well.
- *Impersonal.* Speaker did not seem to be personally involved and passionate.
- *Artificial.* Speaker seemed to be acting rather than speaking genuinely from the heart.

Well-done extemporaneous speaking takes time. Our outline needs to be excellent. We need to rehearse enough so that we know what we are going to say and how we are going to say it. If we are unprepared, it is easy for us to say things we did not intend to say, come across as disorganized, and simply make fools of ourselves.

Extemporaneous speaking is worth mastering if we are willing to take the process seriously. It carries significant potential advantages.

When *manuscript speakers*—those who read a prepared speech manuscript—realize they are going over time, they start looking through their manuscript to determine what to eliminate. Audiences can usually tell what is happening. Some manuscript speakers even unnecessarily announce that they are running out of time and

SERVANT SPEAKING TIP

When preparing to speak extemporaneously, plan on rehearsing three to five times over a few days.

An Extemporaneous Speech Outline

- *MAIN IDEA*—exact wording
- *Introduction*
- *Outline points*—single-sentence or single-phrase statements
- *Example and illustration reminders*—words or phrases to remind us of each one, listed under each outline point
- *Quotes and definitions*—written definitions and source quotations that we will need to read precisely
- *Timing notes*—specific times indicating where we should be at the end of each outline section
- *Conclusion*

Advantages of Extemporaneous over Manuscript Speaking

- *Internalized content.* We know our content better, in our hearts as well as minds.
- *Body freedom.* We can better attend to using our bodies, including facial expressions and gestures.
- *Eye contact.* Instead of looking down at our text, we can spend more time looking at our audience.
- *Flexible length.* We can more easily adjust content to stay on time, such as expanding on or not using particular information.

will have to "skip some material"; the audience wonders what it will miss.

When we write an extemporaneous outline, we prepare for such situations by including items that we can expand on or ignore when delivering our speech. I prepare a slightly longer outline than I will need, knowing I can cut back to stay on time. I mark on my outline which points are optional, in case I need to delete material along the way. I can also adjust how long I take to tell a particular story.

Learn Extemporaneous Skills

Probably no speaking skill has served me better than extemporaneous speaking. But I had to learn a set of four skills to do it well. Too often, speakers use extemporaneous methods just because they are too busy or lazy to prepare a manuscript. That does not work well. Developing an extemporaneous speech can take just as long as writing out an entire speech manuscript.

When we speak extemporaneously from an outline, we rely primarily on four skills: (1) memorization, (2) elaboration, (3) reflection, and (4) audience affirmation.

Memorize an Outline Visually

I asked a terrific extemporaneous preacher how he did it. He showed me his messy one-page outline. Not just sloppy handwriting but colored lines and circles, highlighted phrases, double and triple underlining, cursive and block writing, upper- and lower-case words and phrases. I could not believe he used such a messy page, until he explained it to me.

Most of us remember visually. When we look at something repeatedly we can recall it better. As the pastor worked on his outline, he began to visualize what was on the page, with all the visual emphases. He said that a purely textual page was not easy to "see" for recall.

Creating a double-spaced, one-page outline helps us remember what to say and even how to say it. But we need to mark it up for personal memory.

> **SERVANT SPEAKING TIP**
>
> Mark up your extemporaneous speech outline with different colored inks to make it easier to see and track at a glance where you are on the outline while speaking. As you speak, note which color you are speaking about.

I write out by hand a two- or three-page outline with my points, transitions, and brief descriptions of my examples and illustrations. Then I rework it three to five times. Each time, I recite parts of the speech to myself out loud.

Eventually, I reduce the outline to one fairly clean, handwritten page with numbering, underlines, and some yellow highlighting. That is what I use for visual memorization.

A day or so before the speech, I summarize my outline on one side of a small index card, which I use for the speech. By that time I have memorized visually what goes in the gaps between the brief points on my index card. Even just one word on an index card will remind me of an entire paragraph on the full page. I add a few handwritten marks on the card to help me see the card in my memory. Using color-coded outline sections helps.

Elaborate on Memory

Usually we use concrete quotations, examples, and illustrations in our speeches. When we speak extemporaneously, we elaborate on them without the help of extensive notes. If our example is a story, for instance, we can use a one-word cue on our outline to remind us to tell that story ("party story"). Similarly, we can use a one- or two-word note to remind us what we intend to say about a quotation we will be reading ("loud music").

To elaborate well, however, we have to rehearse without notes. We keep rehearsing until we know that we can elaborate on each illustration, quote, and the like. Eventually, we feel confident. Then, while speaking, we simply tell the audience what we have been reminding ourselves for days or weeks.

Sometimes it helps to practice elaboration with friends along the way. If we keep a copy of our outline with us, we can glance at it and decide which parts we need to practice delivering to others during a ride home or over a meal.

Reflect while Speaking

While speaking extemporaneously, we glance occasionally at our outline. As we look at our outline, we recall from memory what we need to say. As we look back at our audience, we think about what we recall from memory.

In practice, we reflect on the next outline point while the audience is still thinking about what we just said. We do not need to rush. It will seem totally natural to the audience if we are glancing around the room while reflecting on how to express our next point. The audience is not worrying about what we will say next and exactly when we will say it. If we are speaking well, the audience members themselves will be reflecting on what we last said, not merely awaiting our next point. We actually serve them by giving them time to think.

Our goal throughout our extemporaneous speech is to reflect before speaking. If we are engaged conversationalists in life, we already do this. We think about what to say before saying it.

Affirm the Audience

An advanced skill for extemporaneous speaking is affirming the audience's fitting emotional and intellectual responses to our speaking. When we see audience members moving their heads up and down in agreement or understanding, for instance, we want to acknowledge and affirm it by doing the same, but usually more subtly. When we see and hear the audience laughing at something we said that is meant to be funny, we smile in order to both confirm that the audience understood our humor and to stir listeners to laugh even more deeply.

Once we realize that we do not have to rush, we can be more interactive, even playful, as appropriate. We not only speak *to* the audience but also spontaneously interact *with* the audience. We acknowledge that our audience members are serving us—just as we are serving them. The audience's responsiveness helps us communicate more effectively.

It is like comedic speaking. Most comedians use timing along with verbal and nonverbal cues to signal when they have said something funny and the audience should laugh. Then comedians signal with their faces that the audience correctly laughed—perhaps with a smirk or grin.

A few comedians take it one step further, affirming the audience's response verbally. For instance, if a comedian comments humorously on a silly human habit, she might wait for the laughter to begin, and then say, "It's crazy. [Pause] We're all goofy." The audience laughs more.

I simply look at the audience with the same kind of nonverbal emotion that I see emerging on listeners' faces—assuming they are responding appropriately. I smile if they are smiling. I look mildly astonished if they seem to be looking likewise. I even laugh a bit if they are laughing. I let their responses affect me so I can affirm them. It is very natural, especially in extemporaneous speaking, which is more interactive than read-manuscript and memorized-manuscript speaking.

Conclusion

As I discovered with the sociologist who gave an amazing lecture, extemporaneous speaking can be extremely effective. But it takes effort. We should not try to speak from an outline without practice. And it helps to use a personalized outline with visual markups.

American writer Mark Twain humorously said it took him several hours to prepare a good impromptu speech.[1] It takes even longer to prepare, outline, and practice an extemporaneous speech. And it is well worth it. No type of speaking gives us more self-confidence for all of our spoken communication.

FOR DISCUSSION

1. Why might it be easier or more difficult for you to speak extemporaneously rather than to read a manuscript?

2. From your own experiences listening to manuscript versus extemporaneous preaching or teaching, which type would you say tends to be more effective? Why?

3. What is your greatest fear about extemporaneous speaking versus just reading a manuscript? How might you address that fear in speech preparation and practice considering the four essential skills: memorizing, elaborating, reflecting, and affirming?

4. How would you mark up a one-page outline to make it easier to use for delivering a speech extemporaneously? Why?

SIX

Anticipate Challenges and Opportunities

When I was speaking at a convention of agricultural bankers, my opening lines went like this: "I'm delighted to be here today to address those of you who work in the world's oldest profession." I waited about four seconds, then added, "Agriculture! What do you think Adam and Eve were doing back then?"

No one laughed. The audience just stared at me. I received no response to anything else I said the entire speech. No laughter. No applause. Nothing. The applause I received at the conclusion of my speech was probably meant to celebrate my departure.

I thought I was being clever, referring to the world's oldest profession (usually said to be prostitution) as agriculture. I was speaking in the South to a group with significantly rural and presumably Christian roots. Surely, I figured, they would find my reference humorous. They did not.

This chapter addresses important aspects of speech planning and delivery that require us to not only anticipate but also remain flexible. Both opportunities and challenges arise unexpectedly in servant speaking.

Monitor the Time

We need to see our audience's time and attention as gifts. Time is on our side only when we use it well. Being trite and boring, or going over time with an audience-irrelevant speech, is awful. I have done it. I still feel badly about it, years later.

It might be that time—and the accompanying attention—is the most precious thing any of us can give God and others. Our listeners grant us their time and attention; we are morally obligated to use the gift well.

> **SERVANT SPEAKING TIP**
> Two essential rules for servant speaking: Never go over time. Never waste the audience's time.

In my view, we should plan for a slightly shorter speech—but then monitor our progress along the way. We can nearly always finish a bit before our deadline without a problem. Also, assuming our outline includes a couple of optional items, we can fill in the remaining time with one or two of them if needed.

When we practice a speech, we should speak at the same pace we expect to use. We often speak too quickly during practice, especially as we get more comfortable with our material. After practicing, we know the material so well that we forget to include appropriate pauses between major points, and time for audience reflection and reaction. We need to time ourselves delivering the speech exactly as we will deliver it at the event.

As a general rule, then, I plan to speak about 10 percent less than the time I have been allocated. I can always slow down a bit or expand the post-speech time for questions.

The ideal way to monitor our progress is to use a timer at an easy-to-see, nondistracting location. We ought to avoid looking at a clock that the audience can see. The audience will tend to follow our glances at the clock. This distracts the audience and gives the impression that we are worrying about time, and perhaps that we just want to finish and leave.

I add times to sections in my outline. Then I stick to them, using a timer on my phone or, if available, a clock behind the audience.

Attend to the Moment

Staying on schedule is essential in servant speaking. But what if our creative thinking, conscience, or maybe even the Holy Spirit seems to be telling us to say something beyond what we had planned? In my experience, this happens regularly in extemporaneous speaking.

> **SERVANT SPEAKING TIP**
> Practice speech timing with an audience of a few friends who can give you feedback about your pacing.

For instance, what if while delivering our speech we get a new idea—maybe a fitting example or illustration that had not occurred to us previously? Or suppose we unexpectedly think of an opportunity to better serve our audience by including some personal thoughts that might move listeners' hearts? We feel like we should speak up, but also fear saying something that we have not evaluated.

This frequently happens when I am speaking about résumé writing. I might recall working on a particular résumé issue with a particular student. I had not planned to use the example.

Should I ignore a new idea or consider using it? Both options are risky. I might say something foolish. Or I might miss out on making a great contribution to my speech.

In the modern world, we think of time chronologically (the Greek *chronos*), such as yesterday, today, and tomorrow. Another Greek understanding of time is the right and fitting moment (the concept of *kairos*). Scripture does not use the concept of *kairos* for speaking, but uses it more generally as a way of indicating God's appointed time, according to God's purpose. It is God-created opportunity (Gal. 6:10; Eph. 5:16).

As servant speakers, we will have unexpected opportunities while we are delivering speeches. It is not easy to evaluate such opportunities, partly because they also involve understanding the developing situation—our audience, message, and purpose. I have said things that I thought were opportune but I later regretted. I have said things spontaneously while speaking that vastly improved my speeches.

When I feel called to speak to an apparent opportunity, I take a few moments to review the idea in my mind. If it sounds like something that is more than just my ego—that will simply make me look good or clever—and something that will truly serve the audience, I usually speak up. But even then, I might frame my comment tentatively, such as, "I also wonder if . . ." or "Another possibility is . . ."

Plan for Questions and Answers (Q&A)

After-speech Q&A teaches humility. Sometimes my heart sinks when I hear questions that I already answered repeatedly in my speech. Also, I occasionally receive questions that are so obvious and important that I wonder how I missed addressing them in my speech; I get embarrassed. The larger the audience, the more likely that someone is going to point out what I missed, how I confused listeners, or even what I got wrong.

Other times, I am both humbled and delighted by questions that reveal ideas better than my own. I have even felt, after listening to some lengthy comments and questions, that some members of the audience could have delivered a better speech on my topic.

The complicated nature of Q&A, then, shows that we need to prepare for it.

Prepare Emotionally

A Q&A period is a conversation about our speech and the audience's reaction to it. We need to keep in mind that it is not a conversation about us as speakers; we need not take the conversation personally. Sometimes we will not even know the questioners personally, so we have no way of understanding their style of questioning. Their questions might reflect their own life experiences and personalities.

If we receive a seemingly disrespectful question, we need to answer it as if it were asked appropriately, even courteously. In these cases, we have to resist responding in kind.

Audience members have later apologized to me for the way they asked a question or made a comment. They genuinely felt bad. We all understand that kind of situation. We have our bad days. If we feel threatened or challenged by what someone else says, we are inclined to respond emotionally. We need to prepare ourselves to avoid hasty responses.

Preparing emotionally for delivering a speech is not the same as preparing emotionally for the Q&A. The latter requires special patience, humility, and graciousness. We can prepare ourselves to be even-tempered, to take nothing personally, and to always respond kindly.

Admit Ignorance

Ignorance is not stupidity or foolishness. Ignorance is simply not knowing. We might overlook important information in our research. Moreover, we cannot become fully knowledgeable about any topic. As a result, we will face questions that we cannot answer. What shall we do?

First, we can make sure we have understood the question correctly. One way is to ask for clarification: "Thanks for your question. Would you please say a bit more so I can be sure I understand?"

In most cases, the questioner will begin to answer his own question as well as expand on the meaning of the question. This gives us more context and substance. We might then be able to answer part or all of the question. Or we might say that we too have thought about the question but still have not come up with an answer: "I agree with you. I wish I could answer your question well. I need to research it."

Second, we can defer to the rest of the audience. As soon as we say "I don't know. I wish I could answer your question," we are ready to seek help: "Would anyone else like to address the question?"

Third, we can deflect an obviously irrelevant question. Generally, when we receive an irrelevant question, the audience knows it. Sometimes we can see audience members' eyes roll when the question is being asked. We can respond, "Thanks for your question. I have thought about a similar issue. . . ." Our "similar issue" is something that we know about that is somewhat related to the question. In effect, we are asking our own, new question triggered by the irrelevant question. We then answer our own question and move on to other questions.

Anticipate Questions

It is difficult for us to anticipate likely questions because we already know so much about our topic. So we need to invite some friends to attend our rehearsals, prompting them at the beginning to remember any questions that come to mind. Then we can have them write down the questions even before we answer them so that we have a list of questions to practice with later. Sometimes the questions will be so helpful that we revise our speech to take them into account.

Determine a Process

There are two primary ways of conducting audience-serving Q&A. One is to call on those who wish to ask questions. In larger venues, it can be difficult for everyone to hear questions, so it is a good practice to repeat each one before answering. If asked a long and rambling question, we can just summarize it.

The other method is handing out index cards in advance and asking attendees to write down questions to be collected for Q&A. We ask someone to begin collecting the cards for us when we are ready to start answering them. The rest can be collected during the Q&A. Some speakers use text messaging instead of index cards, but I prefer to protect questioners' anonymity, so I use cards. Also, if using cards is not possible, I ask an audience member in advance to take notes for me on the questions and my answers so I have a record for evaluating and later revising my speech.

Recover Graciously

We all make mistakes and embarrass ourselves. We lose our place during a speech. We suddenly realize that we skipped an important section. We stumble through reading a lengthy quotation as if we had never practiced it. We make ourselves look foolish and ill-prepared. Sometimes we even unintentionally offend audiences. I sure did that with my remarks about the world's oldest profession. There are two ways to deal with our speaking mistakes: ignoring and correcting.

Ignore Minor Mistakes

If the mistake is minor, we can ignore it and keep going. In most cases, this works splendidly. When we dwell on our mistakes, we draw more attention to them and divert the audience's attention from our message. For example, if we lose our place in the speech, we can take a few seconds to find it and then keep going. If we accidentally repeat ourselves, we do not need to mention it.

IN THE SPOTLIGHT

Advantages of Using Index Cards for Q&A

- *Brevity*. Written questions are short and direct, whereas some people who ask questions orally take a long time, making their own speeches and frustrating the audience.
- *Relevance*. A quick review of the cards identifies the most relevant questions and enables us to ignore irrelevant ones.
- *Directness*. Questioners are more likely to be blunt.
- *Anonymity*. Questioners will be less inhibited if they know that no one else will know that they asked the question.
- *Evaluation*. Reviewing the cards later helps us evaluate how well we communicated in the speech.
- *Revision*. Keeping and later reviewing the cards equips us to revise the speech for use again.

Correct Substantive Mistakes

If our mistake is substantive—such as misstating a fact or mispronouncing a name—we can just restate the information correctly and continue.

Sometimes we realize that we are off track while delivering speeches. For instance, we might suddenly notice on our outline or manuscript that we missed a section or forgot to include a key example or illustration. Here we need to correct our speech as we continue, usually informing the audience. In effect, we need to add a new transition to accomplish our correction.

Without making a big issue out of it, we can just tell the audience what we are going to do and then do it. We do not need to offer any excuses or explanations, which will be further disruptive. We can offer corrective transitions such as these: "I just realized that I forgot to share with you a wonderful anecdote." "I would like to back up for a moment and mention something I overlooked." We just need to make sure the audience can follow us as we make the correction and then continue where we left off.

These might seem like major corrections to us as speakers, making us anxious or embarrassed. To audiences, however, they are insignificant. We ought not make them bigger than they already are.

Accept the Benefits of Mistakes

We tend to think of our mistakes as problems. Who wants to look foolish? Actually, seemingly embarrassing mistakes can benefit our ethos by helping the audience identify with us. When we do something embarrassing, the audience feels embarrassed along with us. Highly polished speakers often find it more difficult to create audience identification. They seem less relatable to listeners.

Instead of fearing embarrassment, we can embrace it as an unexpected gift. The audience will listen even more closely and openly. Later, we will probably laugh about it—and rightly so.

Beware of Possible Offense

A good friend and effective preacher whom God uses mightily tells his audiences that he gives all the glory to God. Then he adds this, "If God can speak through a jackass, he can speak through me" (referring to Num. 22:21–31). I suggested that he might use the word "donkey" instead.

An amazingly gifted, well-known Christian speaker intentionally uses a few potentially offensive words such as "damn" and "hell" in some speeches addressing Christian apathy toward injustice. After pausing, he adds something like this, "You are probably more concerned about the language I just used than you are about the poor and exploited in the world." It is a bit gimmicky and potentially offensive, but also effective.

At the event where I offended the agricultural bankers with my joke about the world's oldest profession, I should have tested my opening line with a few convention attendees when I arrived the day before. I was upset with myself for not doing so. I felt ashamed.

Also, when I realized that I had offended the audience I should have briefly apologized before quickly moving on. I could have said something like, "Wow, that was a poor joke. I guess I just demonstrated why Adam and Eve got into trouble with their egos." Instead, I continued without addressing it. From what I could tell, I never connected with the audience.

If we offend and realize it, we can quickly apologize and then continue. If we discover later that we offended, there is no reason to dwell on it. We speak and learn.

Prepare for Technological Problems

Using technology like PowerPoint is a way of asking for trouble in public speaking. Sometimes it will not go smoothly even if we practice well in the same room.

 IN THE SPOTLIGHT

Common Situations That Can Offend Audiences

- *Cleverness*—trying to be ingenious or shrewd to impress audiences
- *Humor*—trying to be funny with jokes and puns
- *Criticism*—pointing out others' hypocrisy, ignorance, and disobedience
- *Pride*—speaking overconfidently and even arrogantly
- *Exaggeration*—making obviously exaggerated claims, usually because of poor language choices

With technology, small problems become bigger ones. If we have trouble advancing slides, the digital sound malfunctions, batteries die in a remote control, or the projector light goes out, the audience perceives the problem as significant—compared to mispronouncing a word or losing our place. Technological snafus are nearly always disruptive.

So preparing a backup plan is essential. We prepare by assuming that the worst might happen. For example, I always prepare printed copies of anything I will show on the screen that is vitally important for the audience to be able to read—such as lengthier quotations.

Finally, we should not fuss with the technology if it stops functioning. We need to keep speaking as if nothing happened. Normally it is up to someone at the venue to fix the problem as unobtrusively as possible, but we cannot depend on others. We need our own backup plan. If necessary, we can just continue without referencing the problem.

Conclusion

The time that I offended the agricultural bankers at a major convention really shook me up. I wondered how I could have been so insensitive. I had a wonderful opportunity to serve a group that serves many people. Instead of seizing the opportunity wisely, I turned it into a seemingly impossible challenge that at the time I could not overcome.

Servant speaking is an art to be learned and practiced so we can minimize our mistakes and maximize our effectiveness. We should prepare well but not expect perfection. Instead, we should learn to anticipate wisely, apologize quickly, and continue calmly, even when the technology dies.

FOR DISCUSSION

1. What would you have done if you offended a group, such as with the joke about the world's oldest profession?

2. Should the possibility of offending our audience lead us to avoid all risky language or stories? Is the speaker who verbally shocks audiences to get them to consider the plight of the poor justified in doing so?

3. What do you think about the practice of planning speeches to be a bit short so you do not go beyond the allotted time? Why is that a good or bad idea?

4. How could you determine if a new idea that came to you while speaking might be from the Holy Spirit?

SEVEN

Think Biblically

How is servant speaking different from Christian teaching or preaching? Should all our speeches be anchored in God's Word?

When we speak about social issues like poverty or immigration, a biblical perspective seems essential. If our audience is Christian, we might even use explicitly biblical language to persuade them to adopt a particular view on our topic. But what about an informative speech on making the perfect cheese omelet?

This chapter addresses how we can think biblically about our speech topics, particularly when addressing Christian audiences. Such thinking requires humility as well as biblical insight. We need to know what we believe and why we believe it. We should seek to avoid misusing Scripture but strive to think biblically about even seemingly nonbiblical topics.

Admit Personal Limitations

The best way to begin thinking biblically is through self-examination. One biblical truth is that our knowledge is limited—and it will always be. None of us can know everything about any topic.

Moreover, we misunderstand some of the things we would like to share with others in speeches. We might even misinterpret Scripture. We see "through a glass, darkly" (1 Cor. 13:12 KJV).

Worst of all, we are sinners. We procrastinate until the last minute, inadequately preparing to serve our audiences. We use data that support our

SERVANT SPEAKING TIP
Avoid composing a MAIN IDEA before thinking biblically about the topic. A biblical perspective might be subtle but essential.

claims while ignoring contrary information. We pretend to know more than we really do.

Finally, we are quick to criticize other speakers but slow to evaluate our own speech preparation and delivery. We tend to think that we are all above-average researchers and speakers. So we might judge others without considering the logs in our own eyes (Matt. 7:3–5). We are not responsible for everyone else's public speaking, but we can be responsible about our own.

Perhaps we Christians should be the humblest public speakers even though we know Jesus as the way, truth, and life (John 14:6). Our biblical faith tells us to speak carefully and honestly as representatives of Jesus and the church. We use our freedom in Christ not to boast but to serve one another (Gal. 5:13).

Use Scripture Carefully and Appropriately

Some speech topics do not seem to require deep biblical insight. A speech on a technical topic like how to write a successful cover letter for a job application probably does not require citing Scripture. Yet the Bible still addresses how we should represent ourselves. I heard a terrific student speech on how to tell the truth in résumés without being either deceptive or too humble. Deceptive résumé writing is a major issue in society, including among Christians. Other Christians undersell themselves.

In other words, topics that are not addressed directly or practically in Scripture often can be enhanced by general biblical insight. For example, speeches on leisure activities can be contextualized with a healthy understanding of Sabbath-keeping. God calls us to rest and to delight in the creation, not just to work (Exod. 20:8–11).

Similarly, if we are speaking to non-Christians about ways to reduce stress, we could simply place our speech in the context of self-care—the love of self—without using explicitly biblical language.

When we speak to civic or business groups, we normally refrain from explicit "God talk" unless we are asked to give a more personal or faith-related presentation. We need to use language that connects with less religious audiences. Here are some examples of religious terms translated for nonreligious groups:

- Jesus Christ = God
- sin = brokenness

- religion = spirituality
- obedience = responsibility
- salvation = reconciliation
- sacrifice = selfless love
- church = faith community
- guilt = conscience

> **SERVANT SPEAKING TIP**
>
> "I am not sure" is the truest thing to say when we are uncertain about a biblical perspective on our topic.

If we try too hard to speak biblically, we might misuse Scripture. We should avoid *proof-texting*—using Bible verses out of context to make biblical claims. We will be tempted, especially when speaking to Christians, to use Scripture to gain credibility rather than to use it only to make valid points.

Some parts of Scripture stand on their own without a lot of context. Usually these verses tell us how to live, including how to communicate. For instance, we should not speak hastily (Prov. 29:20). The books of James and Proverbs are particularly helpful for practical and wise advice on communication. The advice applies widely to our everyday communication in church and society and often does not require deep contextual analysis.

Often Christians disagree on how to think biblically about the most pressing issues in church and society. Biblical insight is not always straightforward, because Scripture is not a topical handbook. It is a record of God's works over the course of history—through creation, fall, redemption, and renewal.

Identify Tribal Correctness

We humans sometimes accept uncritically what others assume about a general or a distinctly biblical topic. We practice *group think*—avoiding conflict by agreeing with our *tribe*, our own group. For Christians, a tribe could be a congregation, tradition, or denomination.

We tend to accept our tribe's biblical perspectives on topics without personally conducting biblical research. We practice *tribal correctness*—assuming that the correct biblical view must be the one held by our Christian group. We confirm our existing biases, rightly or wrongly.

After studying Scripture and consulting with biblical authorities, we might confidently affirm our tribe's perspective on a topic. We can still respect the right of other Christians to disagree, but we can then speak confidently about our own tribe's beliefs.

Confirmation Bias and "Itching Ears"

For the time will come when people will not put up with sound doctrine. Instead, to suit their own desires, they will gather around them a great number of teachers to say what their itching ears want to hear.

2 Timothy 4:3

When Paul and Silas visited the new believers at Berea, they found a group eager to hear the message. Yet the "noble" Bereans still "examined the Scriptures every day to see if what Paul said was true" (Acts 17:11). They made sure as a tribe that they understood Scripture rather than just accept Paul's interpretations.

When we speak to a diverse Christian audience on explicitly biblical and theological topics, we ought to be especially careful to identify and explain our own tribal assumptions. Christians reasonably disagree about topics such as baptizing children or adults (or both), how frequently to celebrate the Lord's Supper, and God's sovereignty in predestination versus an individual's choice to follow Jesus.

Know Christian Nonnegotiables

Thinking biblically also requires us to affirm *Christian nonnegotiables*—the core beliefs of the Christian faith. This helps us remember that, beyond our nonnegotiable beliefs, Christians can fairly disagree on "disputable" issues (Rom. 14:1).

Of course, Christians might disagree about nonnegotiable beliefs as well. But by identifying our own nonnegotiables, we will become much more charitable and sensitive while addressing potentially divisive topics.

When speaking to Christians, I frequently use elements of the Apostles' Creed, one of the oldest statements of faith (ca. AD 400), originally adopted to dispel challenges to Christ's divinity and the doctrine of the Trinity. Not all Christian groups fully endorse this creed, so I also put it in historical perspective and admit that it is a summary of biblical essentials, not Scripture itself.

 **SERVANT SPEAKING TIP**

Discuss your speech topic with a trusted Christian leader, mentor, or role model to see how you might approach it biblically.

We need to clarify what we believe biblically, but we also should consider when and how to engage others in matters of biblical faith. When should we speak about distinctly biblical themes and implications? Why? How?

Offer a Comforting Voice in the Church

SERVANT SPEAKING TIP

Unless speaking about a central biblical and theological belief, such as the divinity or resurrection of Christ, do not automatically assume that you know precisely what the Bible says about a topic. First conduct biblical research.

Our Christian tribes are essential for community even though, in a fallen world, they generate conflicts. Tribe-affirming speech fosters healthy community. We need speakers who provide a *comforting voice*—affirming and deepening what a tribe rightly believes and practices.

Speaking biblical comfort is one of the greatest forms of communication within the church. The psalmist writes, "My comfort in my suffering is this: Your promise preserves my life" (Ps. 119:50). When we affirm one another in God's name, we help one another live together faithfully.

Comforting speech can edify the tribe, deepening its true faith—its belief and practices. All churches and denominations need speakers who help them understand and deepen their beliefs. For instance, the more biblically we understand worship, the healthier our worship will be. Similarly, speaking on a biblical view of forgiveness can be both practical and community building.

Unless we feel called to challenge tribal opinions, we should approach our speech topic in a way that will comfort our audience.

Navigate Tribal Conflicts

As servant speakers, we face complicated divisions within and across Christian tribes. How can we speak nondivisively? Are there times when we should speak up for the sake of unity as well as truth, even in the face of conflicts?

Divisiveness has been an issue since the early church, which was infected by internal disputes. The apostle Paul often addressed such conflicts in his letters. He tried to be pastoral, not just critical, as needed. This is not easy, but it is essential for servant speakers.

SERVANT SPEAKING TIP

Avoid preachy language by humbly matching the explicitness of your biblical language to your audience's level of biblical understanding.

The biblical and theological language we use is critically important for how various Christian groups will interpret us. I got into a thorny discussion after a speech I gave about "common grace" in mainstream mass media content. Common grace is the idea that even non-Christians benefit from God's goodness in creation and some aspects of mainstream culture.

I wish I had been more sensitive to my audience members, some of whom wondered if I was discounting saving grace (God's ultimate grace in our eternal salvation from sin). Instead of using the term "common grace," I could have referred to something like "Christian values" in movies and television programs. Or I could have clarified what I meant by common grace.

A sound biblical approach to speaking amid division in the church is to be humble, sympathetic, and compassionate toward one another. We aim overall to become like-minded (1 Pet. 3:8), but getting there is challenging. In any case, we do not want our speaking to come across as disrespectful.

To the general public, our Christian-to-Christian conflicts look like in-house feuds and tend to discredit all Christian belief. Many nonbelievers today say that Christianity obviously is flawed because Christians do not agree on what the Bible says.

Offer a Critical Voice to Church and Society

Thinking biblically as servant speakers sometimes leads us to question mainstream social values and even our own tribe's beliefs and practices, especially regarding *cultural discernment*—judging the good and bad in culture using biblical standards. For instance, we might disagree about which movies to see, books to read, or websites to visit.

I have heard great student speeches that challenge campus dress codes as too liberal or too conservative. I have heard wonderful speeches on how to make decisions about which mainstream musical groups might be invited to perform on campus—and if the performances should be advertised off campus. I have heard impassioned student speeches on freedom of the press for student media.

Should we ever challenge what other Christians believe or do—especially within our own tribe? The whole idea of planning a speech in order to criticize other believers seems wildly wrong. But an important form of speech is helping Christians live *in* the world without being *of* the world (John 14:14–17; 15:19). We need speakers who provide a *critical voice*—challenging our nonbiblical beliefs and practices. It takes courage, sensitivity, and deep biblical insight.

Jesus and the Old Testament prophets proclaimed unpopular truths that upset the religious establishment. In the Sermon on the Mount, Jesus repeated, "You have heard that it was said," and then criticized tribal untruth, nonbiblical practices, and hypocrisy (Matt. 5). Such biblical criticism of church and society is sometimes called a *prophetic voice*.[1]

Aiming to be as inclusive as possible to spread the gospel, Paul challenged how some Jewish Christians were requiring particular tribal practices, such as not eating sacrificed meat (Rom. 14:1–4) and circumcision (1 Cor. 7:19). Paul was a critical voice on behalf of the gospel; he spoke the truth even when it might lead to being beaten or jailed.

A prophet such as Amos spoke to his tribe directly on behalf of God, often delivering the bad news that the tribe was unfaithful. We do not have Amos's direct line to God, but we have his words and the rest of Scripture to help us think and speak critically to our tribes.

Sometimes—after our careful research, prayer, and consultation with trusted friends—we might conclude that we are being called to speak against particular tribal beliefs or practices. For example, we might conclude that our church or Christian school is hypocritical or just misguided. Critical speaking is important for the spiritual health of our tribes. It can be a community version of our own personal self-assessment before the face of God. We all need to identify our sins, confess them, and grow out of them. And we need people who will persuade us to do so. Otherwise we will probably stay silent. As Frederick Buechner says, "No prophet is on record as having asked for the job."[2]

Finally, we can consider how to speak critically in ways that can comfort our tribes as well. We can aim to build up our tribes even as we tear down some false teachings, poor attitudes, and improper practices. We will not gain a fair hearing and change others' hearts unless we also lovingly advocate for what is right and true in community.

The Prophet Amos's Greatest "Hits"

Hear this word, you cows of Bashan on Mount Samaria,
  you women who oppress the poor and crush the needy
  and say to your husbands, "Bring us some drinks!"
    (Amos 4:1)

I hate, I despise your religious festivals;
  your assemblies are a stench to me. (Amos 5:21)

Seek Biblical Wisdom

One of the highest aims in biblical thinking is *wisdom*—enduring and often practical truth from God's Word that we come to understand as a result of our faith in Jesus Christ. Today, people sometimes refer to such wisdom as a biblical *worldview*. But wisdom is more than just theoretical or systematic thinking. Wisdom is understanding God's Word and how to apply it fairly, sensitively, and discerningly in our lives.

For instance, wisdom is partly about making good judgments about our speaking. Not speaking hastily is biblically wise (Eccles. 5:2; Prov. 29:20). How about a speech on not texting hastily—why we do it, why we should not, and how to avoid it?

Our wisdom comes with the fear of God (Prov. 9:10). Only when we trust and believe the Lord, especially God's Word, do we begin gaining deep and true wisdom for life. Personal pride—belief in ourselves—competes with biblical wisdom. A healthy fear of the Lord opens our hearts and minds so we become humble learners (Prov. 11:2).

When I began speaking on the topic of raising children in a media-filled world, I desired biblical wisdom. I had researched the impact of media on children. I knew parents' challenges. I knew my own parenting experiences. But I needed biblical wisdom. I asked God for it. I read books and spoke with pastors.

I discovered that the key in parent-child communication about media usage is threefold: (1) being patient with children, (2) gently encouraging children to think about their media decisions, and (3) creating warm, open dialogue within the family. Biblically speaking, parents need such wisdom in order to avoid embittering, exasperating, and discouraging children (Eph. 6:4; Col. 3:21). I based my church presentations on such essential wisdom. I respected different parenting styles while advocating for a climate of healthy family communication and media discernment.

Some parents wanted me to provide specific lists of what to do and not do with their children's media choices—such as which technologies or

---

Paul on Speech, Love, and Wisdom

If I speak in the tongues of men or of angels, but do not have love, I am only a resounding gong or a clanging cymbal. If I have the gift of prophecy and can fathom all mysteries and all knowledge, and if I have a faith that can move mountains, but do not have love, I am nothing.

1 Corinthians 13:1–2

media content to make available to their children. But such decisions can be made differently among families, partly because children, like adults, vary in their personal susceptibility to culture (1 Cor. 12:22). I saw my servant speaking task as imparting biblical wisdom about the parenting process, not mandating specific cultural-discernment choices.

Focus on Biblical Themes

We also think biblically by focusing on Scripture's overarching themes. These include creation, fall, redemption, and renewal. Related to each of them is a host of essential biblical themes about goodness, faithfulness, responsibility, discernment, reconciliation, peace, justice, humility, and the like. We often need to interpret the particulars of Scripture in tune with such broader biblical themes.

One of our tasks as servant speakers, then, is to determine how our speech topics and MAIN IDEAS relate to biblical themes, not just to particular Bible verses. Since I speak frequently about communication, I developed questions that help facilitate discussion of related biblical themes.

When I speak to Christians about public speaking, I explicitly define and advocate for servant speaking as one solid biblical theme. I make my case persuasively because I want to help equip Christians to use the gift of communication wisely as God's responsible stewards of language. For instance, I say, "We should learn to love our audiences as our neighbors and be virtuous as well as effective servant speakers. We should speak life over death" (see Prov. 18:21).

When we express biblical themes in a speech, we should also give concrete

IN THE SPOTLIGHT

Defining "Christian Speech" in Terms of Biblical Themes

- defines reality in tune with the Word of God (John 7:18; 1 Pet. 4:11)
- demonstrates accountability to neighbor, self, and ultimately God (Eph. 4:25; 1 Pet. 4:11)
- imitates Jesus and his godly followers (1 Cor. 11:1)

IN THE SPOTLIGHT

Questions to Discuss for Biblical Themes about Communication

- Why did God create in us the *ability* to communicate?
- What is the *nature* of communication for humans created in the image and likeness of God—even different from other creatures?
- How does the *fall* from grace affect human communication?
- How does (or how should) salvation renew our *motive* for communicating with God, others, and ourselves?
- How should we *renew* our communication as redeemed persons living in community?

> ## Augustine on Biblical Research and Speaking
>
> There are two things on which all interpretation of scripture depends; the process of discovering what we need to learn, and the process of presenting what we have learnt.
>
> Augustine, *On Christian Teaching* 1.1.1, trans. R. P. H. Green (Oxford: Oxford University Press, 1997), 8.

examples and refer to specific Scripture if possible. For instance, Christians might disagree about exactly how to practice servant speaking, but the biblical concept can still guide us with relevant Scripture: "Whoever would love life and see good days must keep their tongue from evil and their lips from deceitful speech" (1 Pet. 3:10).

Let Faith Guide Biblical Understanding

Gaining biblical understanding of speech topics involves more than knowing *about* the Bible. It includes knowing God personally (John 14:7; Phil. 3:8), speaking the truth from the heart (Ps. 15:2), and putting God's Word into action (James 1:22).

In other words, we gain biblical insight through faith; faith precedes wisdom and wise action. Our faith in Jesus leads us to know God and to know how God would have us think and act as speakers. We interpret Scripture through the lens of faith—not merely through logic. And we nurture our faith together in community so we do not think we are personally inerrant.

In a sense, our faith controls our worldview. Our personal devotion to God—nurtured through individual and tribal practices like worship, prayer, and study—creates the heartfelt desire to gain and apply biblical wisdom in our lives. It also leads us to share wisdom within and beyond our tribes.

Conclusion

When we plan and deliver speeches, we should remember our responsibility as servant speakers to think biblically. Our Christian tribes give us biblical insight and direction, but they, like us individually, are imperfect. Thinking biblically includes admitting our fallenness so we can be humble learners, fully open to God's Word, and learning within a community of faith.

When we desire to think biblically and to surround ourselves with faithful followers of Jesus, we are charting a journey of servant speaking. We gain both humility and wisdom, speaking in the context of biblical themes. We thereby serve God, neighbors, and self with the gift of speech.

1. Identify one or two aspects of your church, Christian school, or group of friends that seem particularly good and fitting from a Christian perspective. How might you speak comfortingly to this tribe on one of those topics?
2. Identify one or two aspects of the same group that seem misguided or inappropriate from a Christian perspective. How might you speak to the group critically but lovingly?
3. Identify and discuss one section of Scripture that might appropriately help guide your biblical thinking on the topics you identified in question 1 or 2—without proof-texting.
4. How would you answer the questions in "Questions to Discuss for Biblical Themes about Communication"?

EIGHT

Research the Topic and Audience

I was trying on new eyeglass frames similar to my old ones, but I feared radically changing my looks. Then it occurred to me that I was evaluating frames based on my personal opinion. What if I tried an audience-centered approach?

As I was the only customer in the shop at that time, I asked the three saleswomen to work together to help me look good. They liked the idea and soon agreed on a pair. I tried them on. What a difference!

"Sold," I said.

I received more compliments on my new glasses than for any previous pair. Instead of assuming I could determine which frames looked best on me, I consulted with people who knew current fashion and who could evaluate the frames on me better than I could by looking in a mirror without my own corrective lenses.

This chapter discusses the importance of topical and audience research. It also considers the problem of information overload as well as the joy of topical revelation. Research can help us find the best information for serving specific neighbors.

Consult Topical Authorities

When I asked the saleswomen to give me eyeglass advice, I was seeking expert opinions. They taught me what to look for in terms of my facial features, skin complexion, hair color, and head shape. I was amazed.

As servant speakers, we normally have to conduct topical research because we are not authorities. Topical experts might include individuals and organizations dedicated to being informed about a subject. Their solid information could include such sources as books, lectures, periodicals, research journals, video recordings, podcasts, and specialized websites.

Our goal in consulting topical authorities is to become educated enough that we can speak knowledgeably beyond just our personal opinion and experience. Even if we already know a lot about a topic, we need to consult authorities to validate our assumptions and identify credible sources to use in our speech.

Consider Knowledge Gaps

How long should an entry-level résumé be? One page, right? Not necessarily. When I was giving presentations on résumé writing for college students and recent graduates, I researched all the articles on the topic in scholarly journals. I also interviewed résumé-writing experts, including the heads of human resources departments. I eventually wrote a book on writing résumés.

Among other things, I discovered that it was not necessary to limit a résumé to one page. Many technical fields welcome longer résumés that include related university course content, projects, papers, and presentations. Also, most authorities say that extracurricular and nonpaid work experience such as volunteering and cross-cultural travel are worth including on résumés, even if they require two pages. My one-page assumption was erroneous. Research proved me wrong.

Know Personal Biases

Never underestimate the power of personal biases, which I address from several angles in this book. We all believe many untrue things.

We live in the midst of *misinformation* (unintentionally erroneous information) and *disinformation* (intentionally erroneous information). Many websites and blogs disseminate unproven knowledge. We all fall victim to *confirmation bias*—seeking and believing information that confirms our existing assumptions about a topic. This is why we should not finalize our MAIN IDEA until conducting adequate research. We might be telling ourselves just what we want to hear, not what is accurate.

Whatever topic we eventually adopt for a speech, we have to become knowledgeable. Otherwise we too might spread false or misleading information.

If I were giving a speech today on résumé length for recent university graduates, my informative MAIN IDEA might be: "Research shows that it is advantageous to use a two-page résumé when the type of job and the extent of our extracurricular and life experiences warrant it." My MAIN IDEA could be refined for a persuasive speech (e.g., to change my audience's largely negative assumptions about using two-page résumés).

Moreover, I would quote some specific authorities who surveyed employers and published the results in respected publications. I would expect that my audience might not believe my word alone. After all, the one-page résumé bias is widely held and taught.

Refine and Change Topics

When we research a topic, we almost always discover unexpected insights. In fact, if we have not discovered anything new, we probably have not adequately researched our topic. Topical research is like digging into the Greek or Hebrew text to understand a Bible passage. We will be surprised.

Two common results from our speech research are (1) *topical overload*, or far too much information on a topic for us to deal with, and (2) *topical revelations*, or unexpected truths about a topic that might even challenge our assumptions.

General and Specific Speech Topics	
General: fixing a bicycle **Specific:** truing bicycle wheel rims	**General:** forgiveness **Specific:** forgiving a former friend
General: how to study **Specific:** how to study for a reading quiz	**General:** Facebook **Specific:** Facebook privacy settings
General: Disney World **Specific:** the best rides at Disney World	**General:** eating out on a budget **Specific:** the best under-$5 take-out breakfasts
General: sin **Specific:** the sin of pride	

Overcome Information Overload

When we search the internet for topics like résumé writing or stress reduction, we will be overwhelmed with information. Even just trying to figure out who the authorities are is challenging. This is not all bad. We want to make sure we are casting a wide enough net so we do not overlook essential information.

We need to refine our topic enough that we can become well informed—both for the speech and the follow-up Q&A. The earlier we conduct research in our speech-preparation process, the better. Our speech needs to be narrow and specific.

Gain Aha Insights

Often, boring speeches are the ones that merely tell the audience what it already knows about a topic. They lack new and interesting insights.

As servant speakers, we look to offer the unexpected. We aim for an "aha moment" (*Wow, I didn't know that!*) that will gain audience attention and keep the audience interested (*Tell me more!*). The point is to be insightful, not gimmicky. Such unexpected speech content can be a revelation to the audience.

One young man's speech to other university students started like this: "I'm a shy guy. I hate asking women out in person. So I decided to learn how and when to do it effectively using text messaging. Here's what I discovered."

He had four main points, all of which he tested out: (1) don't text the request late at night (too creepy), (2) never ask specifically for a date (too forward), (3) suggest meeting for coffee or dessert at a public place off campus (for privacy from nosy and gossipy students), and (4) say that she can bring a friend if she wants to (she will not, but it gives her the option if she is uncomfortable). They all struck me as aha moments. The Q&A discussion was wonderful.

Perhaps the most audience-engaging aha moment I regularly offer in speeches is an expression from ancient monasteries: "Speak only if you can improve upon the silence." I always hear immediate audience responses to that single sentence—typically a chorus of soft laughter.

Then I say something like this: "Imagine if politicians lived by that rule!" The audience erupts. That aha moment sets me up to answer

SERVANT SPEAKING TIP

Write down your aha moments: those times when you run across information that challenges your assumptions.

a question: "How can we determine when our own speech is better than our silence?"

The eyeglass experts revealed to me how to match frames to facial features. I had naively assumed that if the frames looked good to me in a two-dimensional mirror, I had done my research. They taught me that other people will perceive my glasses differently than I will and that I should not depend too much on my own viewpoint.

How can we know if a fact or idea we discover in our research would actually be an aha moment for our audience? We can test it with a few people who represent our likely audience. Even just bringing it up in conversation can help us determine potential audience interest.

I aim for two or three aha moments in each speech. When I speak informally with audience members after the Q&A, they nearly always tell me that they "really liked" those particular points. We all appreciate learning something new, especially if it is counterintuitive but does not fundamentally challenge our existing beliefs.

Assess Recent Information

We often serve our neighbors by offering a fresh perspective on a proven topic of interest. It is not always easy to offer something fresh about a stale topic, and we might find that we have to be very careful about using the latest research.

Suppose we are going to give a persuasive speech about a new weight-loss diet. We discover current research about using nutritional ketosis to lose

IN THE SPOTLIGHT

Checklist for Topical Research

- I narrowed my speech topic so I could research it well without being swamped with unmanageable quantities of information.
- I found aha material to give my audience fresh ideas, a new perspective, or an unexpected example/illustration.
- I refined the topic as I reviewed primary and secondary sources.
- I made sure that the refined topic is relevant to representatives of the likely audience (i.e., I discussed the topic with people who represent the audience, or I found secondary sources that discuss the relevance of the topic for this kind of audience).
- I searched relevant secondary sources (e.g., books, professional journals, magazines, newspapers, reference works, and the internet).
- In the case of information found on the internet, I verified the sources and evaluated their credibility.
- Where relevant, I sought information and perspective from Christian as well as mainstream authorities on the topic.
- I found and considered information contrary to my Main Idea.
- I gained enough knowledge of the topic that I know what I am talking about and what I should not talk about.

weight and fight type 2 diabetes. The basic idea is to eat more "good" fat while drastically reducing carbohydrate intake with only moderate protein. Our MAIN IDEA would defy everyday assumptions about the value of consuming low-fat products. It would be an aha moment for most listeners. But would they believe us? Should they?

We would have to be very careful about our research on this topic. Moreover, as medical researchers continue their work, they might discover that such diets have other problems. We ought to indicate that our findings are new and not completely proven—but worth consideration.

Conduct Audience Research

Another form of research in speech preparation focuses on our likely audience. To whom will we be speaking? What do we need to know about the audience in order to settle on a topic, compose a MAIN IDEA and outline, and adapt our speech to serve the particular group? We also need to know what our audience already thinks and believes about our topic—its assumptions and biases.

If we cannot talk directly with likely members of our audience, we can learn from *representative* members of the audience—people who are like our audience.

When I speak in chapel and classes on various university campuses, I prefer to arrive a day early so I can chat with people. I nearly always spend time at a campus café, introducing myself to some students and asking them confidentially what students are thinking and talking about on campus. I then borrow some of those themes for my speaking, using examples that will fit with my overall

 IN THE SPOTLIGHT

Checklist for Audience Adaptation

- What do audience members already know about the topic?
- What concrete examples or illustrations would most interest them?
- What are their existing feelings, attitudes, and beliefs (predispositions) toward the topic?
- What might they assume about you and your motives—i.e., what is your relationship to some or all members of the audience?
- What are the relationships among members of the audience—i.e., are they friends, colleagues, or perhaps even representatives of different groups with contrasting views of you and your topic?
- What might they expect to hear or not hear about the topic, given the event or occasion—and how will you address such expectations?
- Are they likely to be sensitive—for good or bad—to a faith perspective?
- What kind of rhetorical style would be proper—e.g., strongly encouraging, mildly questioning, wondering out loud, or directly challenging? How would a particular style fit with your speaking purpose—to inform, persuade, or delight?

SERVANT SPEAKING TIP

A good rule of thumb is to do enough audience research to determine the assumptions the audience members likely hold about your topic.

speech. In other words, I fine-tune my chapel addresses with local, relevant, audience-related examples derived from firsthand conversations with likely members of my audience.

Even if you are going to be speaking to a public-speaking group or class, ask them what they think about your topic and approach. If you know a half-dozen people in the group, send them an email to seek their opinions or ideas. Chances are they will ask your advice about their topics as well. This kind of communication contributes to group trust and makes for more audience-focused speeches.

The apostle Paul typically visited churches before he began writing to them. His letters, which were read out loud in churches, referenced many of the relationships he formed through church visits. The visits were his audience research.

IN THE SPOTLIGHT

Checklist for Audience Research

- I described the profile of my audience-neighbors in one sentence with enough specificity that I can imagine who they are (e.g., their demographics, interests, values, and concerns).
- I determined why this audience would want to listen to me, what it would assume about me, and what it might expect from me in the situation.
- I spoke with people who represent the audience (according to the above profile), asking them for their feelings about the topic, how I might serve them, and what they would say if they were to give the speech.
- I searched secondary sources for information about what the audience likely knows or assumes about the topic. If the information seemed contradictory or incomplete, I shared it with likely representatives of the audience to gain their insights.
- If possible, I spoke in advance with someone who will be in the actual audience.
- If possible, I shared an outline of the speech in advance with representatives of the audience to get their feelings about how I could better serve them.
- I reviewed the language and visual illustrations in the speech to make sure that none of the material might offend the audience, seeking advice as needed from representatives of the audience.
- If appropriate, I considered the feelings of the audience toward issues of faith.
- As I became more audience focused, I imagined myself as a member of the group and sought to serve my audience-neighbors as I would want to be served.

When I asked the eyeglass saleswomen to give me feedback, I was using them as representatives of my everyday audience—not just as professionals. Although they were limited demographically—all younger women—they could better represent my eyeglass audience than I could. They worked with male customers. They had to accept returns from unhappy ones. They served me as members of the public as well as authorities on the topic.

Although we often think about public speaking as a one-way presentation, we best serve audiences by conducting our research as informed dialogue. In effect, we aim to join the conversations that are already taking place among members of our likely audiences. Audience research helps us do this.

Use Personal Knowledge

We are usually better off speaking about topics and to neighbors already familiar to us. Thoroughly researching a topic we know little about can be difficult and time consuming. Throwing a big net around a huge, unknown topic can also be frustrating.

When we speak instead on familiar topics, we do not have to burden ourselves with extensive research. Moreover, we can more easily determine audience needs, interests, and likely biases. After all, we can identify with the audience because we are also speaking to ourselves.

In other words, we can consider the needs and interests of those around us, whom we are more familiar with and can more personally serve as our audiences. These might include the needs in our own school, community, or church—even the needs in our own hearts. Then we can think about how we might research such needs, and perhaps offer more immediately helpful insights or even solutions. I find that almost anything that is either delighting or worrying me is also of interest to others.

When I start preparing a new speech for a new audience, I first look for topics that I know about and that the audience would likely be interested in. For instance, I still perform quick online searches using the topic (e.g., "storytelling") and my audience (e.g., "university students"). I know a fair amount already about using stories to engage students, but I want to make sure that I am familiar with newer theories and research. Then I feel confident that I can serve university students with stories. I deepen my personal knowledge and experience.

Conclusion

Research is a form of listening. To my benefit, I listened to the saleswomen at the eyeglass shop. They taught me about facial aesthetics and served me with an excellent frame selection. We humbly listen to authorities and audiences so we know what we are talking about, what our audience already knows and believes, and eventually how to craft our message.

Research can be overwhelming. But nothing destroys our credibility faster than being ill-informed, let alone wrong. Research can also give us (aha!) insights that make our speeches engaging. When we get enthused about our findings, we gain passion that will make us more compelling servant speakers.

FOR DISCUSSION

1. If you were giving this chapter as a speech, what one idea or quotation would you use as an aha moment in your speech? Why?

2. Imagine that you are in a speech audience. How would you go about researching the preexisting attitudes of people like you toward a given speech topic (make one up), using both primary and secondary sources?

3. What do you think would be the most important thing to research about any audience's receptivity to the gospel? Why?

4. How would you go about determining who the authorities are on a non-Christian faith?

NINE

Find and Evaluate
Online Sources

How might we cite a biblical passage in a speech when translations vary considerably? According to some Bible translations, for instance, the apostle Paul says that wives should "fear" their husbands. Others say that wives should "respect" them (Eph. 5:33). Should we select the translation that best supports our MAIN IDEA?

This is not just an issue regarding Bible knowledge. It pertains to all knowledge. As I said in the last chapter, we usually need to consult authorities on our topic. For instance, we should consult experts on topics like climate change, social media addiction, and fake news. But who are the authorities? How can we know for sure?

The easiest way for most of us to access information about nearly any topic is through online research. But the internet is peppered with biased and false information.

This chapter addresses both how to find and evaluate credibility, especially for online sources. As servant speakers, we need to rely discerningly on the most credible authorities.

Step 1: Define Topical Language

Initially, we need to explore how others, especially authorities, talk about our topic. This helps us clarify our topic before doing more in-depth research. We define our topic as clearly as possible.

Sources use different language, often with subtle but important meanings. For example, what is the difference between "global warming" and "climate change"? Similarly, what does the word "addiction" mean in a phrase such as "social media addiction"? What is "online bullying" or "online dating"? Experts do not always agree on terminology. Generally speaking, the sources who define terms clearly are more credible. The less credible sources use similar language loosely, without definitions.

In a speech on casual business dress, a student found various definitions online and then checked with some area companies' human resources departments. He discovered that organizational policies differed, as did online definitions. His MAIN IDEA was that even before going for a job interview, one needs to check with people who work at the location about appropriate dress. And he explained how to use a university alumni database to connect with current employees to ask them what attire they would recommend for interviewees at their companies.

IN THE SPOTLIGHT

Initial Online Research

- How do Wikipedia and other websites define my topic?
- What are the existing conversations or debates about my topic?
- Who seem to be the experts or authorities on the topic?

Wikipedia is one of the best places to begin exploring topical definitions, but we should not use it exclusively or cite it as a credible source since it relies on other sources. Wikipedia publishes information contributed by various individuals, some of whom are experts. Also, material submitted for particular topics is reviewed by experts and revised as needed. Wikipedia's footnotes, "Further Reading" sections, and "External Links" provide additional sources.

Step 2: Consult with Research Experts

Once we have defined our topic with preliminary research, we need to make sure that we know how to research it well. We might ask two or three knowledgeable people how they would research the topic before we get too deeply into our own online research. Otherwise, we might waste considerable time searching the internet.

Research Librarians

Research librarians offer excellent advice. Library websites often list staff with contact information. Library information desks are staffed with people who can answer our questions or direct us to others. Some have research librarians available online for immediate chat.

> **SERVANT SPEAKING TIP**
>
> Always do preliminary research to define your topic before seeking expert advice on the best ways to research it. Otherwise, it will look like you are just trying to get others to do the research for you.

Instructors

Many teachers are helpful sources for the best research methods. If we have already done our preliminary topical research, and consulted a librarian, most instructors will gladly suggest how we might proceed. They might recommend specific books, articles, websites, or other people to consult.

Experts at Teaching Skills/Processes

When we are speaking informatively to teach a skill or demonstrate a process, our research might include how to teach our topic. Some experts on our topic might not know how to teach it well. A great chef is not always a terrific cooking teacher.

The phrase "how to teach," used with our topic (e.g., "how to teach personal finance"), usually produces valuable online results. When I searched that topic online, the first listing that came up was a *Forbes* article titled "How to Stop Boring Students When Teaching Personal Finance."

Sometimes we can interview local experts who teach particular skills. If there are significant differences of opinion about how best to instruct others on our topic, we can ask experts to help us understand and evaluate the variations. We might be able to use them as primary research sources for our topic as well. A professor of personal finance or a financial adviser probably has helpful tips for teaching the topic.

Step 3: Find Authoritative Sources

Most persuasive and informative speeches are based partly on secondary research about what others say about a topic. We need to locate the most trustworthy secondary sources. By citing them, we gain audience credibility.

Broadly speaking, secondary research includes public websites, periodicals/media websites, and perhaps some scholarly/research publications and books.

Search Public Websites

The easiest way to research speech topics is on the open internet. We need to find information on trustworthy websites and beware of personal websites, such as many blogs, podcasts, and video materials produced by nonexperts. Adding "edu" (educational websites) or "org" (nonprofit websites) to our searches often helps. Most search engines' "advanced search" options also provide a way to find recently published information. We can also return to Wikipedia and further explore footnoted sources.

Search Fee-Based Periodicals/Media Websites

Not all websites are fully accessible, even though links to the sites might appear in our online search results. Some allow a limited number of free monthly searches—such as the *New York Times*, *Wall Street Journal*, *Washington Post*, *Atlantic*, and *Medium*. Many of those that charge for access are available free at libraries.

Search Books

Books are among the best sources for servant speakers. They can provide depth, analysis, and bibliographies. Many authorities write books.

SEARCH A LIBRARY

We should search a nearby library's book catalog, in person at the library or online via its website, using our topical keywords—such as "social media addiction" or "how to do a video interview." Then we can note the Library of Congress (LOC) call number for each book on the topic. Finally, we can go directly to the library's bookshelves where those books are located and see what other books are available on the same shelves.

If we are having trouble finding relevant books via LOC numbers, we can search the US Library of Congress book catalog, which is one of the largest collections of English-language books in the world.[1] Many libraries can borrow books from other libraries for us. We might discover the one book that is exactly what we need.

SEARCH GOOGLE BOOKS AND GOOGLE SCHOLAR

Google Books (https://books.google.com) is a major collection of searchable books and other print materials. Most book and many periodical publishers allow their material to be searched on the site. The "advanced book search" feature includes ways of searching by author, topic, and publication. Google Scholar is a similar database focused primarily on scholarly sources.

Some publishers allow only short book excerpts to be displayed in Google Book search results, but usually we can access enough context to know if we ought to track down a copy of the book at a library.

SEARCH AMAZON

Online bookseller Amazon (http://amazon.com) is searchable both for books and within most individual books (the "Look Inside" feature). The website's "Advanced Search" for books includes keywords for author, title, publication dates, and more. Often, only the first part of a book is fully readable, but usually authors summarize their MAIN IDEAS in an introduction or first chapter. Moreover, publishers provide book endorsements on Amazon as well as on most back covers, viewable on the site. The endorsements help us evaluate an author's credibility.

Step 4: Evaluate the Credibility of Secondary Sources

When we use secondary sources, we need to evaluate their *credibility* (trustworthiness). Are they honest and truly knowledgeable—even legitimate experts? If we are speaking about Scripture, for instance, we need to consult biblical authorities rather than just popular writers or speakers. Instead of merely accepting the validity of all the information we find, we should focus on information from the most respected and authoritative sources.

If we are persuading our audience to support a public referendum on a voting rights proposal, we need to know whom we can trust on the issue, especially related to the likely impact of adopting or rejecting the proposal. If we are informing our audience about diet programs, we need to find the most objective sources, even if they disagree.

This is not easy. Surfing the internet can be like walking through a supermarket and asking the average customer for advice on purchasing the most nutritious bread. We need to know what we mean by nutritious and find nutritional experts who can help us.

> ## Quotations on the Internet
>
> Not long ago I was talking to Abraham Lincoln and he told me, "The thing about quotes on the internet is that you cannot confirm their validity." My reply to him was that I thought C. S. Lewis had actually made that statement! Of course, I'm making this up; I've never spoken to Lincoln and I don't believe Lewis ever said it. However, there are many quotations floating around online that are attributed to Lewis that he actually never wrote.
>
> "Quotes NOT by Lewis: A Preliminary Examination," *C. S. Lewis Minute* (blog), January 26, 2014, https://lewisminute.wordpress.com/2014/01/26/quotes-not-by-lewis-a-preliminary-examination/

Check the Sources of Quotations

Popular quotations are notoriously suspect. Just because a quotation appears in a print publication or online does not mean that it is true, accurate, or properly attributed. Even well-known books of quotations do not confirm the quotation's validity. Two respected collections are the *Oxford Dictionary of Quotations* and the *Yale Book of Quotations*. The internet includes websites run by experts dedicated to determining if quotations attributed to particular well-known persons are true and accurate.

I have been unable to document the source of a quote frequently attributed to St. Francis of Assisi: "Preach the gospel always; if necessary, use words." From what I can tell, variations of the quotation have been used in thousands of books and many more articles, as well as on plaques, in greeting cards, and even on T-shirts. Ironically, during his lifetime Francis was better known for his preaching than his lifestyle.[2]

Check Sources' Credentials

When we quote others directly or use information from them, we need to consider their *credentials*—their qualifications or achievements related to our topic. What makes them an authority on our topic?

This is critically important for online research. The visual attractiveness of a website and its high search-engine ranking do not guarantee credibility. Neither does an apparent authority's notoriety, including how often the person is quoted.

Credibility includes four major criteria: educational background, professional membership, publications, and endorsements.

Educational Background

What is the person's education? Did they attend a university? What level of education do they have—perhaps a master's or doctoral degree? What fields are their degrees in?

Professional Membership

Is the person a member of and presumably involved in a professional association? Normally their biography would indicate such activity. We can visit the organization's website for information.

Publications

Has the person published any articles and books, or only a blog? Are the person's articles/essays in popular magazines and newspapers or in scholarly journals? Articles in the latter are generally reviewed by other authorities and demonstrate accepted expertise on a subject.

Just because a book is a best seller does not guarantee that the ideas in the book have been reviewed by experts. If the person has written books, are they for a general public audience or for other authorities? Among the most authoritative publishers are university presses (e.g., The University of Chicago Press) and other academic publishers. Among the least-respected publishers are so-called vanity presses like Amazon's own CreateSpace, which essentially lets anyone publish a book. Some self-published books are excellent; we just need to determine the credibility of those who have endorsed the book. Amazon lists publishers and the major endorsements for most books.

In general, books by Christian authors and Christian publishing houses need to be similarly scrutinized.

Endorsements

Who has recognized the author's work? Often endorsements are listed on the back of books or on the author's or publisher's website. Sometimes there will be additional endorsements in the book's first few pages, which can be previewed on Amazon. If the endorsers are themselves experts who meet the above criteria, chances are the author is a credible source.

Examine Websites' Credibility

The existence of a website does not make the content credible. Websites' credibility includes three major elements: personal versus organizational sponsorship, the quality of writing, and sources.

Personal versus Organizational Sponsorships

Many websites are essentially personal blogs that may not be credible. Some experts do have their own highly respected websites that help general readers understand their work. If the personal website does not provide a substantive biography, chances are the person is not an authority on the topic.

Organizationally sponsored websites are more likely to be authoritative. For instance, the prestigious Mayo Clinic's website has more credibility than one for an individual physician or a local medical practice. Similarly, the website for the National Communication Association is more authoritative than one for any individual communication expert.

Quality of Writing

The quality of writing on a website often reflects the quality of thought. Highly personal and opinionated writing suggests a lack of thoughtfulness. Grammatical errors and awkward prose suggest that the writer is not a careful thinker.

Sources

What secondary sources does the website cite? Does it use specific, verifiable citations, including publications with page numbers? Or does the site seem to speak only in generalities, suggesting that the writing is not based on careful research?

Step 5: Use Sources Honestly

Our own credibility as servant speakers includes not just our speech content and style but also how we use sources. The sources we cite, and what we claim about them, can lead our audience-neighbors to accept or question our trustworthiness.

Identify Plagiarism

Plagiarism is passing off someone else's ideas and expressions as our own. Failing to give credit to the source of an idea, let alone for specific quotes or data, is plagiarism. So is using ideas from someone else's publications or speeches without acknowledging them as a source. When we plagiarize others, we fail to respect them as our neighbors. We become poor stewards of knowledge.

Avoid Fabrication

Fabrication is making up data, examples, findings, or other information. Not only should we never fabricate but we need to cross-check our sources against other sources to make sure that we are not victims of others' fabrication.

Unintentional fabrication includes uncritically accepting and then passing along as fact what someone else says or writes that is objectively false. For instance, is a company's logo truly a satanic symbol? Do microwave ovens actually cook food from the inside out? Can music affect us subliminally? What does the Bible say about drinking alcohol?

No matter how many times people claim something is true, we still need to verify it in order to avoid unintentional fabrication.

One way to avoid even unintentional fabrication is by checking secondary sources against primary ones. If one source quotes another source, verify the original. When this is not possible, acknowledge that the quotation is from a secondary source: "Author and communication professor Quentin Schultze, PhD, quotes Augustine as saying . . ."

Step 6: Cite Sources in Speeches

We usually should cite our sources in our speeches. Some audience members might want to follow up with their own research on our topic. And we gain credibility by citing credible sources.

In most cases we will not be able to cite in our speech all the credible sources we examined during our research. Speeches that continually cite sources are boring and awkward. We probably do not want to cite more than two or three sources per minute in a typical speech. If needed,

IN THE SPOTLIGHT

Citing Sources and Using Quotations in Speeches

- Cite the source at the beginning of a quotation (e.g., "Dr. James Footnote, author of the recent Texas University Press book *Citations Are a Hassle*, says . . ." or "Our own campus professor and citations expert Dr. David Originales says that when quoting a source, cite the source first and then read the quotation, pausing at the end of the quotation instead of saying 'quote' or 'unquote' at the beginning or end of the quotation").

- Give only the essential parts of a citation, such as author name(s), credentials/position, publisher (such as a journal, podcast, website, or book publisher), and the general date (usually the year).

- Cite primary research as your own work (e.g., "In a recent video interview I conducted with Professor Lactose from our Nutrition Department, he said . . .").

we can quickly summarize our main sources in our speech introduction, but that is awkward as well.

One option is to list on a screen projection or distribute on a printed handout the full citations for our research sources. Then we can simply direct our audience to the list and use only the last names of our sources when we refer to them.

Normally, however, we adequately cite sources, with their credentials, when we refer to them in our speech.

Conclusion

Researching our speech topic is somewhat like studying the Bible. We need to avoid letting our own assumptions and superficial conclusions dictate how we understand a topic. We are not biblical authorities, so we depend on experts to help us. Otherwise, we might just pass along our ignorance to others. In effect, we have to become mini-authorities on our narrowed-down topics.

FOR DISCUSSION

1. How would you go about using the internet to begin researching a currently controversial news topic for an informative speech?

2. Can you think of any speech topics where the experts would not be scholars or researchers or where scholarly journals and prestigious university press books would not be helpful and credible sources?

3. Use three different search engines (e.g., Bing, Google, and DuckDuckGo) to search exactly the same words/topic. What do the different results/rankings suggest about the objectivity or subjectivity of such results?

4. Search YouTube for two videos on using credible sources in public speaking. What do those videos suggest? What do they use as sources for their own claims? Are the producers of the videos themselves credible sources? How do you know?

TEN

Be Trustworthy (Ethos 1)

"What is truth?" That was Pontius Pilate's line to Jesus just before freeing Barabbas and sentencing Jesus to death. Pilate found "no fault" with Jesus (John 18:38). That finding was true even if Pilate did not believe it.

As servant speakers, we claim to speak truthfully. But do we? Is it just about being factual? What about speaking the whole truth? Or exaggerating a little?

Truth-telling is not just about what we say but also about how we relate to people. In public speaking, truth-telling reflects our respect for the audience. Are we true to our audiences? Do we honor them as God's image bearers? How we think about and act toward our audience establishes part of our *ethos*—our perceived credibility.

Servant speaking requires us to be true to God, our audiences, and ourselves. Avoiding lies is only the beginning. This chapter addresses trustworthiness as an essential part of servant speaking. It considers being true persons, lying, privacy, the whole truth, exaggeration, and personal opinion.

Be True

As servant speakers, we are true to our audience. We do not want merely to give a truthful impression. We want to build trust by being trustworthy. "Being true" is a relationship built on trust.

In other words, when we speak to an audience, we take up a moral relationship of mutual trust. It is similar to the trust in a marriage or personal friendship. Our audience rightly wants to trust us.

> **SERVANT SPEAKING TIP**
>
> To become a thoroughly truth-telling public speaker, think of your life as a testimony to truth. Be truthful in everything you say and do. Deceptive speakers live deceptive lives; deceptive persons become dishonest speakers.

When we listen to a sermon, for instance, we expect that the preacher has dug deeply into Scripture and is sharing biblical truth. Presumably the preacher aims to meet our expectation.

One student gave a passionate and moving class speech on abortion. She opened by revealing that she had had one a year earlier. After her speech, however, she admitted to some students in the room that she had made up the personal abortion story to gain audience attention and credibility. Her technique initially worked, but her admission destroyed trust.

In short, we need to know that we can depend on a speaker to be informed, candid, and straightforward with us. It is not personally up to the speaker to decide if the audience deserves the speaker's trustworthiness. That would be disrespectful. We are called to be stewards of trust.

In order to build true relationships, we implicitly promise others what they can rightly expect from us. The same holds implicitly true for our speaking. We do not need to take oaths because a mere oath does not guarantee our trustworthiness. People can swear (or promise) many things but never live up to them. Our yes should be yes, and our no should be no (Matt. 5:37).

Being trustworthy or untrustworthy is an attitude toward others that takes root in our hearts, where our God-honoring and sinful desires both reside. We can easily say to ourselves that we wholeheartedly deserve our audience's trust. But do we really? Will we ever be tempted to tell half-truths or just bend the truth a little? Will we ever say things designed to make us look good rather than to serve our trusting audience?

Behind all of our speaking is our own untrustworthiness. It is like the camel's nose in the tent of our heart. After a while, the camel can move in and take over the entire tent. If we claim to be without sin we are deceiving ourselves, and the truth is not really in our hearts (1 John 1:8).

As we research information, we can ask God to search our hearts and test us (Ps. 139:23–24). Are we honestly aiming to serve God and our audience as best we can? If so, we are not just preparing to be a true speaker; we are also preparing for a true life.

Reject Lying

According to Augustine, a lie is never acceptable.[1] Even if speaking the truth might cause harm to others, he argued, we must tell that truth or remain silent. But what if a democratic leader lies in a public speech in order to confuse an authoritarian enemy in the midst of military battle? Would that be unethical?

In ethics, a lie has a narrow but essential definition. A *lie* is a statement intended to deceive. To lie, we have to know that what we are saying is untrue when we say it. Intentionality reveals our motive. We might be sloppy speakers who unintentionally pass along nonfactual information. But that does not make us liars.

Scripture, including one of the Ten Commandments, affirms that we should not make statements we know are untrue. For instance, we ought never give false testimony against our neighbor (Exod. 20:16). We should speak only truthfully about others.

In public speaking, truth-telling is essential for trust. Even if we *misspeak* (unintentionally make a false, misleading, or at least confusing statement), and someone in the audience assumes what we said is false, that person might lose trust in us.

IN THE SPOTLIGHT

Tough Questions Regarding Truthful Speaking

- *Should we ever lie—or at least bend the truth?* Is it okay to change someone's name to protect their privacy in a story we tell about them? What about exaggerating a bit?

- *Should we always speak the whole truth?* What if a hundred books are written on our speech topic? Do we need to examine all of them? Should we ever leave out of our speech something that is true but contrary to our MAIN IDEA?

- *Should we ever express personal opinions in a speech?* If so, should we reveal to our audience our opinions on our topic even if speaking informatively?

- *Should we consult different interpretations (versions) of Bible passages?* Is it acceptable in a speech to use only the interpretation that we prefer?

If we thought that what we said was accurate, we might be able to regain some trust. If during the Q&A, for instance, an authority on the subject corrects us, we can simply admit that we were wrong, but add that we thought we were accurate—perhaps by giving the source of our misinformation.

We need to be as informed about our topic as possible, given the time we have to prepare for speeches. If anything sounds even a bit untrue to us, we can check it out thoroughly with adequate research. If we are using facts and quotations, we need to confirm them.

Protect Privacy

A difficult issue in public speaking is protecting others' privacy. Should we ever reveal personal information about another person? What if the information is a concrete story that will effectively engage our audience and make our point? Can we legitimately bend the facts to protect privacy?

We first might seek permission to use a person's name. Even without using a name, however, listeners might be able to identify the person. I struggled with this over the years because I had so many great examples of good and poor communication from my own family, students, and friends.

If a person will not give us permission to use a terrific story, we might alter the story enough to protect privacy. If I believe that I will best serve my audience by using a particular story, but I do not have permission to use it, I consider making it more generic, without identifiable details.

I needed to consider privacy issues while I was deciding what to include in this book. I have had to adjust students' and colleagues' anecdotes in order to protect the particular people involved. If the person is a close relative, for instance, I might instead refer to the person in my speech as a friend. If the setting is a particular location, I might change it to a similar place.

Some servant speakers are not comfortable with altering story details. They believe it is lying. In defense, I say that I focus on the truth of the lesson behind the story, not on the details of the story. I use a fictionalized story to convey my message. Am I justified in doing so?

Seek Nearly Whole Truth

Courtroom dramas capture the promise people make when giving testimony: "Do you swear (or promise) to tell the truth, the whole truth, and nothing but the truth, so help you God?" Can we possibly meet that standard in our servant speaking?

Capturing the whole truth is impossible for us. No matter what we are speaking about, our knowledge is limited. Even topical authorities cannot know everything. While working on a speech, we will often uncover far more helpful information than we can possibly use. We might examine only the parts that seem most topically relevant.

Writing speeches involves a lot of informational pruning. We are guided by both our speaking purpose and our emerging Main Idea. No two people who research the same topic will end up with the same speech. Yet we have to make

IN THE SPOTLIGHT

Avoiding Deceptive Use of Sources

- Have I used all sources fairly without twisting their words or including only the material that supports my Main Idea?
- Have I researched and examined sources that hold views contrary to my Main Idea?
- Have I represented my sources' credentials fairly?

sure that we are not intentionally or unintentionally leaving out relevant and important information from credible authorities on the topic.

When pressed for time, we will be tempted to use information that supports our MAIN IDEA and simply ignore material that does not. This is not itself lying but can be deceptive. It also disrespects our audience. One way to address this problem of not being able to know or tell the whole truth from credible authorities is to admit to our audiences that there are other views, arguments, and data. To some extent, audiences already assume that we are being self-selective about what we cover in a speech. Still, making this explicit is important for credibility.

Exaggerate Fairly

Speaking publicly to his disciples and crowds, Jesus said, "The greatest among you will be your servant. For those who exalt themselves will be humbled, and those who humble themselves will be exalted" (Matt. 23:11–12).

Then he turned to the teachers of the law and Pharisees, delivering a brutal attack in the form of seven "woes." Jesus said they "strain out a gnat but swallow a camel" (Matt. 23:24). He meant that the corrupt leaders tended to focus on relatively minor parts of the law while ignoring the greater ones—like justice, mercy, and faithfulness (v. 23). He criticized the legalists and literalists who intentionally avoided the very heart of God's law in order to look more righteous. Jesus used figures of speech—such as metaphors and similes—to speak powerfully.

Use Figures of Speech Carefully

In servant speaking, we often use *figures of speech*—language that is figuratively (or metaphorically) rather than literally true. None of the Pharisees could actually swallow a camel, but the imagery is striking. Similes, metaphors, and other literary techniques can sometimes get at the truth better than straightforward literal language can.

Exaggeration—especially *hyperbole*, exaggeration for effect—is an important technique in servant speaking.

Scripture is filled with hyperbolic language. The Psalms, in particular, stretch us beyond our earthly understanding. They use figures of speech that greatly enrich our faith with the deep truth of our sinful condition and the reality of God's inestimable love for us even before we were born. Our tears are our food (Ps. 42:3). The heavens declare the glory of God;

they "pour forth speech" and "reveal knowledge" even though they "use no words" (Ps. 19:1–3).

In other words, using figures of speech is not itself lying. The issue is when and how to use them so our audience will understand our meaning.

Use Precise Language

We serve our audience by using language precisely. As a colleague put it, we aim for "instant intelligibility." Our audience should not have to work at understanding exactly what we mean.

Figurative language can be a problem, especially with non-native English speakers. For instance, if we use the word "everyone," will the entire audience know that we mean only "most people" rather than literally everyone?

The language we use about our MAIN IDEA is particularly important. When we say that our research *proves* our MAIN IDEA, do we literally mean it? Or does our research merely *support* our MAIN IDEA? Will our audience understand the distinction?

Most linguistic confusion is caused by either the wrong word/phrase choices or by using language with multiple meanings depending on context. So we have to be precise, using all language carefully for shared understanding, taking our speech context and audience's level of English experience into account.

In a speech on gun laws, a student repeatedly used the term "assault weapon" interchangeably with "automatic weapon." During the Q&A another student pointed out that the word "assault" refers to what a weapon looks like, not whether the weapon is automatic. At that point, I think most students were completely confused.

Use Appropriate Flattery

Another aspect of trustworthiness is *flattery*—insincere and usually excessive praise of others. We all want others to like us, so we tend to say positive things about them. We even expect the same in return. But we can overdo it.

The apostle Paul said that some people in the early church used "smooth talk and flattery" to "deceive the minds of naive people" (Rom. 16:18). He said he never used flattery—and that God was his witness (1 Thess. 2:5).

We rightly could say good and positive things about others, but flattery can come across as insincere and reduce our overall credibility. We might use mild flattery when it is expected, such as when introducing someone. It would be disrespectful not to praise the speaker with some flowery language.

Some speakers try to increase their credibility by speaking glowingly about their sources. But is a particular source really an expert? *The* expert? A world-renowned authority? A leading authority? If we can document these kinds of claims, we can use such language appropriately.

For instance, perhaps a major professional association has given an award to one of our sources; we certainly might consider using that fact in our presentation. As much as possible, we can indicate why our sources are credible and authoritative. If we cannot, perhaps we are exaggerating the status of our sources.

Control Opinions

We all hold many personal opinions. For instance, we think more highly of some people than others.

I hold opinions about different Bible translations. I am not able to say professionally that one translation is definitely more accurate than another. I do not make Bible recommendations in my speeches even though I usually use my favorite one.

When I am not careful, I pepper my extemporaneous speeches with personal opinions. Sometimes they are unrelated comments about politics, education, popular books, celebrities, sports teams, movies, and the like. I am an opinionated person. Given all of my education and experience, I feel like I deserve to be. Arrogance is one of the camels poking its nose into my heart, waiting to take over the whole tent. It gets me into trouble. I identify with the apostle Paul: "For I do not do the good I want to do, but the evil I do not want to do—and this I keep on doing (Rom. 7:19).

Distinguish between Informed and Uninformed Opinions

Sometimes we hold opinions that we just pick up from others, with no basis in life experience or informed sources. Often our strongest uninformed opinions are attitudes, including prejudices.

Expressing uninformed opinions usually reduces our credibility. We come across as arrogant or foolish rather than understanding. The writer of Proverbs says, "Fools find no pleasure in understanding but delight in airing their own opinions" (Prov. 18:2).

If our speech-related opinion is informed, especially through personal experience and research, we might want to use it. Informed personal opinions can serve our audience well if we also use expert opinions. Still, opinions should be directly related to our topic.

Acknowledge Semi-informed Personal Opinions

Sometimes we have topic-relevant opinions that are reasonable even if not fully informed by extensive research or life experience. For instance, I have opinions on effective teaching based on years of experience, but they are not grounded in research.

When we express such semi-informed opinions, we can simply be transparent and humble: "This is my view, and I might be wrong."

Conclusion

We servant speakers are called to be trustworthy, which requires far more than just not lying. Before we consider what to say in our speeches, we have to examine our relationships with God, others, and ourselves. We need to make sure we are being true followers of Jesus Christ. Otherwise, the kinds of charges Jesus leveled at religious leaders in his day could be directed at us today. A clean heart with godly desires is essential for servant speaking.

Then we can focus on treating our audience respectfully as our neighbors. We will not do what is merely in our own interest but what is in the service of our audience, including how we reject lies, tell truth, protect privacy, exaggerate cautiously, speak precisely, and control our opinions.

FOR DISCUSSION

1. When might it be unethical to alter the details of a "true" story in a speech in order to protect the subject's privacy?
2. If a lie is a "statement intended to deceive," what exactly is a "statement"? Could it include an image, such as a photo?
3. How much research do you think we must do before concluding that we have more or less reviewed the "whole truth" about a topic? How shall we make that kind of decision?
4. How can we make our language most precise when speaking to an audience from various cultural backgrounds?

ELEVEN

Be Virtuous (Ethos 2)

A friend attended a lecture by a prominent biblical creationist who believes the earth is less than ten thousand years old. After being introduced, the speaker rapidly delivered a well-rehearsed slideshow that did not address disparities between scientific findings and a literal reading of the Bible.

During the Q&A, my friend asked, "Could you address the current disagreements between many scientists and creationists? For example, what about using scientific techniques to determine the age of the earth?"

"Those are irrelevant findings," replied the presenter. "After all, who speaks the truth, almighty God or secular scientists? The Bible is our textbook. Next question."

The Q&A pleased some attendees and frustrated others. Whether the creationist's arguments were right or wrong, my friend worried that the speaker's dismissive attitude toward critics would discredit Christianity.

This chapter addresses the importance of being *virtuous speakers*—speakers of good character with a positive ethos. We servant speakers aim to be not just effective but also worthy of imitation. We lead others partly by following Jesus Christ. We especially seek to conform our speaking to the fruit of the Spirit.

Imitate the Ethos of Jesus Christ

In *Rhetoric*, the ancient philosopher-rhetorician Aristotle identifies ethos as a critically important means of persuasion along with *logos* (logic)

SERVANT SPEAKING TIP

Avoid expressing your MAIN IDEA dogmatically, creating the impression that you are closed-minded.

and *pathos* (emotion). *Ethos* is the audience's conception of a speaker's character, especially their credibility.

The great Roman educator and orator Quintilian (35–96) said that rhetoric is a morally good person speaking well, or speaking carefully.[1] We make a good or bad name for ourselves partly through our communication. Whether we are posting on social media or teaching at church, we create an ethos that defines us in others' eyes.

As Christians, we speak in the name of Jesus as well as in our own names. Our ethos reflects Jesus's ethos. When we speak unkindly about others, for instance, we tarnish Jesus's and our own names.

Every phrase we utter, each of our bodily gestures, all of our rolling eyes and smirks, "speak" to our own and Jesus's perceived character. Our speech honors or stains Jesus's name and our own. Unlike the general rhetorical understanding of ethos, then, ours as servant speakers is grounded in a moral sense of responsibility to God.

Of course, just because we communicate like Jesus as persons of good character does not guarantee that others will agree with us or even like us. Jesus was crucified in spite of his praiseworthy character.

Be Worthy of Witness

Successful evangelism is complicated. But one rhetorical truth is that others will be more open to us if we are personally worthy of their attention. How we listen and speak to others is part of our witness. The apostle Paul wrote to the Colossians, "Let your conversation always be filled with grace, seasoned with salt, so that you may know how to answer everyone" (Col. 4:6).

Many religious leaders in Jesus's day were judgmental. They aimed their guilty verdicts at Jesus as well. They expected others to respect them, but they did not respect others. This attitude infected the church. Paul wrote, "Get rid of all bitterness, rage and anger, brawling and slander, along with every form of malice" (Eph. 4:31). This was preceded by these wise words, "Do not let any unwholesome talk come out of your mouths, but only what is helpful for building others up, according to their needs, that it may benefit those who listen" (4:29).

SERVANT SPEAKING TIP

Ask someone to read your speech outline or complete manuscript to see if any of the language seems disrespectful.

If we come across as critical persons, we will not gain listeners. We all tend to turn away from those who demean us. Shaming others, in particular, shuts down communication. It undermines our message of love. It gives others the impression that Jesus is a messenger merely of judgment and guilt, not of forgiveness and redemption.

Speak to Enemies as to Self

The word "enemy" seems militaristic and defamatory. Should we ever refer to people as enemies? Many psalms do (e.g., Ps. 35:1; 59:1). Jesus says, "But to you who are listening I say: Love your enemies, do good to those who hate you, bless those who curse you, pray for those who mistreat you" (Luke 6:27–28).

Some people are highly critical of Christians and the church. They use Jesus's name only in vain. A few YouTube speakers apparently enjoy belittling Christians. Some claim to be former believers. In short, our enemies are among our neighbors. We need to listen and speak to them just as we want to be listened to and respected. We are to be known in the world by our love (John 13:34–35).

We tend to assume that our enemies are unlike us. We feel threatened and grow fearful when we listen to those with different values and beliefs. We want to stand up for ourselves, our tribe, and the gospel. Yet our enemies are also God's image bearers.

Jesus and Paul say that we should be hospitable to the "strangers" among us (Matt. 25:35; Rom. 12:13). After all, we too are strangers who seek hospitality from others. We like to be listened to. We are delighted when nonbelievers listen to our story of faith. We feel respected.

When we stand before an audience, we hope and pray that our listeners will be hospitable toward us and our message. If they are not, we love them anyway. The first Christian martyr, Stephen, cried out after his stoning and just before he died, "Lord, do not hold this sin against them" (Acts 7:60). He echoed Jesus's own words of forgiveness on the cross (Luke 23:34).

SERVANT SPEAKING TIP

Write your speech with the mind-set of a hospitable host who wishes to honor, please, and serve your audience-guests even if they might not agree with you. Do this by imagining how those "strangers"—who might be critical of your MAIN IDEA— feel as guests in your audience.

Speak with Integrity in the Spirit

Servant speakers gain *integrity* by unifying their inner and outer selves. Teachers, for example, "speak" with their attitudes, not just their words. When their character contradicts what they teach, they lose credibility.

Paul describes Christian virtues partly as fruit of the Spirit, including love, joy, peace, patience, kindness, goodness, faithfulness, gentleness, and self-control (Gal. 5:22–23). These inner qualities of character, which ultimately are gifts, shape our outer actions. "May these words of my mouth and this meditation of my heart be pleasing in your sight, LORD, my Rock and my Redeemer," says the psalmist (Ps. 19:14). Our Spirit-led heart and mouth are meant to work together. Speaking with integrity in the Spirit requires Spirit-given inner direction as well as Spirit-motivated action.

Speak with a Joyful Heart

We joyfully serve audiences because we know that our knowledge, skills, and audiences are all gifts. Joy-shaped speech flows naturally from grateful hearts. Proverbs says, "A person finds joy in giving an apt reply—and how good is a timely word!" (15:23). We all prefer speakers who enjoy addressing us. Speakers cannot completely fake a joyful spirit, although sometimes they have to go through the motions because their own lives are so disheartening. When we sense that a speaker dislikes the task, we wonder if they care. Are they grateful for the opportunity? Do they value our attention? Students naturally like teachers who enjoy teaching, just as congregants appreciate ministers with joyful spirits. A person's joyful countenance elicits pleasure in audiences as long as it seems genuine and fits the situation.

Happiness means many different things to people. But perhaps our deepest happiness is a joyful heart that cannot be attained merely by circumstances or accomplishments. James Houston writes that true happiness "can only be complete when it is given to others." He adds, "This is one of the great keys to understanding happiness. It can never be grasped selfishly for our own sake, but must be shared."[2] The gift of language equips us to receive and share joy for real happiness, not just temporary fun. We naturally are attracted to joyful speakers partly because they give us joy.

Speak in Peace

We are called to be peacemakers (Matt. 5:9; Rom. 14:19). Therefore, when we wage verbal war on other persons and groups, we are not exhibiting the fruit of the Spirit.

Even when we disagree with others, we speak truth in love to promote peace. We avoid the temptation to engage in destructive rhetoric toward those we do not like or with whom we disagree. Our own rhetoric should not worsen conflicts and destroy dialogue. We avoid us-versus-them language and speak for shared interests.[3] When we need to speak critically, our words and tone ought never to sound like a battle cry.

Speak Patiently

Those of us in industrialized nations frequently find that day-to-day demands leave little time for cultivating patience. Russian dissident and author Aleksandr Solzhenitsyn (1918–2008) told university graduates that hastiness is a "psychic disease" of our era.[4]

Of course, excessive busyness and the resulting impatience are nothing new. Church critic Søren Kierkegaard (1813–55) wrote that "in the world of spirit, busyness, keeping up with others, hustling hither and yon, makes it almost impossible for an individual to form a heart, to become a responsible, alive self." He added, "It is absolutely unethical when one is so busy communicating that he forgets to be what he teaches."[5]

In the New Testament, the word "servant" partly means "waiting on" others. This language survives in English, such as restaurant servers who wait on customers. We servant speakers set aside time for researching, crafting, and rehearsing each presentation. We also deliver speeches patiently enough so that our audience has time to follow along, gain understanding, and formulate responses.

The opposite of patient speech is hasty, often hot-tempered and ill-considered rhetoric. There is "more hope for a fool" than for someone who speaks hastily (Prov. 29:20).

Of all types of public speaking, persuasion requires the most patience. We cannot easily change peoples' attitudes, beliefs, and actions. We have to aim for small, reasonable goals, sometimes just one step in the right direction.

Speak Kindly

Speaking unkindly of other persons or groups seems to be part of our DNA as fallen creatures. We all do it privately if not publicly. Hostility is especially common today, but we are set apart to be kind-hearted, kind-listening, kind-speaking servants. Kind words are sweet and healing (Prov. 16:24). Unkind words stir up anger (Prov. 15:1).

To foster kindness during Q&A, assume that any miscommunication during the speech was your own fault rather than that of the audience.

If our audience's critical views are similar to our own, we can easily fall into unkind public speaking as well. We are most susceptible to such shared unkindness when speaking on controversial issues.

There will be times when we feel called to be critical—like the Old Testament prophets, or like Jesus criticizing the temple peddlers. But criticism is rarely the place to begin. We start by listening and learning so we know what we are talking about and how to offer truth in love.

In his letter to the Colossians, Paul provided some rhetorical principles for being kind to audiences. "Be wise in the way you act toward outsiders," he wrote. "Make the most of every opportunity. Let your conversation be always full of grace, seasoned with salt, so that you may know how to answer everyone" (Col. 4:5–6).

Our speaking can convey sincere kindness toward others. Public kindness includes *communicative civility*—polite and courteous speech.

Unkind speech commonly includes *ad hominem* arguments—attacks on people's character, such as ridiculing, mocking, and verbally bullying others. Sometimes we question others' motives. It is difficult to know why someone is saying something. Judging others' apparent motives is often just cruel talk.

As servant speakers, we sometimes do expose others' foolishness, but not by unkindly calling them fools. We focus on others' statements, not on their characters. Otherwise we tarnish our own ethos as well.

A non-Christian friend complained to me about a wedding he attended where the pastor pleaded for attendees to accept Jesus or risk going to hell. Did the minister display kindness by preaching damnation at a celebratory event made up of Christians and non-Christians?

Augustine apparently posted the following sentence in large letters on the wall in his room: "Here we do not speak evil of anyone."[6] Augustine likely needed the reminder, because he sometimes spoke unkindly of his theological enemies.

Speak with Goodness

God originally created all things good, for his enjoyment and our flourishing (Gen. 1:31). We glorify the Lord by choosing good over evil. Our speaking is an opportunity to create

Address your opponents' ideas, not their character. Let your audience decide if an opponent is a good person.

goodness, especially when we respect and honor our neighbors.

I grew up in a working-class neighborhood where using obscene and profane language was common, especially among men. I learned how to employ cuss words, sexual innuendo, bathroom humor, and outrageously "funny" profanity. Four decades after becoming a Christian, some awful language still slips into my mind. The good thing is that I understand such language; I am not so quick to judge those who use it.

We do not need to be prudish, but neither should we use inappropriate words and examples that will offend. I used the word "hell" in a speech to a Christian audience, quoting what someone said to me. Some attendees gently criticized me afterward. Perhaps they were overly sensitive. More likely, I spoke inappropriately. I apologized. Every time I used that story in later speeches, I said "the *h* word" rather than the word itself. No one protested.

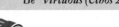

IN THE SPOTLIGHT

Common Types of Unkind Speech

- *Ridiculing*—making fun of others
- *Mocking*—negatively caricaturing someone's peculiarities
- *Bullying*—belittling and even threatening others
- *Gossiping*—talking about people behind their backs
- *Questioning motive*—questioning others' motives and intentions

Speak Faithfully

Every speech is an act of faith, since we cannot guarantee our intended results and we believe that the Holy Spirit is with us. Paul wrote, "My message and my preaching were not with wise and persuasive words, but with a demonstration of the Spirit's power, so that your faith might not rest on human wisdom, but on God's power" (1 Cor. 2:4–5).

Theologian and author Eugene H. Peterson realized as a young preacher that members of his congregation were yawning and sleeping. One woman gave him hope; every Sunday she took extensive sermon notes in shorthand. Peterson eventually learned that "she was getting ready to leave her husband and was using the hour of worship to practice her shorthand so she could get a self-supporting job."[7]

Once I drove several hours to speak at a large church. I was delighted to see a jammed parking lot. I went to the basement fellowship hall, where

IN THE SPOTLIGHT

Common Types of Bad Speech

- *Obscenity*—immodest, indecent talk
- *Profanity*—language that disrespects God and religion
- *Perversity*—corrupt, wicked speech

my three hosts warmly welcomed me. Then one of them apologized for the poor attendance and quickly offered a list of all the ways the publicity team had promoted the event.

"But it looks like a full house," I replied.

"Well," she said sheepishly, "the cars belong to people attending the packed Alcoholics Anonymous meeting upstairs. We are the only ones here for your presentation."

If we believe primarily in ourselves and other people, we are bound to be disappointed. We need more than skill and self-confidence. We need faith in a God who delivers audiences at his pleasure and guarantees results according to his will. Driving home that night, I thanked God for filling the AA meeting and emptying my ego.

Speak with Gentleness

Gentleness is vital for servant speakers. Paul appealed to the Corinthians "by the humility and gentleness of Christ" (2 Cor. 10:1). "A gentle tongue can break a bone," says Proverbs (25:15). Gentle speakers are mild-mannered toward their neighbors, even as they sometimes make forcefully persuasive arguments.

While strolling down Bourbon Street in New Orleans one evening, I came across three young street preachers who were yelling at a drunken college-age man sitting on the curb and desperately trying to stand up on his own. As one evangelist preached, the intoxicated man mumbled incoherently and tried to wave him away. Then the other two evangelists grabbed the reveler by the shoulders to hold him still so they could jam a Bible tract down his shirt. I wondered why they did not just gently try to help the man get home or find his friends. The growing audience was howling in laughter at the spectacle.

A mild-mannered spirit is better than an overbearing one. As Augustine told Christian speakers, a gentle person does not revel in controversy.[8]

---

1 Peter on Sharing Hope

But in your hearts revere Christ as Lord. Always be prepared to give an answer to everyone who asks you to give the reason for the hope that you have. But do this with gentleness and respect, keeping a clear conscience, so that those who speak maliciously against your good behavior in Christ may be ashamed of their slander.

1 Peter 3:15–16

Gentleness is one kind of loving witness. When Peter said that we should be prepared to give an answer to those who ask the reason for our hope, he added that we should respond gently (1 Pet. 3:15). Paul encouraged believers to make their gentleness evident to all (Phil. 4:5).

SERVANT SPEAKING TIP

Especially when speaking impromptu, go slow enough to think before you speak. Be your own best censor.

Speak with Self-Control

It is difficult to practice self-control in a provocative rhetorical climate where so many people are quick to speak and slow to listen. We can get caught up in the kind of rapid-fire rhetoric used in social media and on TV.

When someone disagrees with us, especially during our Q&A, we naturally become defensive and feel like we have to challenge our accuser. Yet that is when we most need restraint.

Even our hasty research and outlining can reflect a lack of self-discipline, including a negative tone. Before we know it, we will have written a speech out of self-indulgence rather than self-control. Our egos constantly challenge our self-control.

God's own self-control with us is beyond measure. We probably speak daily in ways that dishonor him. Who are we to lose control with others' speech?

With self-control, we speak apt words and offer others a timely, life-affirming reply (Prov. 15:23). Without it, we multiply words and crush people's spirits (Prov. 10:19; 15:4). Our uncontrolled tongues can control us (James 3:8). Our tongues are restless; they seem to have a will of their own, causing us to say things we will regret.

Every speech is an opportunity to regulate our communication. We get to self-censor what we say and how we say it. Without self-control, we are prone to trouble. For instance, we might say too much, violate others' privacy, belittle people, and twist the truth, sometimes even with admirable motives.

Simply put, we servant speakers think before speaking in order to conform our words to our faith. James warns us, "Those who consider themselves religious and yet do not keep a tight rein on their tongues deceive themselves, and their religion is worthless" (James 1:26).

Impromptu and extemporaneous speaking especially require self-control. It is so easy to

SERVANT SPEAKING TIP

After writing your expanded outline or first draft, put it away for a few days before revising it. Then review it with a fresh heart and open mind to determine if it reflects the fruit of the Spirit in your life.

let our egos run like wild horses. We avoid saying anything that our own conscience is questioning. Self-control requires listening to ourselves as we speak, editing ourselves as we hear the words developing in our minds before we utter them.

An ancient Jewish teaching says that human speech is like an arrow, not just a sword (Ps. 57:4; 64:3). A rabbi explains, "If a man unsheathes his sword to kill his friend, and his friend pleads with him and begs for mercy, the man may be mollified and return the sword to its scabbard." Once an arrow is shot, however, "it cannot be returned, no matter how much one wants to."[9] Without self-control, we become verbal archers who regret that we did not put our arrows back into our quivers.

Conclusion

If we are not careful, we will communicate like the world around us rather than in distinctively Christian ways that build our positive ethos, honor God by loving even our apparent enemies as ourselves, and open dialogue. Perhaps the creationist or his questioners spoke too hastily. Maybe they could have opened up a fruitful dialogue by speaking in tune with the fruit of the Spirit.

The church itself ought to be the most striking example of a community of virtuous communicators. In fellowship, we together imitate the Lord we follow. The fruit of the Spirit are gifts to speakers. We accept and nurture them in our hearts as people of Christlike character.

FOR DISCUSSION

1. How would you assess what happened in the Q&A with the creationist as described in the introduction to this chapter? Was anyone at fault? Could either the speaker or the questioner have acted more virtuously? If so, how?
2. What difference might it make if we thought of our audience members as "strangers" in the biblical sense (e.g., see Matt. 25:35 about welcoming the stranger)?
3. Explain and critique this claim: "How we listen and speak to others is part of our witness."
4. What have you most liked and admired about your favorite pastor or teacher? Are those outward attributes related to the internal work of the Spirit, as described in the fruit of the Spirit? If so, which fruit?

TWELVE

Convey Ideas Passionately

God told the prophet Jeremiah to show the Judeans a clay pot and then smash it to pieces to illustrate how God would deal with their disobedience (Jer. 19). Jeremiah would draw attention to God's forthcoming justice.

As servant speakers, we communicate passionately, using all the appropriate verbal and nonverbal means available. Augustine said that we should never "bore our listeners" and "stifle their desire to believe."[1]

Communicating well requires passionate verbal and nonverbal expressiveness. A speech is a performance, not merely a manuscript, an outline, or slides. We can offer a lively performance, not a lifeless presentation.

This chapter is about expressing ourselves passionately, using various means to create memorable as well as effective speeches. We can do this by creating identification and expressing ourselves passionately, both verbally and nonverbally.

Create Identification

One of the most powerful ways for us to connect passionately with an audience is *identification*—helping the audience identify with us and others. If audience members cannot identify with us, they will not listen as attentively and openly. If we are aloof and impersonal, we might quickly lose audience identification for the rest of our speech. Similarly, if our audience cannot identify with the characters in our stories, we will lose audience interest.

Use "We" Rather Than "You"

Every time we practice a speech, we play two roles—the role of ourselves and the role of an audience member. We get to listen to ourselves speak as if we were also in the audience.

One simple technique to help us accomplish identification is using "we" instead of "you" in our speeches. The "we" includes us as speakers. In some cases, "we" seems awkward because we have not written the speech for adequate audience identification.

Using "you" to refer to our audience can be just as appropriate, especially when we mean to include everyone in the audience. We can include "we" as well: "You all know how it feels when someone criticizes you harshly. We usually feel angry and defensive." But we should not use "you" so much that it disengages us from the audience completely.

Empathize with Neighbors beyond the Audience

As servant speakers, we need *empathy*—seeing things from others' perspectives. Ideally, we have done enough audience research that we can empathize with our audience as we compose our speech.

If we are speaking on behalf of a group of neighbors beyond our audience, however, we need to empathize with them as well. We need to demonstrate through what we say and how we say it that our hearts have connected with our neighbors in need.

Nothing communicates such empathy better than passionately told personal stories. We might use one or more autobiographical stories of how our engagement with our neighbors created empathy for them in our hearts. In effect, we are using our identification with others to help our audience identify with both us and those we are speaking about.

When I speak about cross-cultural communication, I use the example of being invited to a family's hut near a garbage dump outside Guatemala City. The woman sent her young son to trade some bottles from the dump for a few eggs and a tomato to make scrambled eggs for us over an open fire. Her husband had abandoned her.

She was gracious and easy to commune with, largely because we shared a common faith. Our communication occurred authentically from our hearts—not artificially from our external differences related to our native tongues, races, or financial prosperity. She seemed to live with a level of spiritual peace that was hard for me to imagine, given all the things she could reasonably worry about. I found myself desiring her level of faith—not pitying her. I realized how essential cross-cultural communication is for our own living faith, no matter our own culture.

I empathized enough with my Guatemalan friend that some thirty years later I can still talk passionately about her—and what she taught me about faith. She showed me that the Holy Spirit transcends culture. That material possessions can be stumbling blocks to wholehearted faith in Jesus Christ. And that I need to thank God for all good things, especially those that I take for granted. Cross-cultural communication can help us identify with others and thereby learn more about ourselves.

Use Audience-Relevant Examples and Illustrations

The most effective way to help our audience identify with us is to use audience-relevant examples and illustrations from our own lives.

For instance, when I speak to teachers, I begin with my own educational journey, using a story from my successes or failures. I want my audience to know that I am one of them, and that they can identify with me as a fellow teacher rather than just as a lecturer.

When I speak to young professionals about finding and using a mentor, I start with an illustration about my own mentoring. I tell the story of a new mentee who needed a father figure as much as a professional mentor. I explain that the mentee taught me to be the kind of person who is worth imitating, not just a source of professional advice.

When my students speak to classmates, they learn quickly that they have to identify with the students—not necessarily with me. Then classmates

---

Jesus the Servant Identified with Us

In your relationships with one another, have the same mindset as Christ Jesus:

> Who, being in very nature God,
>> did not consider equality with God something to be used to his
>> own advantage;
> rather, he made himself nothing
>> by taking the very nature of a servant,
>> being made in human likeness.
> And being found in appearance as a man,
>> he humbled himself
>> by becoming obedient to death—
>>> even death on a cross!

Philippians 2:5–8

will begin identifying with them, and the amazing gift of real communication occurs. No matter how enthusiastically class speakers come across, they need to create identification in order to cultivate passion among classmates.

Mutual identification between us and our audiences is an amazing gift. We have to look for and use points of identification, especially illustrative stories. As servant speakers we become Christlike, taking on the heart of Jesus, who passionately identifies with us. We speak from and with passion.

IN THE SPOTLIGHT

Tropes—Unusual, Symbolic Uses of Words

- *Hyperbole*—exaggeration for emphasis: "Many of the Samaritans from that town believed in him because of the woman's testimony, 'He told me <u>everything</u> I ever did'" (John 4:39).

- *Metaphor*—an implied comparison, usually highly symbolic: "You <u>are</u> the salt of the earth" (Matt. 5:13).

- *Simile*—an explicit comparison of two things, usually with the words "like" or "as": "The hair on his head was white <u>like</u> wool, <u>as</u> white as snow, and his eyes were <u>like</u> blazing fire" (Rev. 1:14).

- *Personification*—giving human traits to nonhuman things: "Let the rivers clap their hands, let the mountains sing together for joy" (Ps. 98:8).

- *Irony*—words that suggest the opposite of their meaning: "Pilate had a notice prepared and fastened to the cross. It read: JESUS OF NAZARETH, THE KING OF THE JEWS" (John 19:19).

Use Words Creatively and Evocatively

Our everyday language is not particularly interesting or engaging. In a speech we use language more creatively. We can employ literary devices that generate interest and make our words come alive in listeners' minds and hearts. Scripture gives us wonderful examples of such devices, which can make reading the Bible out loud a more engaging experience.

We can also order our words creatively. It is hard to give examples from English translations of Scripture because they do not capture all of the unusual word ordering in original texts.

We can stylize for speaking. We should speak in a style that is comfortable for us personally, but some common stylistic conventions are helpful. Often style involves the difference between written and oral modes.

Express Verbally

We speak passionately to engage our audience with our message. We never want to bore our audience. Our voices are critically important. How we speak is just as important as what we literally say. We need to be expressive without seeming inauthentic.

Why do most speakers fail to speak passionately? First, because they fear looking and sounding foolish. Actually, they will look and sound more foolish if they speak to an audience just like they would converse with friends.

Second, some speakers simply have trouble hearing what they actually sound like. They cannot tell how boring and uninteresting they sound—until they record and listen to themselves (even more

IN THE SPOTLIGHT

Common *Schemes*—Unusual Ordering of Words

- *Repetition*—repeating a word or phrase: Listen empathically. Listen sympathetically. Listen, listen, listen.
- *Parallelism*—two or more phrases or sentences with the same grammatical form: "Ask and it will be given to you; seek and you will find; knock and the door will be open to you" (Matt. 7:7).
- *Alliteration*—repeating a consonant sound: Savvy servant speakers are slow to speak.

than just watching a video, although that is important as well). In their hearts and minds they might be engaged and enthused. But not in their speech. They are trapped inside themselves without even knowing it. They think that their mild expressiveness is major expressiveness.

Once a semester I used to hear students screaming in a nearby classroom. If it was the classroom next to mine, I could barely conduct class

IN THE SPOTLIGHT

Stylized Language

- *Active voice*—with the sentence subject carrying out the action: "Paul encouraged Timothy" (active voice) rather than "Timothy was encouraged by Paul" (passive voice).
- *Vividness*—language that appeals to the human senses, including sight, sound, touch, and smell: "A great sign appeared in heaven: a woman clothed with the sun, with the moon under her feet and a crown of twelve stars on her head" (Rev. 12:1).
- *Incomplete sentences*—sentence fragments that provide emphasis and variety: "Speak slowly. And more quickly. Depending on the situation."
- *Concreteness*—specific rather than general language: "This is how you are to build it: The ark is to be three hundred cubits long, fifty cubits wide and thirty cubits high" (Gen. 6:15).
- *Variable sentence length*—using shorter sentences for emphasis: "Jesus wept" (John 11:35); Paul uses a 167-word sentence in Eph. 1:15–21; it is hard to imagine how listeners could fully take it in with one oral reading.

IN THE SPOTLIGHT

Common Vocal Problems

- *Vocal upticking*—ending sentences on a higher note, as if asking a question
- *Sing-songing*—raising and lowering pitch predictably, like singing a song's harmonic tune repeatedly
- *Fading out*—dropping volume and sometimes pitch at the end of sentences, including the speech conclusion

through the racket. A colleague who taught public speaking for years used to hand out newspapers to his students, ask them to roll up the papers, and then encourage everyone to start banging and shouting. His goal was to get students to become outwardly expressive. The exercise opened them up to see that when speaking publicly they have to reach beyond their everyday expressiveness.

To prove his point, my colleague would ask his students, "Have speakers ever bored you?" All hands would go up. Then he would ask, "Have you ever seen speakers make fools of themselves by speaking too enthusiastically and passionately about a topic?" No hands would go up. Case closed. We all tend to be far too worried about what we think we will look and sound like, and not enough about how the audience will perceive us. Time to roll up a newspaper and express ourselves.

Vary Vocal Range—Pitch and Tone

Audiences dislike monotones. No matter how great our ideas, if we do not vary the pitch and tone of our voices, our audiences probably will tune us out. Our own voice is like a musical instrument. We can learn to play it skillfully.

The easiest way to learn vocal range is to listen to ourselves singing. We all have a natural range we can sing as well as speak, without straining our voices. We can speak effectively across that range, enhancing our own expressiveness.

Vary Vocal Pace

The problem with speaking rapidly is twofold. First, we end up delivering the entire speech at the same pace in a race to finish. Second, we confuse our audience because one steady, speedy pace creates the impression that everything we are saying is equally important. We lack vocal periods of emphasis.

Normally, vocal pacing is slower at the beginning of a speech and faster toward the conclusion, with variations along the way for emphasis.

The most difficult pacing is during storytell-ing. We need to keep the story moving along but also gradually build anticipation, leading the audience's imagination.

If we find ourselves getting out of breath while speaking, we are probably speaking too quickly, without variation.

> **SERVANT SPEAKING TIP**
>
> If you know that your audience will include non-native speak-ers with limited vocabulary, use common language, avoid vernacular expressions, and be-ware of figurative (nonliteral) phrases.

Vary Volume

Speaking more loudly and softly is essential in every speech. The best way to emphasize a point is to express it more loudly and then repeat it more softly. In effect, the second, softer vocal expression further empha-sizes our point and gives the audience a chance to think more about what we are saying.

Also, we need to vary our volume in tune with our meaning. Shouting is generally a bad idea, although it is essential as part of a story when a character actually shouts, or when delivering some quotations. Whisper-ing works well if we can get extremely close to a microphone. Then a whisper can effectively draw in the audience, as if we are sharing a vital secret.

Vary Vocabulary

We cannot communicate passionately by using the same few words repeatedly. We need to express ourselves using a reasonable range of vo-cabulary that matches audience interest and ability. Adjectives and adverbs are notoriously very overused, and frequently excessively repeated (as I just demonstrated).

We might consult a thesaurus when writing a speech so we can deter-mine the best words for expressing our meaning. One rule: write with a dictionary and edit with a thesaurus. Then we can speak like we are performing jazz, with variations on a theme. Use fresh but understandable language.

Avoid Verbal Fillers

A bad habit is using verbal fillers, such as *um, ah, y'know, like, kinda, so, sorta, just,* and sometimes *and*. The most common ones, *um* and *ah*, are nearly always meaningless

> **SERVANT SPEAKING TIP**
>
> Determine if a word or phrase is merely a verbal filler by singing the complete sentence. Verbal fillers awkwardly interfere with the flow of the lyrics.

SERVANT SPEAKING TIP

Replace verbal fillers with silence, which respectfully gives the audience a chance to think. It also gives you more time to recall or plan your next point, renew eye contact, and observe audience reactions.

distractions. They are like vocal hiccups, detracting from the significance of the adjacent phrases. They, um, create choppy delivery.

Consider this public prayer: "Like, you know, Lord, we're just kinda grateful."

Now contrast it with this one: "Lord, we are grateful."

Perhaps the first version, with verbal fillers, sounds more authentic to some audiences. Maybe it connotes humility and sincerity to those who speak that way in everyday life.

But what would happen if the first prayer continued that way for two minutes in a public setting? Would a congregation find it more meaningful than one with few verbal fillers? Would the fillers distract from the meaning of the prayer?

The best way to avoid verbal fillers in our public speaking is to eliminate them in our everyday conversation. It takes about two weeks with the help of a couple of friends who also want to stop using them. Agree to point out each other's fillers. We can also post notes to ourselves as reminders—on our phone, computer, dining table, dashboard, and the like: "NO FILLERS!"

Our friends catch us when we use fillers. We catch them. Soon we begin catching our own fillers. We become so conscious of fillers that we cease using them. Then we need to beware of self-righteousness; people who have given up verbal fillers love to point out the problem in others.

Express Nonverbally

Human communication is so wonderfully rich that we can even speak without saying anything. Medieval monks, who lived by vows of silence, developed elaborate sign languages to communicate inaudibly. Signing is a powerfully nuanced form of language.[2] So is eating cold French fries at 8:00 a.m. (see the sidebar that follows).

When God instructed Jeremiah to smash the clay pot, he gave the prophet a lesson in nonverbal expression. It was one thing for Jeremiah to speak passionately to a disobedient people. It was even more for Jeremiah to nonverbally illustrate God's anger.

We are multimedia creatures. Not one of us expresses ourselves only with spoken words.

The Student Who Ate Cold French Fries While Speaking

A student showed up for an early morning speech class looking like he had been up all night. Unshaven. Ratty hair. He was sweaty and smelly. He was carrying a bag of fast food and eating French fries. The classroom smelled like a combination of sweat and fries.

Most amazing of all, he was supposed to be the first speaker that morning. He walked up to the front, placed his bag of fries on the podium, looked across the room, stuffed another fry into his mouth, and began.

"I am here to tell you that you can graduate from college debt free. I am also here to convince you not to do it. Unless you like working all night, eating fries for breakfast, and having no social life."

After telling us about his two jobs and complete lack of a social life, including weekends when he worked overtime for a freight company, he simply said, "Don't do it. Debt is better than constant exhaustion and no friends."

He smiled slightly, ate one more fry, sat down at his desk, and drifted off to sleep.

Was the whole thing an act? Not really. He looked like that every time I saw him on campus. I suspect other students joked about him.

He was more than just prepared for that speech. It came from his heart. It was clear and organized—point by point. And all his nonverbals naturally reflected his MAIN IDEA.

His nonverbal communication—the looks and smells—were so effective that I could not imagine anyone in the room wanting to work so hard to stay debt free, while missing out on much of the fun of university life.

Manage First Impressions

Creating a "good" first impression includes being authentic. If the French-fry-eating student had gone home, showered, shaved, and gotten dressed for class, he would not have been nearly as effective. His first impression was deceptive, at least when he walked into class; I and others assumed he had just stayed up all night working on his speech. In fact, he was dressed to show us what his life was actually like. If he had just spoken about being tired, unclean, and smelly all of the time, without being himself as he presented, he would not have communicated as well.

When we speak publicly, our verbal and nonverbal messaging represent two parallel languages. Even before we speak, our audience is sizing us up nonverbally, making assumptions about our appearance, including our clothing. Do we seem personable? Aloof? Uncomfortable?

Our intended and unintended nonverbals affect audience perceptions. They inform and misinform.

Integrate Nonverbal Cues with Intentional Words

Our *cues* (unintentional nonverbals) might not match our intentional words. We might unintentionally be creating conflicting messages—what we display versus what we say.

The solution is to be as conscientious as we can about how others might interpret our nonverbals. We want to integrate our appearance and mannerisms with what we are intentionally saying. We turn our cues into intentional expressions.

Consider the Interpretive Context

The *context* (situation) in which we are speaking tends to shape others' interpretations of our nonverbals as well as our verbals. Speaking in a church setting differs from speaking at a civic event. Speaking in a class carries significantly different audience assumptions than speaking at work.

Presumably Jeremiah's audience knew what to expect from public prophets like him. By adding the clay pot demonstration, however, God was probably getting across a point even more passionately in a public context. Jeremiah could have used only spoken words, but his multimedia demonstration helped the Judeans see, hear, and perhaps even smell God's displeasure as the dust rose from the ground.

Using unexpected nonverbals can greatly confuse our audiences. We ought to avoid gimmicky visuals and exaggerated actions that seem out of context, and instead visually draw our audience in to the meaning of our words. Our nonverbals need to fit with our MAIN IDEA, purpose, and situation. The sleepy and exhausted student did it well.

Speak with the Body

Like Jesus, God incarnate, we use our bodies as well as spoken words to convey what we mean. We give physical birth to a speech while delivering it. Our speech becomes a living, bodily performance.

The twentieth-century American rhetorician Kenneth Burke said that humans speak like dancers. He suggested that "beneath the dance of words" always lies a "dance of bodies."[3]

Augustine offered a wonderful metaphor for nonverbal expressiveness based on Psalm 149. He encouraged Christians to "praise the Lord" with their "whole selves," not just their voices.[4] In the same way, servant speakers can use their physical presence to connect with audiences. "The soul speaks in the movements of the body," St. Ambrose (340–397) told young priests.[5]

Facial expressiveness is vital. In the Old Testament, God rarely shows his face to people because it is so personal and holy. But Jacob gets to see God in person. The astonishing event changed how he perceived people too. After being received in friendship by his brother Esau, Jacob declared, "For to see your face is like seeing the face of God, now that you have received me favorably" (Gen. 33:10).

IN THE SPOTLIGHT

Managing Nonverbals

- *Facial expression.* Do we seem unhappy or grateful to serve?
- *Posture.* Do we appear stiff and uncomfortable, or poised and confident?
- *Eye contact.* Are we looking interestedly at the audience, or disinterestedly at the floor or our notes?
- *Attire.* Do we seem dressed to impress others, or is our clothing fitting for the event?
- *Gestures.* Do our arms and hands reinforce what we are saying, or are they visual distractions?

A welcoming *countenance* (facial expression) is a nonverbal invitation to relationship. Warm facial expressions suggest favoritism, which literally means "lifting up" our faces to one another. An audience wants to see, not just hear, a speaker's favor.

The Roman orator Cicero argued that "all depends on countenance; and even in that the eyes bear sovereign sway."[6] From the moment a speaker enters the room, the audience begins interpreting the speaker's face.

As we begin speaking, our facial expressions continue to be important. If we fail to look at the audience, we might convey shyness or indifference. When we use eye contact and smile genuinely, we express care.

Conclusion

I wonder what it was like to be near the prophet Jeremiah as he spoke to God's people. He used satire, rhetorical questions, and condemnatory language. Was he always shouting? Perhaps screaming at times? Whispering? We have little to help us hear him. But we can imagine him breaking the clay pot to demonstrate God's anger and justice.

Created as multimedia creatures, we have many ways of using nonverbals to support our verbal expressiveness. To paraphrase Augustine on Psalm 149, we should be alleluias from head to toe.

FOR DISCUSSION

1. Why do you suppose many speakers do not express themselves passionately?
2. If Jesus identified with us in our sinfulness, should we identify with our audiences in their sinfulness? Also, should we encourage our audiences to identify with our sinfulness? If so, when and why?
3. Are verbal fillers ever appropriate in a public speech or other presentation? If so, when and why?
4. What is the difference between a nonverbal cue and an intentional symbol? Which do you think is more important in servant speaking?

THIRTEEN

Speak to Inform Dramatically

A student dumped his course notebook into the metal trash can after finishing my final exam. The remaining students chuckled as he left the room. I felt hurt, embarrassed, and even angry.

Now I thank that student for waking me up. I committed myself to finding a way of teaching that might persuade some students to keep their class notes for the rest of their lives. It was an outrageous goal, but it gave me direction.

Speaking to inform—*informative speaking*—is a challenge. How many times have informative speakers bored us? How often have we daydreamed during lectures or sermons?

This chapter offers effective ways of informing audiences. It explains how to find and use the audience-focused drama in a topic and describes the major forms of informative speaking.

Determine and Address Audience Interest

A major challenge in informative speaking is being interesting and engaging. We all are programmed to assume that anything like a lecture will be dull. In fact, our audiences might not care about what we have to say. Why should they? That is always a question in informative speaking.

After we select an informative speech topic, we need to verify that our audience truly is interested in it. Even so, we might still have to convince our audience to pay attention to us. That is what happened with my own

SERVANT SPEAKING TIP

Come up with three topics that you could use for an informative speech. Then ask ten people who are representative of your likely audience to rank them from most to least interesting. Consider speaking only on a topic that at least seven of the ten people rank as the most interesting one.

teaching. I had to figure out how to get students to care enough to keep their course notes for years.

It is simply not enough that we are passionate about our topic. Why would anyone else be passionate?

Address Audience Needs

The beginning of all effective informative presentations is communicating the value of our information to our audience—how our information will address the audience's needs. Sometimes the needs are obvious. People looking for a job already feel the need for information about how to find one.

Other times we have to first explain the need. Suppose we begin a speech intended to teach a skill this way: "I would like to show you how to produce a video résumé." If our audience feels a need to learn that skill, our rhetorical task is easier. But what can we do if the audience feels like our topic is irrelevant to its needs?

First, we can briefly make a case in our introduction for why the audience might care about our information. In this case, we can cite data about the growing use of video résumés for job applications. We might say, "This is an important skill if you want to be competitive in the new economy. For larger companies, it might become as important as the traditional résumé. We can beat the competition with well-produced video résumés."

Second, we can offer a very concrete example or illustration that shows what the audience will gain from the information. Usually we would tell a story, perhaps about ourselves, that shows how our speech will highlight our audience's need for information.

A student gave an informative speech to classmates on cooking omelets for breakfast, demonstrating with an electric fry pan. He began, "I live off campus and used to eat sugary cereal for breakfast. I was hungry again by the time I got to campus. So I figured out how to make a tasty omelet while getting dressed. It's fast and cheap. Keeps me going until lunch. I plop it on bread and eat it like a sandwich while driving to school. It's great. I'd like to show you how to do it—with my clothes on." In other words, the student was going to demonstrate not just how to cook an omelet but how to meet a need for a fast, cheap, and healthy breakfast.

When I speak on the topic of how to get good grades, I tell the story of being a thoroughly mediocre student my freshman year. I felt like I was an academic failure, but I did not know what to do. Then one day I learned a secret. It made all of the difference. So simple. But no one ever told me that I should . . .

SERVANT SPEAKING TIP

At or near the beginning of your informative speech, either explain or illustrate how your information will meet one or more needs—why the audience should care.

Find the Human Drama at the Intersection of Needs and Information

I left you hanging in the last paragraph in order to make my point. Information can have perceived value to people. All of us are motivated to learn something that we believe will benefit us.

Speaking on the topic of getting higher grades, I begin like this: "I learned a simple way to boost my grades from Cs to nearly straight As in one semester. I would like to show you how to do it."

I continue, "I took good lecture notes and rewrote them for comprehension the same day. And if my notes did not make sense, I asked the instructor for clarification at the next class session. Then I just quickly reviewed the well-organized, easy-to-read notes once a week. It really worked for me and it will work for you. Here's exactly how to do it." I entice students into a drama at the intersection of their academic needs and my information.

The great American playwright Neil Simon said that all drama involves people wanting something.[1] We all desire relationships, skills, success, and so forth. Christians want faith. Our lives are dramas of wants that we often perceive as needs.

As informative servant speakers, we can address our audiences' ongoing life dramas. We can invite our audience-neighbors to learn how to meet their needs. But we first have to explain or show why they might desire what we have to offer.

When I speak to university seniors and recent graduates about résumé writing, I typically begin with the story of a former student with average grades, no paid professional experience related to her academic major, and no internships. She felt like a failure with an embarrassing résumé.

Once I showed (informed) her how to examine her academic and non-academic experiences more carefully, she realized that she already had considerable relevant experience. She just needed to learn how to (1) identify her many life experiences and (2) show how those experiences demonstrated the skills, knowledge, and traits required for specific jobs. Even her travel and cross-cultural experiences were relevant.

For instance, the student's work as a restaurant server, which she was hesitant to put on her résumé, actually demonstrated many career-related skills, knowledge, and traits. She learned about memorizing, cross-cultural communication, small-business operations, stressful working conditions, overcoming conflicts, flexibility in hours, and dedication. When I start an informative presentation with that story, students become very interested in what I have to say. They care about the information because they see the need in their own lives.

As we touch on the needs of our audience early in an informative speech, we generate interest. We are no longer just passing along information. We are telling the story—the drama—at the intersection of our information and the audience's needs. If the audience does not entirely feel the need, we have to explain why the topic is important.

Choose a Form of Informative Communication

Informative speaking includes at least four major, somewhat overlapping forms of communication: describing, instructing, reporting, and explaining. Focusing on one of them can help us find the inherent drama and adapt our content to our audience. Usually our topic best fits with one of them, although we can dip into the others as needed.

Describe Someone or Something

Some of the most interesting informative speeches involve telling audiences about events, devices, people, animals and plants, and the like. Such descriptive speaking often takes the form of a story—the story about or behind our topic, or at least the story of how we discovered the topic and developed our knowledge of it.

We can describe what happened to us once—and what we learned about it. We can describe the life of a particular kind of animal, even our pet. We can describe the story behind how a technology works or fails to work for us. We can describe the tales of places we have visited.

The goal is to focus on description, not analysis, evaluation, or opinion. We certainly can offer our perspective, but if we find ourselves advocating for something, we are moving closer to persuasive speaking. We might describe the pros and cons of competing phone apps, for instance, but the point of our informative speech would not be to persuade others to use one app.

We all like hearing about interesting people, particularly if they are well known or historically significant. Among the most intriguing for various audiences are celebrities, athletes, political leaders, business innovators, and inspiring religious figures. Such people usually have life stories with interesting experiences.

I have learned that on every university campus there are well-known persons—staff, faculty, or administrators—who are well liked by just about everyone. They are fine people who help others and have a pleasant demeanor. Most people on campus would like to know more about them. What makes them so joyful? Encouraging? Friendly? What are their lives like off campus?

In addition to reviewing important aspects of a person's life, we might suggest why the individual is significant. What about the person's life is relevant for our audience today? What personal practices, mental or spiritual habits, and other descriptors come to mind? What did the person have to overcome to be successful? In short, what lessons can we learn from others' lives?

Teach a Skill or Other Process

We all like to learn how to do things well. Public speaking itself is a skill worth learning. So are talents related to getting along with others, cultivating a vibrant spiritual life, developing professional abilities, and communi-

IN THE SPOTLIGHT

General Forms of Informative Speeches

- *Describing*—telling an audience about an event, person, place, plant, animal, or thing. Often this is storytelling—perhaps even the underlying story of why and how we became interested in the topic.
- *Instructing*—demonstrating a process, sharing a skill, showing how to interpret a biblical text, or teaching others how to follow procedures. This is usually like focused training, not a lecture, and can include how and why we learned about the topic.
- *Reporting*—informing others about the results of our research, a planning meeting, an experiment, or an investigation. This is like objective journalism and sometimes can be the story of what we discovered.
- *Explaining*—defining and clarifying an idea, theory, social or political issue, theological or doctrinal belief, or Bible passage (not advocating a position/perspective, which would be a persuasive speech). This can include the story behind our interest in the topic, such as needing to know what the Bible really says about a topic that affects our lives and perhaps even leads to tension within families and the church.

cating cross-culturally. Sometimes we would like to learn something highly practical, like budgeting, finding a reliable used car, or grilling corn on the cob.

Moreover, most of us learn skills better when others demonstrate them for us. Reading about skills is not usually as effective as being taught them. This is one of the reasons why YouTube has become a major place to learn skills.

Every process that we learn involves a skill. The process of interpreting Scripture is a skill. So are teaching, Bible study, prayer, and listening—including to sermons. Perhaps churches could offer workshops on how to listen to sermons. Doing so would at least acknowledge listening as an essential skill.

The drama in teaching a skill or process involves addressing the gap between what audience members already can do and what they would like to be able to do. How can we appeal to the audience's desire to close the gap? What does the possible benefit look like from the audience's perspective? We need to ask ourselves such questions as we select a topic and then begin preparing an instructive speech.

Explain Something

We all are confused about many things. We would like to better understand ourselves, others, and the world around us. As Christians, we are especially interested in knowing God's will and living faithfully amid conflicts and disagreements. We go to public lectures partly to reduce our confusion. Except for sermons, lectures are probably the most public form of explanatory speaking—even if the lecture is called a "speech" or "presentation" so it does not sound too academic. At some churches, sermons are called "talks."

Peter was direct with Jesus: "Explain the parable to us" (Matt. 15:15). After suggesting that Peter was still "dull," Jesus explained the meaning. A major part of Jesus's speaking was explaining his ministry to his uninformed followers. Most of the time Jesus did not explain his parables, but when he did, he was short and direct.

Explanatory speaking informs audiences about confusing or unknown ideas, issues, conflicts, and the like. When we ask someone to explain something to us, we do not want to be lectured. We are not seeking to be persuaded—just to be enlightened. Why are my science grades so poor—and what can I do about it? How can I find the right kind of people for informational interviews for a career I would like to pursue? What really is the Trinity—and why do we believe it when the word is never used in Scripture?

Even if we have strong personal opinions on our topic, we need to avoid letting them dictate how we research, write, and deliver an explanatory speech. I prefer to let the audience know my opinion so they can better judge if I am being fair-minded: "This is how I think about it, but I could be wrong."

Why should our audience care about what we are explaining? Our task is to make it clear from the beginning that we are explaining something of potential value. This is why social and theological issues can be great topics for explanatory speeches. Often the audience already feels confused and would like greater clarity. We can explain the tensions and disagreements over the topic without having to take a stand. We can facilitate healthy discussion and contribute to shared understanding.

Explaining to others what we know often requires us to begin with the basics. It is like explaining the rules of a particular board game to people who have never played it before. If we begin teaching game strategy, they will get confused. If we start with the essential game rules, they can begin playing and will soon begin to understand strategy.

Report a Discovery

Much of the world revolves around people discovering things and reporting their findings to others. Such reports are at the core of fields such as journalism, education, business, science, and biblical archeology.

A critically important type of informative speaking is essentially reporting. Reporting is not meant to be persuasive, even though it can change peoples' minds and actions. When news reports emerge about health and diet, some people adjust their eating accordingly, without even consulting a doctor. They feel such a strong need to improve their health that they accept and use the latest reported information.

The best informative reports are forthright and brief. The reporter normally has too much information to present. Yet the audience wants to know the truth, and we have a moral obligation not to edit the information for persuasive effect. The journalistic analogy is particularly fitting; reporters who get caught bending the facts lose credibility, and the audience is not really served. Brevity is not an excuse.

I encourage public speaking students to read at least one news source daily through the semester—even just a Yahoo or Google news feed. Some of the stories are actually reports about new discoveries in the sciences and humanities. The news feeds can be personalized by key words such as "university," "jobs," "depression," and "Christianity."

As I am writing this book and checking some news feeds, I see articles on college students' debts, dorm requirements, campus speech issues, graduate school admissions trends, difficulties international students face, challenges encountered by students moving back home after college, how instructors catch students who buy essays online, and more—all of them related just to

> ## A Speech on Why Some Graduates Are Unprepared for the Job Market
>
> A student gave a speech to communication majors on why many such majors may not be prepared to get good jobs after graduation. His Main Idea was to explain that communication majors need to take the right kinds of noncommunication courses to prepare themselves for communication careers.
>
> He examined actual job descriptions from the internet for people in fields like journalism, social media, and public relations; nearly all of them required knowledge about particular communication content—communicating about something and for particular audiences. For instance, public relations jobs required not just communication skills but also knowledge of fields that use public relations, such as healthcare, government, sports, and education.
>
> He concluded along these lines: "Maybe a key to getting communication jobs after graduation is taking the right noncommunication courses."
>
> It was a solid speech that prompted considerable discussion. It offered a fresh perspective aimed at students' perceived needs. He also could have used his findings to develop a persuasive speech to convince students to take specific actions, such as taking particular types of courses.

a "university" keyword feed. Most of the articles cite studies and interviews that could be bases for informative speeches.

Reports tend to have a newsy quality with implicit drama: "Here is what I found that you will find interesting and helpful. You don't want to miss this information." If we set up the drama, the audience hopes that we will deliver on our promise. The audience will care, and we need to care enough to deliver.

Conclusion

When the student threw out his course notes at my final exam, I knew I had to become a servant teacher. Instead of shoveling information, I needed to find the student-focused drama in my lesson plans. It transformed my teaching career. Both my students and I were more interested and motivated. One student told me twenty years later that she still had my course notes.

We all know about ineffective informative speaking because we suffer from it regularly. With care and imagination, we can be part of the solution.

Perhaps our audiences will even want to take notes on our presentations and review them later. It is a worthy goal for informative servant speakers.

FOR DISCUSSION

1. Why are so many lectures boring? What could a typical lecturer do to make a lecture more engaging and interesting?
2. How might we address the inherent drama in an informative speech about the creation of the universe to religious skeptics?
3. Identify one of your own informational needs and imagine how to begin a speech on the topic that was aimed at you. What would quickly engage you in the topic?
4. Identify a well-known person you admire. Then ask yourself what you would like to know about that person's life. Why? How would you begin a descriptive speech about the person that addresses your own curiosity?

FOURTEEN

Tell Stories (Mythos)

The first time I told a story well in a speech, it scared me. It was a true tale about my son's love affair with a pair of He-Man underpants. The audience was first silent. Then giggling. Then laughing uncontrollably. Then silent again. I felt like I had emotional control over them.

Stories can be powerful tools for engaging audiences' emotions. A major part of Jesus's earthly ministry was using stories to engage, explain, convict, and sometimes even intentionally confuse audiences. His two-dimensional stories—parables—used everyday situations to help listeners understand God's kingdom.

Stories gave Jesus—and they give us—a powerful way of engaging our audiences. Statements generally prompt audience thought, whereas stories often elicit wonder even as they entertain: "What did that story mean?" "What does it say about me—or us?" This is why we like to discuss movies, plays, novels, and even our own storied lives. We seem to be created to tell, enjoy, and ponder stories.

This chapter addresses storytelling in servant speaking. It considers how narratives work and how we can use them, especially as illustrations, testimonies, and humor.

Identify Mythos

Whether real or imagined, stories can move our hearts, making us sympathetic and empathetic with the characters. When we read the parable of the prodigal son, we are moved by the father's love and the son's redemption (Luke 15:11–32). And we might wonder if we are like the angry brother.

Moreover, the Bible is the overarching story of our faith. It is God's story and our story. In it, we discover who and whose we are, and how we should live. The Bible's *narrative* (story) draws us in.

Aristotle added *mythos* (story, sometimes translated as "plot") to his three means of persuasion—logos, pathos, and ethos.[1] He recognized the distinctive power of "mythical" tales to move audiences.

Today we tend to think of a myth as a false belief. But myths can also be stories that express both true and false claims about reality. A major myth is a powerful story that can give life meaning and purpose. Perhaps everyone lives by such mythic tales—even the most seemingly secular persons and groups. We just seem as humans to transfer religious faith and hope to other "gods," such as technology, science, and human creativity. For instance, the myth (story) of technological progress suggests that technology always improves the human condition. Most news reports about new communications technologies retell the story of technological progress, wowing us with descriptions of the latest features.

Meanwhile, everyday stories can give us joy and delight. There are proverbial tales, like the one about dogs supposedly eating students' papers the night before they are due. I have heard many variations over the years.

Then my dog ate a couple of my students' papers and peed on the rest of the pile spread around my living room floor. I did not know what to do. I did not want to return the awful-smelling essays. Also, I had used a water-soluble gel pen for comments and grades; the gel had run all over the papers. I just told the students what had happened and gave everyone an A for the assignment. Students laughed about it. I never again piled student papers on the floor as long as we had that wire-haired fox terrier.

Ponder Our Storied Lives

We are storied creatures. We dwell in narratives that instruct, persuade, and entertain. Most of our everyday conversation includes sharing our life stories. Why go to a coffee shop with someone, except to share personal stories? Most of the media we consume—from advertising to news and drama—employ stories. We are drawn to use social media to track one another's life stories and to participate in them.

IN THE SPOTLIGHT

Benefits of Learning How to Tell Stories

- speaking more self-confidently with less speech apprehension
- using stories as effective illustrations and examples
- speaking well from memory (picturing and telling a rehearsed story, especially one that we have told repeatedly in other situations)
- engaging audiences (audiences participate with us in a story)
- adjusting the length as needed for the overall speech duration
- making our own speaking more enjoyable

After Mary heard from the angels and the shepherds about the good news, she "treasured up all these things and pondered them in her heart" (Luke 2:19). Mary had much to think and wonder about. She had heard that she was part of a much greater story than just her own life with Joseph.

Speak with Narratives

As servant speakers, we instruct, persuade, and delight one another with the essential help of narratives. We borrow them from our own experiences, others' experiences, fictional stories, and our imaginations. We use stories that are true and make believe, current and historical, personal and common.

Most of our storytelling emerges naturally from everyday events. A eulogist recalls an episode from a deceased person's life. Dinner guests swap anecdotes about raising children. College roommates laugh together about professors' absentmindedness—like the time one of my colleagues gave the same lecture two weeks in a row without realizing it; not a single student had the courage to tell the instructor what was happening at the time. It was probably fun for the students, waiting to see when the instructor would realize what he was doing.

Engage Audiences

In my experience, no form of communication better gains audience attention than a well-told story. Stories engage audiences more effectively than questions, information, and visuals. I learned as a teacher to have appropriate stories ready when students' attention started fading. I learned as a parent that children would stay at the table after eating if we told stories about our day. Opening our speech with a story is probably the single most effective way of initially engaging our audiences.

Audiences may not recall most of what we say in a speech. They will soon forget much of our content, even important information. Chances are, however, that they will recall our well-told stories. We remember storied events more than anything else.

Stories often have a parabolic quality that beckons listeners. We want to know what the story means. Stories "illuminate an inner meaning which calls for a response from the hearers."[2]

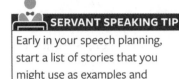

SERVANT SPEAKING TIP

Early in your speech planning, start a list of stories that you might use as examples and illustrations.

Exemplify and Illustrate

We serve our audiences with concrete examples and illustrations. If we speak too theoretically, our audiences might not understand us and will probably be less interested in what we have to say. If we are delivering an informative speech, we almost always need specific examples.

Data and statistics are important ways of illustrating what we mean to say. But they cannot substitute for stories. Stories are intimate, pertaining to particular people and situations that cannot be summed up by facts and figures. Stories give us a very personal way of being known and sharing what we know. As Wendell Berry puts it, people are best "known by their names and histories, not by their numbers or percentages."[3]

When I speak about interviewing for jobs, I use concrete examples reported to me by students and friends. I first explain how to answer interview questions with personal stories. Then I tell one or two stories that illustrate my point clearly and compellingly. Every job interview is a story. I ask students to prepare personal stories for every point on their résumés. The stories are, like parables, what they learned from each experience.

Sometimes we can use a story example or illustration first, and then explain it. This creates audience interest, especially if we suspend our storytelling before completing the tale.

I tell this story with more elaboration: "A student excitedly went to an interview for the ideal job. After introductions, one of the three interviewers asked, 'So, why do you want this job?' She was caught off guard. Getting increasingly nervous, she thought about her options."

That story immediately engages a student audience and illustrates the importance of being prepared to answer a number of standard questions. Members of the audience identify with the young woman and begin thinking about what they would do in that situation even before I explain how to prepare for it.

SERVANT SPEAKING TIP

If possible, prepare a story as an example/illustration for each outline point in your speech, with an additional one for the speech introduction.

Use Humor

Humorous stories have an amazing effect on audiences. They can open up hearts and minds. By relieving our tension and creating a sense of community, humorous stories can prepare audiences to learn, be persuaded, and celebrate. At the same time, they can reduce our speech anxiety because we too get caught up in the story. If we have told the story repeatedly, we do not have to prepare as much for that part of our speech.

One way to use humorous stories is *comedy*—stories with happy endings. When everything seems to work out well in a story, the audience is emotionally satisfied. As Christians, we can relate comedic stories to God's provisions, recalling times when things worked out for good in spite of human weaknesses and confusion.

A second way of using humorous stories is *tragedy*—stories with unhappy endings usually caused by foolishness. The primary form of humorous but tragic storytelling is *satire*—using irony and exaggeration to criticize others' stupidity or vices. Late-night television comedians and many popular YouTube producers use it frequently. Old Testament prophets employed satire to attack wretched leaders and unfaithful groups.[4] Jeremiah 10 is largely a satire on idolatry; the prophet compares the "way of nations" with a scarecrow who cannot speak, walk, or do any harm or good (Jer. 10:1–5).

The overworked and stressed-out student who gave the speech about how to graduate from college debt free located himself in a personal tragedy. He had no social life. He had stopped caring for his spiritual needs. He said he wished he had taken on debt instead. He satirized himself in front of an audience.

As Christian satirists, we use stories to expose the effects of the fall on persons, groups, and institutions. We show our audience what is wrong in church or society, and what might occur if people and organizations do not change their ways.

Some "tragedies" are just personal missteps. For instance, being unprepared for standard job interview questions is foolish. Yet we all do it. We tell ourselves that we will give a good interview just by showing up. Also, we spend more time worrying about the interview than preparing for it. What is wrong with us?

When asked by the hiring committee why she wanted the position, the student said, "Well, I guess I need to start paying off student loans

SERVANT SPEAKING TIP

Use humorous storytelling to be self-critical as well as satirical. Make fun of yourself in ways that your audience can identify with.

and move out of my parents' place." Everyone laughed. It was not a great answer, professionally speaking, but it was honest and funny. She got herself out of a sticky situation by telling a bit of her own story.

When I use her story as an example in a speech, everyone laughs. The audience immediately relates to it. But the audience wants to know how the story turned out. Was it a comedy or tragedy? She got the job, so it was comedic.

Nevertheless, a more professional answer would have involved explaining how she wanted to serve the organization and grow professionally. But in this case her authentic humor and quick wit served her well. Interviewers probably saw her answer as both candid and honest, and they may have assumed she would be a fun colleague.

Tell Personal Parables—Testimonies

From a Christian perspective, humor runs deep into the meaning and purpose of life. Jesus Christ humbled (same root as "humor") himself to take the form of a servant on earth. We humble ourselves before the cross. Life is a laughing matter for us because we know that our sin does not have the last word.

In other words, the gospel is what the Christian poet Dante (1265–1321) called a divine "comedy." By grace, all things work together for good for those of us who love God and are called according to his purpose (Rom. 8:28). The gospel is the ultimate comedy for those who believe.

We all are living parables whose lives point to the reality of our fallenness and God's redemption. In a sense, our lives speak about where we are in the journey of faith. We have "seen and testify" that God sent his only Son to save us from our sins (1 John 4:14).

Therefore, we share the good news, sometimes using our own life stories as comedic illustrations of God's mercy. We can be more or less explicit, depending on our audience and our speaking purpose. Teaching about the gospel is not the same as persuading people to believe the gospel or delighting people with stories of the impact of the gospel on our lives.

Moreover, every truthful tale we tell about how we have fallen down and God has picked us up points to our personal need and the entire

SERVANT SPEAKING TIP

Start keeping a list of personal stories (parables) from your life and practice telling them with friends, family, coworkers, and classmates. God will provide opportunities to use them in many different speaking situations, from job interviews to speeches.

SERVANT SPEAKING TIP
Learn to tell the story of your faith humbly and honestly, as appropriate. Focus on how God's love turned your tragedy into a comedy.

human race's need for God. We servant speakers are all called to be comedians, inspired and directed by the Holy Spirit as witnesses to both human fallenness and God's love.

Throughout this book I have used personal stories as examples and illustrations, hoping to inspire as well as teach readers. My stories are parables. They carry meaning, even lessons. They point—sometimes directly and obviously, other times indirectly and implicitly—to the gospel metanarrative, the overarching story of creation, fall, redemption, and renewal.[5] As servant speakers who follow Jesus, we find the meaning of our stories ultimately in the gospel metanarrative. A *metanarrative* is a story that helps us make sense of other stories—like a story-based worldview that explains the meaning of life's events.

At a large conference of Christian men, the speaker got the audience involved by asking them to shout out all their denominational and independent church affiliations—Baptist, Lutheran, and so forth. It sounded like chaos. Then he asked everyone to shout "Jesus." It was the sound of unity.

When we share testimonies—when we honestly open up to others—we create memories that give life to relationships. Every speech we give becomes the story of our relationship with a particular audience. Moreover, the stories we tell within each speech often carry more of our meaning than anything else we say. They build connections with our audiences. They reveal what we are really like and amplify what we mean to say. Without stories, speeches come across as transfers of information that lack a relational bond. As Wendell Berry suggests, we cannot really trust one another unless we share our stories.[6]

We can overdo stories about ourselves. But we can also fail to tell stories that give God the glory for leading us through difficulties. As Frederick Buechner says, the Christian faith is a tragedy (sin) before it is a comedy (salvation).[7]

The Psalmist Urges Biblical Storytelling

Let the redeemed of the Lord tell their story—
    those he redeemed from the hand of the foe,
  those he gathered from the lands,
      from east and west, from north and south.

                    Psalm 107:2–3

The best humor, well expressed, opens our audiences' hearts. When our audience laughs with us, we create a special human bond. That is probably what happened with the job interviewee who unexpectedly told her story about having to pay back student loans and move out of her parents' home.

Tell Stories Well

Storytelling is a unique skill that does not always come naturally. For instance, we might think that a personal story is engaging, but when we actually tell the story it falls flat. As we say, "You had to be there." Our task is to help audiences *experience* stories, not just to *hear* stories. We have to help them experience stories *vicariously*—as if they are the characters.

Earlier I addressed this as a form of identification unique to God and his image bearers. In storytelling, using our voices and bodies, we lead our audience to identify with one or more characters—even with us if we are speaking in first person.

The oldest memory I have of successfully telling a story to a church audience was when I first described my young son's obsession with superhero (He-Man) underpants.

He had one pair and wanted to wear them every day, without washing them. When I confronted him about not letting me wash them, he cried, "But Dad, when I wear them, I am He-Man." I could not have asked for a better illustration of how we humans identify with substitutes for God. In a sense, mass-media stories often compete with our pursuit of Jesus Christ. We spend far more time with media stories than biblical stories.

While telling the He-Man tale, I suddenly realized that everyone was paying close attention, including the adolescents. They all could identify with me or my son—or both of us. I knew after that speech that I needed to work hard to make my stories interesting, engaging, and relevant.

When I finished telling the story at the church that day, I said something like this: "We all are like my son, trying to become heroes. We do it with our autos, clothing, technology, and more. We comfort ourselves by thinking we have mastered our own little world. But down deep, as followers of Jesus Christ, we know that we are frauds. We play at being heroes, chasing false gods. Sooner or later the game is over." There was silence.

When we tell a story really well, we barely have to explain what it illustrates or exemplifies. For the most part, the story speaks for itself. This is especially true in informative speaking. The audience will get the meaning

Telling a Story Well

- *Setting*. Describe vividly where and when it takes place.
- *Characters*. Paint visual images with your words and body to illustrate how people look and act.
- *Motivation*. Explain what the characters are trying to accomplish or overcome—what they want or need—and what is holding them back.
- *Timing*. Keep the story moving, delivering key lines at the right places and concluding the story before it wears thin or dominates the entire speech.
- *Anticipation*. Keep listeners wondering what will happen next and how the story will turn out.
- *Relevance*. Make sure to tell the story to illustrate the point being made in the speech, not just for entertainment.

if I have selected a relevant story and told it well. We have the capacity for understanding the speaker's intention without needing to be told.

In persuasive speaking, however, we usually want to tell the audience specifically what to think or do. I informed the church group about the importance of role models for human identity. But I also wanted to direct my audience away from worldly role models and toward Jesus, the true master of the universe. So I needed to be a bit more explicit about the meaning of the story.

Those of us who grew up in storytelling families are inclined to practice at mealtimes and during special events such as reunions, weddings, and funerals. But we still need to remind ourselves that well-crafted stories are rarely just entertainment. They implicitly teach us.

Conclusion

The He-Man story scared me when I first told it effectively. The power of a single story to captivate an audience was amazing. To have such power in my own hands both delighted and concerned me.

Delivering well-crafted speeches requires storytelling skills. When we stand before an audience, we are not only preparing to tell stories about a topic but also participating with the audience in giving birth to a meaningful experience. Later, someone will ask members of our audience about our speech: "How was it?" Whether or not that person can respond with one of our stories partly indicates how well we crafted our speech.

If God had given us only the moral law, including the Ten Commandments, we probably would not be so attracted to biblical faith. The Spirit works through our hearts, not just our minds. And our hearts desire stories that help us understand God, others, and ourselves.

1. What was the last play or movie you saw? Try telling the story briefly (no more than thirty seconds) in an engaging way. Do not include how you feel about the story—only the story itself. What makes it easy or difficult to tell the story? What is the most important part of the story? Why?

2. Discuss the validity of this claim: "Good humor is always humble."

3. Identify a story (such as a TV series or movie) you want to see or hear repeatedly. What about that story attracts you so strongly?

4. What might be the most audience-engaging story from your own life that you would be willing to tell publicly? Why do you think it is the most engaging one?

FIFTEEN

Speak to Persuade Logically (Logos)

A Baptist minister invited me to preach at his southern church. I accepted. When he called me a week before the event, he added this: "Of course, don't forget to do an altar call." He wanted me to invite attendees to come forward to accept Jesus Christ as their Lord and Savior.

My sermon on Adam and Eve's fall from grace was already complete. Now I would have to figure out how to persuade attendees to come forward and give their lives to Jesus. Later, I will explain what happened at my premier altar call.

Ethos was covered in chapters 10 and 11. Now we move on to the persuasive appeal of *logos* (logic). Using research and reason to persuade particular audiences are ways of utilizing logos.

Persuade with Logos, Pathos, and Ethos

The ancient Greek philosopher-rhetorician Aristotle developed three methods (or means) of persuasion that can be applied in nearly all situations: logos, pathos, and ethos. They are broad but very helpful categories for assessing possibilities and determining strategies in all persuasive public communication, including most advertising and public relations.

Many of the great theologians and leaders in the history of the church also served as public speakers who wrote about rhetoric and borrowed concepts from ancient Greeks and Romans. They include Tertullian, Augustine, Martin Luther, John Calvin, and John Wesley. We can still learn from their fine examples of preaching and teaching.

The archbishop of Constantinople, John Chrysostom (ca. 347–407), who began his rhetorical education at the age of twelve, believed that an educated Christian must know how to speak well. Otherwise, a Christian's acquired wisdom could be miscommunicated, resulting in spiritual misdirection, errant Christian practice, and false or ineffective witness. Chrysostom realized that even a believer who correctly understands God's Word must be able to express such insights clearly for the church to benefit.[1] He practiced what he preached, earning the name Chrysostom, which means "golden mouth."

IN THE SPOTLIGHT

Aristotle's Three Means of Persuasion

- *Logos*—logical appeals based on sound evidence and clear reasoning
- *Pathos*—emotional appeals, such as love, anger, and shame
- *Ethos*—credible appeals based on the speaker's ethicality and trustworthiness

As Augustine studied Scripture and reflected on his own rhetorical training, he concluded, "Since rhetoric is used to give conviction to both truth and falsehood, who could dare to maintain that truth, which depends on us for its defence, should stand unarmed in the fight against falsehood."[2] He encouraged believers to imitate the eloquence of King David and Paul. Largely as a result of Augustine's persuasive arguments, the fifth-century church began adapting ancient rhetoric to its own good purposes rather than rejecting it outright. Augustine's book *On Christian Teaching*, for example, encouraged Christian pastors and teachers to speak wisely and well. It is still one of the best books ever written about how Christians should practice oral rhetoric.[3]

Identify and Address Audience Attitudes

Especially for persuasion, we need to determine our audience's preexisting attitudes toward our topic. For instance, if we are going to give a persuasive speech about which Bible version our audience might use for daily reading, we need to address our audiences' attitudes about Bible translations. Do daily Bible readers even think or care about which translation is best for that purpose? Perhaps many Christians just assume that "the Bible is the Bible," regardless of the translation.

Audience attitudes include how interested or uninterested the audience is in our topic, and whether the audience feels favorably or unfavorably toward our topic and MAIN IDEA. Attitudes are essentially biases.

We can identify audience attitudes through research. We can determine how many people use the various Bible translations, and probably why they do. Nonprofit organizations that own Bible translations collect such information. So do some of the publishers and retailers who distribute and sell Bibles. We could also conduct primary research by asking people who represent our likely audience about their personal Bible preferences and practices. We might ask them which translations they use, when they use them, and why they use them. Such research would reveal audience attitudes.

We usually discover that logic is not the only or even major reason for particular attitudes and actions. My own primary research over the years tells me that Christians use particular Bible translations because of (1) *tradition*, such as the practices of their family and church communities; (2) *habits*, including short- and long-term Bible use; (3) *authority*, such as the influence of personal pastors and Christian thought leaders; and (4) *emotions*, such as what a particular print copy of the Bible means to them as a gift from a loved one or church.

In other words, audience attitudes about a topic are almost always a mix of logic and emotion. If we are going to use logical appeals, we need to know which kinds of logical arguments will address the audience's attitudes so that the audience is more likely to accept our claim.

Persuade Logically

God created us as thinking creatures with considerable intellectual capacity. For instance, we can compile and analyze data, weigh evidence, and argue opposing ideas. The field of *apologetics*—the defense of the faith—includes such logical argumentation.

One way to persuade is through *simple logic*—developing a persuasive MAIN IDEA with one or more logically supporting points. We make our case logically by appealing to our audience's reasoning capacity. We (1) make a claim, such as which Bible translation is best for daily study; (2) state our reason, such as why a particular translation is best for daily study; and (3) provide evidence to support our case.

Our reasoning must seem logical to our audience—not just to us.

Suppose we want to persuade our audience to use a particular Bible translation. Our persuasive MAIN IDEA might be, "I would like to offer two reasons why you might try using the NIV—that is, the New International Version—for daily reading."

With simple logic, normally each of our two outline points would be supporting evidence. In this example, suppose we discovered research-based evidence that the NIV is good for daily reading because of its (1) reader under-standability and (2) textual-interpre-tive accuracy. These two qualities of the NIV are not just our personal opinions; they are evidence from trustworthy sources, including respected biblical scholars. In effect, we say to our audi-ence, "Don't just believe me. I'm the messenger. Believe me because of the evidence I am presenting from these respected sources."

We could even add our evidentially supported points to our MAIN IDEA: "I would like to convince you to use the NIV for daily Bible reading be-cause you will understand it and it is an accurate translation of the original Greek and Hebrew texts."

We always need to consider our lis-teners' possible *objections*—reasons why they might not accept our ar-gument. In other words, they might conclude that our evidence does not adequately support our claim.

Our audience's objections might seem weak to us, but we still need to consider and possibly even address them directly in our speech; admit-ting contrary claims usually gives our speeches more balance and increases our credibility with even hostile audi-ences. For instance, why would daily

IN THE SPOTLIGHT

Types of Reasoning
(*or* Argument)

- *Inductive*—using specific information to make general conclusions ("The con-version of the apostle Paul on the road to Damascus shows how God works in people's lives.")
- *Deductive*—using a general state-ment or principle to make specific conclusions ("Since all Christians go to heaven, and Augustine was a Christian, Augustine went to heaven.")
- *Causal*—using evidence to say that something causes something else (cause to effect; e.g., "Religious fanati-cism causes terrorism.") or something that happened was caused by some-thing else (effect to cause; e.g., "Terror-ism is caused by religious fanaticism.")

IN THE SPOTLIGHT

Making a Logical Argument

- *State a claim.* State something as true ("The NIV is a good choice for daily Bible reading").
- *Provide reasons.* Provide reasons that support your claim ("Because the NIV is both easy to read and biblically ac-curate, it is a good choice for daily Bible reading").
- *Offer evidence.* Offer evidence/material that supports your claim, preferably from sources that have credibility with the audience ("Bible scholars say that the NIV is easy to read and an accurate translation of the original texts").

SERVANT SPEAKING TIP

When preparing to persuade through logic, list all possible evidence and reasons why your particular audience would and would not be likely to accept your MAIN IDEA. Then use the most strongly supported reasons. If necessary, explain why your reasons are stronger than opposing reasons, given the evidence that you have discovered.

Bible readers not want to use the NIV? Why do they already prefer a different translation? What evidence do they have that a different version would be better for daily reading and study? Whom might they believe more than our sources of evidence?

Use Evidence—Secondary and Personal

Logical arguments are necessarily based on evidence. We cannot persuade effectively just

IN THE SPOTLIGHT

Types of Secondary Evidence

- *Statistics*. Verifiable data from credible sources (not questionable statistics passed along from unknown sources) can support our claims and challenge opposing claims ("The bestselling and fastest-growing version of the Bible in the United States is the NIV").

- *Examples and illustrations*. Particular, relevant examples and illustrations that document exactly what we are claiming—such as the actions of particular persons or groups, frequently presented as events, reports, or stories—can be particularly convincing ("The initial print run of over a million copies sold out before they were even done printing. Such was the demand for an accurate, readable Bible. Dozens of evangelical denominations, churches, and seminaries embraced the NIV as their official Bible translation for preaching, study, public reading, and personal use").

- *Definitions*. Experts' definitions of key words and phrases can help us credibly define, frame, and argue our claims ("The NIV

captures the syntax, grammar, and idioms of Scripture").

- *Testimony*. Just as courts use witnesses' testimonies to determine the truth or falsity of legal claims, we can use other individuals' or groups' testimonies as evidentiary support for our claims ("I preach to thousands of people each year and my NIV Bible is with me every time. . . . It is the version I've used to memorize and internalize God's holy word."—Lysa TerKeurst, author and speaker).

- *Facts*. Although facts can be statistical, most are not. Facts are simply true statements about states of affairs—the way things really are in the world around us. Such facts are the "is" and "are" predicates: such and such *is* true, not opinion ("Genesis is the first book in the Bible"; "A team of fifteen biblical scholars representing numerous denominations created the NIV using the earliest, highest-quality manuscripts available").

by making claims without supporting evidence; unsupported opinions are not evidence. We conduct research partly to gain evidence that we can use logically in persuasive speeches. The Bible, for instance, provides various kinds of evidence for Jesus's divinity, from his miracles and his understanding of Scripture to his death and resurrection. Witnesses to his life on earth after his death provide evidence.

Of course, we have to tune our evidence to our audience. What will our audience consider reasonable evidence? Which types of evidence will help us persuade them? Evidence is often divided into two categories:

Persuasive Claims: Fact, Value, and Policy

Karl Payton
Professor of Communication

As servant speakers, we make and defend claims that we hope our neighbors will adopt as their own. These include claims of *fact, value,* or *policy*.

In a claim of fact, we assert that something is either true or not true: "Christianity has positively affected society."

In a claim of value, we raise moral matters or compare options: "Christianity provides more peace of mind than does agnosticism."

In a claim of policy, we declare that something needs to be done, either by the audience or someone else: "All should accept God's gift of salvation."

The three types of claims call for different persuasive approaches—sometimes called "patterns."

We could organize a speech supporting a claim of fact by listing points of evidence. With this statement-of-reasons (or simple logic) pattern, we could support our claim about the positive impact of Christianity by listing institutions such as compassionate charities, hospitals, schools, and orphanages established by Christians.

For claims of value, we might use a causal pattern to connect good choices to positive outcomes, or bad choices to unpleasant results. We could also use a comparative advantages approach, listing the pros and cons of competing ideas. For instance, we might compare Christianity's assurance of eternal happiness with agnostics' perpetual doubt.

These types of claims and persuasive approaches often involve different ways of organizing our speech. Speech organization and argument work together.

Choosing how to support a claim of policy depends on whether the audience or a third party would be acting on our persuasive idea. If our claim is directed to a third party, we are really just asking our neighbors to agree with us. We can use the statement of reasons, the comparative advantages, or other patterns for this kind of policy speech. If, however, we want our neighbors to act on our claim of policy—to believe or even do something—we must lead them to a moment of decision. Monroe's Motivated Sequence is probably the most widely used approach.

IN THE SPOTLIGHT

Monroe's Five-Step Motivated Sequence Applied to an Evangelistic Speech Situation

1. *Attention.* Gain audience attention by making the speech highly relevant: "People are looking for meaning in their life."
2. *Need.* Show the specific need that the speech addresses: "God gives our life meaning, but sin separates us from God."
3. *Satisfaction.* Offer a means of satisfying the need, a solution for the problem: "God sent his only son, Jesus Christ, to pay for our sins."
4. *Visualization.* Help the audience see and desire the anticipated outcome: "You can have the assurance of everlasting happiness in heaven."
5. *Action.* Directly ask the audience to think or act according to the speech purpose and goal: "I invite you to accept God's gift of forgiveness and salvation."

Adapted from Alan H. Monroe, *Principles and Types of Speech* (New York: Scott, Foresman, 1935).

---

(1) *secondary* or external evidence based on our research and (2) *personal* or internal evidence based on our own life experience. What biblical scholars say about the NIV is secondary evidence. What we say based on our own experience using the NIV is primary evidence. Our actual experience makes our personal evidence more than unsupported opinion, but it might not convince others. Personal evidence can seem highly subjective because it is *anecdotal*—a brief story based on just one or a few persons' experiences.

Primary (internal) sources are particularly difficult to use effectively if we lack authority and credibility. Why should someone be persuaded just because we personally say so? Who are we to claim anything that itself is convincing?

Nevertheless, we know from Christian witness—testimony—that personal experience can be both relevant and convincing in some situations. But in most cases our personal life evidence can supplement secondary evidence. We know what a Christian testimony is and what it means to us partly because of the credible secondary testimonies we find in Scripture.

Use Logic with a Comparative Advantages Approach

A second way of organizing a persuasive speech—after simple logic—is a *comparative advantages* approach (sometimes called a *two-sided* approach). When persuading an audience, we develop both the pros and the cons of our MAIN IDEA in order to show that our claim is more convincing given our evidence. This persuasive approach is widely used in debates, particularly because both sides typically know in advance the strengths and weaknesses of their own claims and supporting evidence.

For example, we could begin to persuade daily Bible readers to use the NIV over the other two most popular English translations by listing the advantages and disadvantages of all three. Then we could argue that the NIV, relative to the other translations, is the logical choice.

SERVANT SPEAKING TIP

When developing a persuasive speech for a Christian audience, consider using a comparative advantages approach because there are often reasonable differences of opinion and behavior across Christian groups.

If the evidence is not in our favor, we might have to consider a different speech topic. We might even want to change our own Bible preference! Our story of personally changing from one Bible translation to another could then be a great opening story for a new speech. However, personal experience (anecdotal testimony) is only one type of evidence, and if our audience does not already know and trust us, we probably would not have enough positive ethos to make our case persuasively.

Similarly, imagine that we are going to persuade Christians that baptizing new adult believers with full immersion is more biblical than sprinkling them with water. Some members of our audience might know a lot about what the Bible says about baptism. Using a comparative advantages pattern, we could first explain the two interpretations of Scripture regarding adult baptism. Then we could argue why our view is more soundly biblical on the basis of evidence.

We have a duty to search for and assess contrary evidence anyway. We might even determine that our MAIN IDEA is logically weak enough—compared with counter-evidence—that we have to change it.

Use Logic with Problem-Solution Organization

A third way of organizing and arguing a persuasive speech—after a simple logic and comparative advantages approaches—is to state a problem that our audience has and then offer the most logical solution. The *problem-solution* approach defines the audience's felt problem and then argues for the best or only reasonable solution.

This approach works best when our audience already feels the burden of the problem. Otherwise, we have to convince listeners that they have a problem. This is a major factor in unsuccessful evangelism, for instance. But it is difficult to convince an audience that faith in Jesus will wash away personal sins. It is probably even more difficult to convince some listeners in the first place that they are sinners who need salvation.

Do most Christians who read Scripture daily feel the need for a better English-language Bible translation? If not, we probably should not use a problem-solution approach to convince them to use a particular translation. In fact, we might not even want to try to persuade them to use any version. We might instead want to prepare an informative speech that merely highlights the strengths and weaknesses of different translations for daily reading. We can use the comparative advantages approach to provide information, and then let the audience decide what to do with the information. In such an informative speech, we do not have to take sides.

Face the Difficulty

As I have said repeatedly, persuasion is difficult. In spite of all the evidence we collect, and regardless of how logically we present it to support

---

A Speech to Persuade Students That They Do Not Really Lie Very Often

A student gave a thoroughly credible speech based on the MAIN IDEA that most of the time when we think we are lying, we actually are not lying. She aimed to persuade students to stop thinking that they lied frequently. Her case rested on two forms of evidence: (1) surveys showing that people think they lie daily, and (2) the historical definition of a lie as a statement intended to deceive.

She said something like this: "Most of the time we think that we are lying, we are just passing along information that we believe is true. We ought to stop thinking that we are terrible liars."

That was an interesting idea for a persuasive speech. In one sense, it seemed to challenge what we Christians believe about sin. We lie all the time, right? Why else would lying—false testimony—be in the Ten Commandments? As she argued, we infrequently lie according to the ethical idea that, in order to tell a lie, we have to know that what we are saying is definitely false.

She was not successful in changing other students' minds. In fact, her classmates challenged her. They accepted the evidence that people lie frequently but rejected the evidence that a lie has to be intentional.

She thought she was doing students a favor by easing some of their guilt. But the audience's preexisting attitudes were so strongly against her second form of evidence that she failed to persuade. She might have been more successful if she had found evidence that few of the many "lies" people tell daily are actually intentional. But persuasion is difficult, and she still might have failed.

our reasons, we face an uphill battle. Most people cannot recall a single instance when they changed someone's mind about something the other person felt strongly about. The easiest persuasion has to do with things that people do not hold strong attitudes about—like how to grill salmon or which bank to use.

When I poll students after a persuasive speech, few of them indicate that the speaker changed their minds. Often the best a classroom speaker can do is get the audience thinking about something that it previously took for granted.

Persuasion usually occurs slowly, bit by bit. We need to set low goals. Even convincing our audience to be less opposed to our position is a notable victory. We are not going to convince most Christians to change the Bible translation that they use for daily reading or study. But we might convince them to explore other options by suggesting they compare translations on websites like biblegateway.com or biblehub.com.

Identify Poor Reasoning—Fallacies

Living in a fallen world, we Christians acknowledge that people say ridiculous things. Christians too make poor arguments based on erroneous evidence and faulty logic.

Nevertheless, we can avoid the most common *fallacies*—errors in reasoning. The more we attend to our own faulty logic, the greater our credibility. Also, we will be better able to identify poor reasoning in others' speeches.

Conclusion

Knowing that I was going to have to call attendees to come forward to begin or renew their personal relationship with Jesus Christ when I was preaching at the Baptist church, I tried to prepare. I considered logical and emotional appeals. Emotional ones seemed manipulative. Or maybe I just lacked the courage to use my own sermon: "You just heard about Adam and Eve's fall from grace. We've all fallen into sin. Now is your chance to avoid eternal hell; please step forward by grace into God's loving arms."

I just could not do it. I wanted to be rational. Logical. To appeal to the congregants' minds. I cannot recall exactly what I said, but it was logical and devoid of emotion. No one came forward. I do not think I would have come forward either. All I could think about at the time was that I never wanted to become a Baptist preacher, let alone an evangelist.

IN THE SPOTLIGHT

Common Speech Fallacies

- *Ad hominem argument*—an attack on a person's character, such as a statement that a particular television evangelist is a crook, without supporting evidence
- *Hasty generalization*—like a stereotype, a broad claim based only on specific cases, such as a statement that Christians do not believe in evolution
- *Red herring*—an irrelevant comment usually based on a sudden change of topic, such as a claim about Jesus's lack of divinity during a speech on the causes of current conflicts in the church
- *Begging the question*—a claim of fact with little or no basis in evidence, stated as if everyone agrees, such as the claim that everyone knows Christians are intolerant of other faiths
- *Circular reasoning*—a claim that begins with what it is claiming to prove, such as the claim that the Word of God is the Word of God because it says so

(Christians take this as a matter of faith, whereas nonbelievers see it as thoroughly circular reasoning)
- *Popularity*—a claim that something is true or right simply because many people believe it or do it, such as the claim that a Christian book is "good" or "authoritative" simply because it is on the best-seller list
- *False analogy*—a statement comparing two things that are not really alike, such as a claim that today's evangelistic campaigns are like the medieval Crusades
- *Either-or*—a claim that there are only two sides or options when in fact the situation is much more complicated, such as a claim that the Christian faith is either rational or irrational
- *Non sequitur* (Latin for "does not follow")—a claim that cannot reasonably be supported by the premise, such as stating that God cannot exist because there is suffering in the world

Learning how to use logic to become a persuasive servant speaker is not easy. There are no simple techniques that fit all situations. And sometimes we need pathos more than logos. I think I could have offered a real altar call if I had been a better persuader back then.

FOR DISCUSSION

1. To be fair and honest with our audience when delivering a persuasive speech, should we always address the arguments against our MAIN IDEA?

2. Which of the common speech fallacies do you think Christian speakers are most apt to use? Why?

3. How would you try to persuade a group of agnostics that the Christian faith is "logical"? What evidence would you use? Why?

4. Can you think of any potentially effective ways of logically persuading a non-Christian that the Bible is the Word of God?

SIXTEEN

Speak to Persuade Emotionally (Pathos)

I f we can touch peoples' hearts with our words, we might be able to persuade them. This is one of the most important things I have learned about public speaking in forty years of teaching and speaking. As servant speakers, we must touch hearts. Otherwise, much of our speaking will fail.

But how do we touch hearts? Not easily. Touching hearts is not a science. It depends on emotion more than on logical appeals. From a Christian perspective, it requires us to appeal to people's loves (or affections).

This chapter considers the importance of emotion (*pathos*) in persuasion. Emotional appeals can seem unethical, even manipulative. Sometimes they are. But we are not merely rational creatures. God has created us as creatures of heart.

Consider the Limits of Logic—Habits and Corrupted Minds

In most cases, persuading an audience purely through logic is insufficient. We humans are creatures of habit and emotion, not just reason. Sometimes we create reasons to believe or do something after we have already started believing and doing it; we *rationalize* our existing beliefs and actions. Then we reject reasons and evidence for why we should not believe or do the particular thing. We even offer ourselves excuses for not listening to people

A Passionate Freshman Lacking Ethos, Logos, and Pathos

The sole freshman in a public speaking class of mostly seniors saw an opportunity to change his classmates' sleep routines. The first-semester student claimed that everyone should start getting up by 7:00 a.m. so they could get more work done. He had no evidence except his own life; rising early worked for him. But he admitted that he had always been an early riser.

The whole situation seemed like a *Seinfeld* episode. Was the freshman expecting to suddenly change seniors' sleep habits? Did he think about the fact that a lot of people actually stay up late to get more work done—and that some people seem to be wired that way?

Moreover, he had little positive ethos because the rest of the class saw him as a naive freshman telling seniors how to live. He had no real logic—no evidence and reasoning. And he had little pathos—except for his personal enthusiasm for getting up early, which was hardly the basis for an emotional appeal to his skeptical audience.

The speech exemplified how not to persuade. The student wrongly thought that his passion and personal experience were sufficient.

who seek our best interest.[1] No wonder it is so hard to persuade people to do things that might even bless them.

We humans are not easily persuaded by logical appeals partly because of our *habits*—our repeated, often unquestioned ways of thinking and acting. Habits can be good or bad, but they generally are difficult to change. A ten-minute speech, no matter how logically argued and passionately delivered, is not likely to change an audience's ingrained habits.

How many times have we promised ourselves that we would pray more? Or that we would no longer engage in a particular sin? In spite of our good intentions, our existing habits hold us back. The apostle Paul summed up our problem when he said, "I do not understand what I do. For what I want to do I do not do, but what I hate I do" (Rom. 7:15).

Persuading people to give up their bad habits for good habits is a noble goal, but it takes a lot of research, planning, and practice. Most of the time we will fail, especially if we use only logic and set a high goal.

We humans also can be difficult to persuade logically because our minds are corrupted by sin. We tend to assume that we are more rational than we really are. We might even believe that we live entirely by a logical set of principles—such as a biblical worldview—that informs every aspect of our lives. But can any of us look honestly at our personal lives and still believe that our thinking and actions are free of sin?

Paul, the church's first great theologian, had not attained moral perfection. Did he lack a biblical worldview? Was he irrational? Paul, like us, was a fallen creature. Our minds as well as our hearts are corrupted (2 Cor. 3:14; 1 Tim. 6:5).

Speak to Preexisting Attitudes

To put it simplistically, we often need to appeal emotionally to audiences' existing *attitudes*—what people believe and especially feel about something. As I indicated earlier, attitudes are biases, often strongly held.

When I speak persuasively about forgiveness, I assume that everyone in the audience knows logically that they should forgive someone who has wronged them. But they are usually held back by resentment. I assume that their attitude toward forgiveness is positive even if they do not want to forgive particular people. I seek to appeal emotionally to their generally favorable attitude toward forgiveness.

I tell the story of when I forgave my alcoholic father for failing to nurture me as a child. I forgave him at his gravesite when I was sixty-three years old—the same age he was when he passed away. I waited decades, but I finally did what was right. It was an emotional experience that required me to change my attitude toward him.

My story helps open up others' hearts to forgive those who have hurt them. It is a strong emotional appeal based on the underlying positive attitudes toward forgiveness that reside in most people's hearts, if not their minds. People might not want to forgive those who wronged them, but most people are nevertheless moved by stories of reconciliation. They positively value forgiveness even if they do not always forgive others.

Face the Challenge

For a couple thousand years, rhetoricians emphasized combining logical and emotional appeals for the most effective persuasion. Contemporary research supports what the rhetoricians claimed long before the rise of modern science. The ancient speech organization patterns and rhetorical techniques addressed earlier in this book are relevant to today's logical and emotional appeals.

We also know that we have to combine logical and emotional appeals uniquely for each persuasive situation. We must examine the particular audience's attitudes toward the topic and perhaps toward us as speakers. The speaking context is essential—where, when, and to whom we are speaking. Then we can begin to get a sense of how we can persuade.

Two general rules about emotional appeals are consistently helpful: (1) use emotional appeals early in a speech to gain audience interest and open listeners' hearts (which is why I open my speeches on forgiveness with my troubled childhood), and (2) use emotional appeals toward the end of the speech to move the audience toward a change in belief or action (which is why I close my forgiveness speeches with the story of my eventual reconciliation with my father at his gravesite). Then I immediately call the audience to do the same—to forgive someone whom they know they ought to forgive.

Understand Affections—Heartfelt Loves

As a Christian scholar-teacher, I like to use the biblical language of "love" (or "affection") to understand how emotional appeals work. We can talk about appealing to people's attitudes, values, beliefs, and the like. But I find both in my faith and from my speaking experience that understanding "affections" helps me appeal emotionally to my audiences.

We appeal to our audience's *affections*—heartfelt loves. Affections are like deep attitudes having to do with what we truly like and desire—even what we most love.

Identify Audiences' Affections

We all live along an "affect continuum," with love on one side and hate on the other side. Lesser loves are "likes," closer to the center of the continuum. Lesser hates are "dislikes," also closer to the center.

In the New Testament, the Greek word *pathos* (emotion) is generally used negatively to refer to humans' mistaken and even evil loves (Rom. 1:26; Col. 3:5; 1 Thess. 4:5). Such corrupted affections are viewed as afflictions, such as lust and other passions that lead to human suffering.

The Gospels show that those who opposed Jesus were looking for reasons to accuse him (Mark 3:2; Luke 6:7), sometimes asking questions to trap him (Matt. 22:15; Luke 20:26; John 8:6). They apparently acted on the basis of negative emotions such as jealousy and pride. Their view of Jesus was on the hate side of the affect continuum.

An Emotional Appeal to Mercy for Neighbors

A student decided to persuade classmates to volunteer as mentors at a public library in a poor neighborhood. He had volunteered there for a semester as part of a service-learning project. Area kids began visiting the library when he was there, specifically to talk with him. As the student told us in his speech, he became friends with children who did not want to go directly home after school because they would be alone or their home life was so stressful.

He needed a way to convince other students to replace him at the library. He was passionate about the needs of the children and the value of volunteering there. At one point, while describing what it was like to meet with such kids and hear about their home lives, he was barely able to hold back tears.

The student speaker figured he should appeal to his classmates' hearts, not just their minds. He could have listed reasons and provided secondary research evidence for the importance of such after-school programs. But he wanted to move other students with an emotional appeal.

He said something along these lines: "If you volunteer just two days a week for one semester, it will change your life. You will be a big brother or sister to disadvantaged kids living in fear and lacking the kind of love you probably had growing up. You will even be Jesus to these amazing kids. Why not share love with them, just by showing up?"

After class a couple of classmates met with him in the hall to talk about his experience.

What exactly did the student appeal to in his classmates' hearts? He appealed to their sense of mercy for others. Mercy is a strong emotion. It is the basic emotion for some of the best, most selfless human love. It is not pity. In fact, I did not get any sense that the student pitied the children who hung out with him at the library. He loved them as an ambassador of Christ.

Along the way, the student had to use the right kind of mercy-capturing language. He did it by describing two of the kids he had gotten to know. He described their difficult home lives. Their smiles. Their laughter. Their joy at having him as an older friend.

He also did it by telling the story of his own volunteer experience. He went to the library largely to fulfill a service-learning credit. Within the first few weeks he considered his visits there the highlights of his week. He felt the kids' love for him. The experience also transformed his view of what it was like to be a child in a broken home in a rough neighborhood. He said that he came to appreciate his own upbringing more, as well as how God can use someone like him to bless others in need. He learned mercy, and he appealed to his classmates' hearts.

So what did Jesus do as a rhetorician? He appealed to his critics' hearts. He said they loved the wrong things, including their religiosity, their legalism, their pride, their social standing in the community, and ultimately themselves. Jesus rarely argued with them logically about the Scriptures.

Use Negative or Positive Appeals

We can use emotional (affective) appeals positively or negatively. For instance, suppose we are preparing a speech to persuade Christians to spend more time daily in prayer. Our MAIN IDEA is "Replace just ten minutes of your daily social media use with prayer for a deeper spiritual life."

We could try a *negative emotional appeal* based on a possible negative outcome: "If you don't trade ten minutes of social media for daily prayer, you might fall completely into sin." That would be a severe, even manipulative, appeal. Would anyone believe us? Logically, probably not. Emotionally, probably not.

We could consider a softer negative appeal: "Trade ten minutes of social media usage for daily prayer before you become a spiritually indifferent person." Still, would a negative, fear-based appeal on this topic work with our audience? Is it even respectful?

The problem with most fear-based appeals is that they do not offer anything appealing. Nothing to love. They tend toward negative emotions such as shame and guilt.

We could also try a *positive emotional appeal*—based on the likely positive outcomes for our audience. We might appeal to our Christian audience's likely desire to love the Lord more deeply. If we can appeal positively to that affective desire, we might be able to persuade our audience at least to try changing daily prayer habits.

One question then is how strongly our audience desires to love the Lord more intimately. Another one is whether our audience would believe what we are offering them. Do they feel, as well as think, that prayer can lead them to a deeper relationship with Jesus? Has their experience with prayer led them at all to love prayer? Or do they see prayer negatively as ineffective and laborious—maybe even just boring? Where is prayer on their affect continuum?

We could testify personally about the positive impact of more prayer in our own lives. Also, we could tell the stories of others who successfully pursued greater daily intimacy with God. We might even record a few short video clips of such people telling their stories. In short, we could help our audience identify with those who have found greater love for God by increasing daily prayer. We could paint a picture of a deeper, more loving relationship with Jesus and then invite our audience to participate in such wonderful love. If our audience already has a desire to be closer to the Lord through prayer, we might be somewhat successful. If not, such an appeal to intimacy with God will probably not work.

From a Christian perspective (borrowing from Augustine), we can say that all of our audiences have conflicted loves. Each of us loves numerous, often conflicting things. Our loves are disordered in the sense that we do not love God first, and then our neighbor as ourselves. We love some things more than God. We love ourselves more than we love others. We love some sins more than others. We are messes. When we use emotional appeals based on our affections, we have to explore such messiness.

IN THE SPOTLIGHT

Using Love in Emotional Appeals

- *Desire*. What or whom does our audience love (its affections) with respect to our topic, especially as reflected in existing attitudes and behavioral habits? Does our audience love prayer or feel indifferent about it?

- *Order*. How strong are existing affections relative to competing ones in the hearts of our audience members? Does our audience love social media more than prayer?

- *Hope*. Given our audience's disordered loves, what kind of right-ordered love might the audience hope to gain through our speech? Could our audience imagine—and perhaps act on—the idea that less time with social media and more time in daily prayer is worth pursuing as a way of putting the love of God first in their lives?

- *Action*. How can we move our audience members to know and act rightly, in tune with affections that will help them flourish as God's image bearers? Would a positive or negative appeal work better? How can we touch our audience's heart with respect to our MAIN IDEA so that they spend more time daily in prayer? Testimonials? Scripture? What kind of evidence—logical or emotional—might help us persuade our audience to believe and do what we are claiming would be good for them?

Appeal Practically to Affections

As servant speakers, we persuade others in order to help them identify and practice right loves—to flourish as human beings made in God's image. This is both our motive and our goal. And it can be enormously practical. We might seek to persuade our audience to exercise more, criticize less, be more patient, or tutor a needy student. We can judge our motives and methods in the light of God's call for us as speakers to love our neighbors as ourselves.

When I speak to college students and recent graduates on the topic of writing effective résumés, I know that I need to do more than simply inform them. I need to persuade them to examine all of their life experience, not just their education and paid employment. In effect, I need to persuade them to love their lives and to see the value in what they have already experienced.

When I speak to Christians on the topic, I take it a step further. I persuade

Evoking Emotions in Speeches

- *Language*. Use evocative language that appeals especially to people's positive desires. For Christians, such language often has to do with grace, love, mercy, and hope.

- *Stories*. Use narratives, including testimonials, to help the audience feel the emotions that characters are feeling. For Christians, such stories are parables that can point to God's kingdom on earth.

- *Vision*. Cast a vision of a positive or negative state of affairs—such as a wonderful or horrible job or relationship—that the audience can identify with. For Christians, the most evocative states of affairs are "hellish" versus "heavenly" relationships and experiences—that is, those that seem to be more like hell or heaven on earth.

- *Body*. Use nonverbal actions that mirror linguistic emotions. For Christians, such actions often involve nonverbals that suggest a hospitable heart and warm embrace versus a closed heart and personal indifference. Widespread, open arms with open hands are among the most effective nonverbals for hospitable persuasion. So are smiles with accompanied with eye contact.

them to consider what God has been doing in their lives, preparing them for more than what they have yet imagined. Writing a résumé can be extremely frustrating and depressing for those who dismiss unpaid work experience. But it can be very rewarding and encouraging for those who are persuaded to look beyond the narrow categories of formal education and professional experience to the nurturing love of God in their lives. So I appeal to students on an emotional as well as a logical basis.

In effect, I appeal to their existing love of and faith in a personal God who as the Holy Spirit is already active in their lives. This kind of positive appeal directs me away from suggesting anything that would discourage such students. I know from experience that if I give them a sense that they are dumb or ignorant about résumé writing, they will not listen to me. My ethos will suffer considerably, and they will tune me out.

Wonder Out Loud

I would like to conclude this chapter with what I call a rhetoric of wonder. My idea is that by nature we humans, made in God's image and likeness, wonder about what we love and should love.

Some of my most persuasive speaking today is like wondering out loud with others. This is a soft emotional appeal to others' desire to wonder about (or imagine) a better life for themselves. For example, to persuade

Christians I often wonder with them about goodness and grace. I do it with curiosity and delight. This rhetoric of "wondering out loud" is personal, invitational, and positive.

I still end with a call to belief or action, but I first paint a picture of goodness and grace. I open my heart and invite audience members to wonder about their affections.

Wondering Out Loud about Hell

When I was beginning a round of impromptu speaking, students asked me to go first. I agreed. I even let them give me a topic. Their choice was "hell."

The only good news for me was that students laughed so long that I had extra time to think. I did not know what to say. I could have offered some biblical references to the concept of hell, but I was not a biblical expert to do it well. Moreover, it can be a divisive topic among Christian tribes. My class included a range of faith traditions from Roman Catholics to Pentecostals to Baptists. What could I do?

I decided to wonder out loud with my audience.

First, I admitted that I was the wrong person to speak definitively on the topic. I said I loved the topic, not the place. And I admitted that I was not an expert they should trust.

Using indirect communication, I then made a metaphorical leap. I talked about growing up in a hellish family situation with an alcoholic father and paranoid schizophrenic mother. I wondered out loud if the relational brokenness and loneliness I felt in that situation might be a small taste of what hell is like.

Students were no longer laughing; they seemed to be wondering.

So then I wondered out loud if the warm and loving relationships I eventually gained through my spouse, children, and grandchildren might be something like a taste of heaven.

I created emotional space for us all to wonder. I did not solve any theological issues associated with the concept of hell. I did not directly persuade anyone to adopt my personal views on the topic. I did not speak prophetically about the need for the students to live righteously or be destined to hell.

Then I said that maybe the ways we humans act toward one another create hellish or heavenly relationships on earth. Perhaps when we love one another as God has loved us, we create signposts to the kingdom of God—tastes of heaven on earth.

We had a great discussion after my impromptu speech. Students openly expressed different Christian perspectives without criticizing one another. They even admitted their own lack of biblical understanding of the topic. We wondered biblically together. In short, we communicated about a potentially divisive topic. And here is the most amazing thing: my own wondering had prepared our hearts and minds to be taught about the topic, even to be persuaded.

Of course, the gospel is the ultimate message for deepening our loves, so that God becomes our first and most intimate love. For us, Jesus is both emotion (*pathos*) and word (*logos*) incarnate. But I think there is something metaphorically important about how Jesus works in our hearts that can help us reach others' hearts: the wonder that the Spirit creates in us so that we want to be closer to God.

A rhetoric of wonder may be one of the most important kinds of emotional appeals we can make in a world of hate and division.

Conclusion

Persuasive appeals are difficult. Emotional appeals are difficult. They have to do with our hearts, not just our minds.

In this chapter I took the liberty to go beyond the typical material in public speaking textbooks about how to write appeals to human emotions. I offered a Christian perspective that might help us all be more effective persuaders in contemporary culture. Although emotional appeals can be powerful, we need to use them cautiously and with respect for our audiences.

FOR DISCUSSION

1. Are human minds really corrupted, making us less than fully rational persons? Can you think of a common belief or action that is not rational?

2. What does it mean to say that God created us as "lovers"? Does this help us understand emotional persuasion in terms of people's different motivations, such as being successful (in a career) versus simply for the love of it (as an amateur)?

3. How might we approach our audiences' affections (deep loves) in a persuasive speech designed to get listeners to volunteer at a local food bank for the poor—using positive or negative emotional appeals?

4. Can you think of a time when you felt you were being emotionally manipulated by a speaker? Describe it. Then explain your feelings at the time.

SEVENTEEN

Share Special Moments

When my mother passed away, I was the only one who offered a eulogy. She was a difficult person because her illness made her paranoid. She criticized even loved ones and rejected her children's spouses and her grandchildren. I gave the eulogy at a gathering of close family after the funeral. I first offered a confession about how difficult it was to love her. Then I thanked God for her, challenges and all.

At the heart of our Christian faith is our gratitude to God for all good things, especially the good news of Jesus Christ. Even life's challenges can be causes for celebration. They help us grow and provide situations where God's glory can be made manifest in our weaknesses. The apostle Paul calls us to give thanks in all circumstances (1 Thess. 5:18).

We gather for important milestones, like weddings, graduations, baptisms, and award ceremonies, rightly expecting one or more speakers. At funerals, we remember and give thanks for the deceased. We need speakers to help us mark the occasions.

This chapter considers speaking at special gatherings. It discusses how to introduce speakers, speak impromptu, and speak at common occasions such weddings and funerals.

Introduce Speakers

I encourage mentees to practice servant speaking by volunteering to introduce speakers, such as in classes, at work and civic events, and in churches.

IN THE SPOTLIGHT

Introducing a Speaker
(select and vary tips based on the situation)

- *Tone.* Determine the seriousness or lightheartedness and the formality or informality of an introduction by considering the occasion and topic as well as your relationship to the speaker.
- *Length.* Since an introduction is not a speech and should not divert attention from the speaker, shorter is better—perhaps thirty to sixty seconds.
- *Pronunciation.* Determine and practice the correct pronunciation of the speech title and the speaker's name, title, affiliation, and geographic place of residence or work.
- *Sponsors.* Give credit and express gratitude to any organizations sponsoring the speaker and event.
- *Purpose.* In addition to identifying the speaker, give the audience a reason to listen well, especially any information about why this particular speaker and topic are important for listeners.
- *Personalization.* Without drawing attention to yourself, explain why you personally are honored to introduce the speaker, such as something the speaker has written or said that has influenced your thought or practices related to the topic.
- *Credentials.* Honor the speaker by reviewing significant credentials, from books and influential articles to major speaking engagements, academic degrees, and special honors and awards.
- *Welcome.* While looking at attendees, invite them to welcome the speaker; then smile, applaud with the audience, and welcome the speaker to the podium with a handshake before returning to the audience.

Few people volunteer; opportunities are abundant. Sometimes opportunities arise at the last minute, even at the event. These are essentially impromptu speaking opportunities. We will not usually volunteer unless we commit ourselves in advance to take advantage of such opportunities.

Speak Impromptu

We all are called occasionally to *impromptu speaking*—speaking on the spot, with little time for preparation. Impromptu speaking is sometimes called off-the-cuff speaking—referring to the practice of jotting notes on one's sleeve.

The first time I recall being asked to speak impromptu was at a wedding. The groom stood at the mic and suddenly asked me to talk about my role in bringing the couple together. I briefly told the story.

Impromptu Speech

- *Gratitude*. If appropriate, thank the person who invited you to speak.
- *Occasion*. Speak to what the audience likely expects at such an occasion (e.g., congratulatory words, memories/recollections, insights, observations, or wisdom and direction).
- *Story*. In most cases, a brief personal story about the topic or person(s) involved is sufficient and effective.
- *Humor*. Many impromptu speaking situations benefit from lighthearted humor.
- *Positivity*. Nearly all impromptu speaking should be upbeat, not critical or negative.
- *Brevity*. Limit the speech length, perhaps sixty to ninety seconds, depending on audience desires and expectations.
- *Relevance*. Speak only to the situation even if you have other engaging ideas or memories.

On another occasion, my church took a congregational vote to offer a position to one of two potential pastors. The ballot counters reported that the two candidates had received an equal number of votes. Elders said there was nothing in the congregation's bylaws about how to proceed. We all sat in silence, stunned and confused.

A founding member of the congregation stood up and gave an impromptu speech, suggesting that we should pray, trust God, and vote again. Who could disagree with such a wise suggestion? He prayed, the congregation voted again, and one candidate gained a majority. A faithful church member saved the day with fitting words. He was just the right person, respected by everyone. As far as I could tell, we all went home in peace and gratitude.

The best impromptu speaking comes from our hearts. We quickly size up the situation and then say something in tune with what people expect.

Speak at Celebratory Occasions

Beyond standard speeches to inform and persuade, we can speak with delight at special occasions—occasions to celebrate, commemorate, inspire, and entertain.

Aristotle and other ancient rhetoricians studied *epideictic oratory*—a broad term that included speaking at many kinds of popular ceremonies in ancient Greece and Rome. Speeches sometimes were designed to criticize opponents as well as to praise friends. The Greek origins of the word "epideictic" suggest something that is fit for displaying or showing off. In other words, a ceremony was a time for impressive speeches.

Identify the Occasion

Occasions mark our lives. We hear that we are receiving an award—or that a dear friend is—and the accomplishment will be celebrated at a special ceremony. We learn that our parents or grandparents are having a special anniversary—with a party that we would not miss. We receive an invitation to a beloved coworker's retirement celebration—and we are eager to give thanks with others. We discover that a couple we admire is getting married—and we want to rejoice with them at the wedding. We mourn a relative's passing, but we know she was a faithful person who served others throughout her life—and we look forward to the funeral as a celebration.

Such important events can convey great meaning and build communities of gratitude. "As human beings," says Frederick Buechner, "we also know occasions when we stand outside the passing of events and glimpse their meaning. Sometimes an event occurs in our lives . . . through which we catch a glimpse of what our lives are all about and maybe even what life itself is all about."[1]

Delight the Audience

Showy rhetoric seems to conflict with servant speaking. How are our neighbors served if we are trying to impress them? On the other hand, some occasions do call us to speak with greater flair and even infectious delight. These occasions usually provide a context and purpose for being a bit showy. We can simply have more fun. Eugene H. Peterson writes, "No lover was ever celebrated enough, no death ever mourned enough, no life adored enough, no achievement honored enough."[2]

When we speak at a graduation party, for instance, we need to be enthusiastic and complimentary. Everyone knows that our job is to praise and highlight the graduate's accomplishments.

Even when we offer eulogies at funerals, we can serve the gathering by speaking emotionally about what the person meant to us. At a Christian funeral, we can simultaneously praise God for the person and draw attention to the ways God blessed us through him or her.

Highlight Endearing Quirks

Often it is fitting to poke fun at some of the subject's quirks. We might playfully point out some of the person's idiosyncrasies or eccentricities, especially if everyone knows about them and they are more endearing than objectionable. We address foibles, not failings.

Imagine a funeral where everyone spoke only glowingly about the deceased. Would it be authentically joyful? Would it be appropriate to address the fact that the deceased tended to be tardy—and that we were glad he

> **SERVANT SPEAKING TIP**
>
> When trying to describe a person's quirks for a celebratory speech, imagine yourself with the same quirks. Would you consider your language endearing or demeaning?

finally showed up on time for an event? Our point would not be to criticize but to remember together that he too was human. Still, we need to be sensitive about whether such a comment is more likely to amuse or offend. By contrast, at a retirement party the same human quirk probably could be addressed anecdotally without fear of offending attendees.

Celebratory speaking, then, can honor both the subject (person or institution) and the audience by capturing everyone's shared humanness as imperfect people who nonetheless bless others. We all are like the honoree in that we too have our quirks. And we all are like the honoree in that we accomplish things and delight others.

Celebrate to Remember

Addressing an audience at a celebratory occasion borrows meaning from ancient forms of worship. The word "celebrate" has religious connections. We "celebrate" the Lord's Supper as a memorial of Christ's death and resurrection.

In other words, when we celebrate an occasion, we join with others in remembrance and thanksgiving. We "perform" the celebration, including our speech. We are somewhat like worship leaders, conducting a ceremony for all the participants. In the Roman Catholic Church and other traditions, a participant in the Mass is called a "celebrant." Celebration suggests a kind of ritualistic remembering, honoring, and praising.

One of the most famous celebratory speeches of all time was given by Jesus at the Last Supper, where he created a new occasion for us to observe. When we celebrate Communion, our leader usually recalls Jesus's words for us. The leader verbally (with words of remembrance) and nonverbally (with the Communion elements) guides us into celebratory participation.

> **SERVANT SPEAKING TIP**
>
> When planning a celebratory speech, use all fitting verbal and nonverbal means of expression to make the occasion memorable. Speak about what you would like to remember, and presumably what others would as well.

Focus on the Subject

When we share special moments, we need to draw attention to the speaker rather than to ourselves.

In one of my commencement addresses, I told stories from my own education. I intended

Jesus's Celebratory Words at the Last Supper

While they were eating, Jesus took bread, and when he had given thanks, he broke it and gave it to his disciples, saying, "Take it; this is my body."

Then he took a cup, and when he had given thanks, he gave it to them, and they all drank from it.

"This is my blood of the covenant, which is poured out for many," he said to them. "Truly I tell you, I will not drink again from the fruit of the vine until that day when I drink it new in the kingdom of God."

When they had sung a hymn, they went out to the Mount of Olives.

Mark 14:22–26

to help the graduates identify with how God used me beyond my educational accomplishments and professional expectations. I sought to paint a picture of God's good plans for the graduates that far surpassed what they believed they could accomplish on the basis of their formal education. But I focused too much on myself and not enough on the graduates.

 IN THE SPOTLIGHT

Celebratory Speech

- *Brevity*. Keep it short and to the point.
- *Pacing*. Speak slowly, savoring responses and letting the audience think and remember; speed up if appropriate for telling an anecdote and toward the conclusion of your speech.
- *Humor*. Be funny, but only appropriately, with honor toward and compassion for the subject.
- *Story*. Tell anecdotes about the subject.
- *Focus*. Focus on the honoree, not yourself; tell your stories only about the subject.
- *Challenges*. Include trials that the person or institution had to endure and eventually overcome.
- *Quirks*. When speaking about a person, add endearing imperfections that are well known and will not come across as criticism.
- *Wordplay*. Use some, but not excessive, creative wordplay, including fitting and imaginative puns or double-meanings related to the honoree and the event.
- *Theme*. Use a short phrase or even one word that captures your MAIN IDEA; use it repeatedly but not excessively, perhaps three or four times.

Similarly, at a funeral, one of the deceased woman's business partners offered a eulogy about working with her. Even though his anecdotes were appropriate, he wrongly framed his remarks in terms of himself. He ended up highlighting what it was like for the deceased to work with him rather than what she was like at work. Because of the way he structured his comments, he became the subject of the eulogy. The audience learned more about him than the deceased.

Use a Unifying Theme

Many of the best celebratory speeches are variations on a theme. When we speak at a wedding, retirement party, or baptism celebration, for instance, we need to focus on one MAIN IDEA in tune with the purpose of the event.

When I spoke at my brother's sixty-fifth birthday celebration, I wanted to highlight his courage and hard work. I chose a theme tied to a popular television series, *Survivor*. I said that my brother overcame far more than most of us knew. He triumphed over deep hardships and became a successful entrepreneur who served many employees and an entire industry.

Add Positive Humor

It seems comical that rhetoricians would actually dissect humor. The more we analyze humor, the less funny it becomes. Comedians work hard on their phrasing and timing, but they still have to come across spontaneously. They need to tell a joke so well that everyone thinks they are the first ones to hear it. And everyone has to get the point of the joke.

Celebratory events cry out for such immediately appreciated humor. We strive to deliver. Our purpose is not just to be funny but also to open hearts.

When pastors tell a funny personal story near the beginning of a sermon, they open congregants' hearts to the sermon and the entire worship celebration. Even unplanned humor opens hearts. An accidental *malapropism*—using the wrong word for a similar one—can open hearts: "King David skillfully played the leer—I mean lyre."

Not all humor is appropriate at every event—especially unfitting satire, off-color remarks, and stock jokes. Thousands of joke books and websites offer poor humor: "One good

SERVANT SPEAKING TIP

When speaking to honor an organization, examine its mission statement for a fitting theme for your address.

thing about graduation is that you get to wear a funny hat that makes your brain look larger than it actually is." "Why didn't the skeleton go to prom? Because he had 'no body' to dance with."

Employ Playful Speech

Closely related to humor is using language playfully. This is tricky. We can easily be silly rather than fittingly clever. Because celebratory events are generally lighthearted even if somber—such as a funeral—we have more rhetorical space for playing with language.

Augustine, like earlier rhetoricians, believed that speakers ought to use any appropriate verbal means to engage audiences. He employed catchy witticisms in sermons. Even when speaking in a "plain style," he wrote, "believers should take steps to be heard not only with understanding but with pleasure and assent."[3]

Celebratory speaking can be like play—open, imaginative, and fun. When we speak playfully, we speak more freely from our deeper feelings. We are less bound by formal rules of speech.

In short, *wordplay*—using words playfully, usually humorously, to delight others—is a significant part of celebratory rhetoric. We might use puns, rhymes, *alliteration* (matching sounds at the beginnings of words), *neologisms* (made-up words), and words with multiple meanings.

Was Jesus a punster? Apparently so. For instance, in the parable of the growing seed, he said, "This is what the kingdom of God is like. A man [*adam*] scatters [*zara*] seed [*zera*] on the ground [*adama*]" (Mark 4:26).[4]

Analyze Occasions

Many speeches occur at *occasions*—common, somewhat ritualistic social events. They include public lectures, business presentations, speaker introductions, wedding toasts, and eulogies. Coaches must be inspirational speakers to keep players

SERVANT SPEAKING TIP

Avoid using the internet to quickly find tired or trite jokes and stories. Instead, use humorous personal anecdotes related to your theme and preferably from the life of the person or the history of the organization being honored.

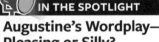

IN THE SPOTLIGHT

Augustine's Wordplay—Pleasing or Silly?

- "Faith must *hold* what it cannot yet *behold*."
- "The fisherman's *scope* is the rhetorician's *hope*" (about St. Peter).
- "The damage is not done by *militia-ness* but by *maliciousness*" (about the military profession not being inherently evil).

Garry Wills, *Saint Augustine* (New York: Viking, 1999), 70.

working hard together. Pregame and postgame speeches are rarely public, but they are important occasions.

One of the benefits of crafting speeches rhetorically is narrowing down our speaking tasks to recurring types of events with established *social conventions*—common ways of speaking, listening, and relating to audiences at specific kinds of occasions. We humans organize the world into occasions that provide guidelines for what to expect and how to act.

Preaching is one of the most common speaking practices in the world and usually occurs as part of a worship service. Yet delivering a sermon in most Protestant services is different than offering a homily at most Roman Catholic Masses. Protestant preaching tends to be longer and more

A Recent University Graduate Gives a Difficult Wedding Toast

A recent Christian university graduate faced a complicated relational context. His mother asked him to give the first wedding toast when she was getting remarried after divorcing his father. His brief speech would involve his relationships with God, guests, family members, and his mother and her new husband.

His biological father, whom he greatly loved and admired, was not invited—although the recent graduate knew that his toast would probably be reported to his father via other relatives. He felt some resentment toward his mother for the divorce, but he still loved her and wanted the best for her.

Moreover, he knew from other weddings that attendees have common expectations for wedding toasts—especially the first toast at the reception. They expect an upbeat, personal toast that sets the tone for those that follow.

He decided that he had to meet audience expectations for a wedding toast, be honest with himself, please his mother, and not offend his father.

He was so stressed-out that he had second thoughts, wondering if he should try to persuade his mother to ask someone else to give the first toast. But he knew that his mother needed his support and encouragement in front of family and friends. She was anxious about her new husband being accepted and loved.

He concluded that he would have to speak more about the future than the past. He could offer hope. He imagined that although some attendees would have second thoughts about the marriage, they all probably desired that everything would work out for good.

He spoke like this, with more elaboration: "Tonight I would like to be the first one to call us together with hope for this new couple's commitment to each other. May their love for each other grow daily."

explicitly exegetical and expository (interpreting and explaining the meaning of Scripture). In both cases, the ministers learn how to preach appropriately for their own traditions' worship occasions.

When we are called on to give an infrequent speech such as a wedding toast, we can research how to speak at such an event. What makes for a good as well as fitting toast? Once we have a sense of the occasion, we can think about how to address our specific relationships within that context.

We might also consider the relationships involved with our audience and us. Perhaps the audience already knows us. Members of the audience might be the honoree's family, friends, colleagues, or even adversaries.

We might need to know about any tension or divisions among the audience. How might we speak across the divisions? How can we speak primarily to one group in the audience without alienating others?

The university graduate who gave the wedding toast (see sidebar) was just beginning a speaking life. He might be called on years later to speak at his mother's funeral—a very different occasion. Or he might end up in a sales career, making client presentations. He might be asked to give his testimony at church. Perhaps his high school would ask him to speak to students about his field of work. These are typical speaking situations. His experience with the wedding toast helped him gain life experience defining an eventful occasion and relating to a particular audience.

Among other things, he learned to be fittingly brief. Long celebratory comments—including toasts—usually defeat our purpose. Rebbe Naphtali of Ropshitz captured the importance of brevity, suggesting that we make the introduction concise and the conclusion abrupt—with nothing in between.[5]

Conclusion

When I arrived at my mother's hospital room the night before she passed away, I took her hand and said, "Mom, it's me. I love you and Jesus does too." She lightly squeezed my hand, opened her eyes for the last time, and slipped into unconsciousness. I went to sleep in peace that night, knowing that I would positively eulogize the mother who caused me and others considerable grief. She passed away that night.

Speaking to close family after my mother's funeral was a challenge. I knew I needed to give thanks for her. She was made in God's image. She tried to love me while struggling with her disease. I spoke from a place of forgiveness. Since we Christians dwell in church cultures of praise and worship, we can be among the most celebratory servant speakers in society.

Blame-free celebration is in our spiritual DNA. We are forgiven. We forgive. We give thanks. Again and again.

FOR DISCUSSION

1. Should Christians really be among the most celebratory people? Is not celebratory rhetoric naturally prideful?

2. Why do we enjoy hearing about others' endearing quirks at celebratory events? Is it healthy?

3. What do you most remember about the last celebratory speaker you heard? What does that tell you about the rhetorical quality if not just the memorability of such speeches?

4. If a pun is fun, why do most people groan when they hear one? Are they only pretending that they do not enjoy them?

EIGHTEEN

Advocate for All Neighbors

Amy King

A church speaker persuaded me to mentor a disadvantaged child at one of the poorest schools in my area. The program matched me with a child for weekly academic tutoring. I soon realized that helping her with schoolwork was only one way of serving an at-risk student. My presence in her life as a caring adult was more meaningful to her than the tutoring itself. One church speaker convinced me to touch the life of one underprivileged child. It became a blessing for the student and for me.

As a matter of biblical justice, we are called to advocate responsibly for people in need, our neighbors in the biblical sense of the Good Samaritan helping his neighbor. Our neighbors might not look like us or share our beliefs and practices. Nonetheless, the Bible morally requires us to love them and even to speak up for them (Prov. 31:8–9). Augustine said that a just society submits to God.[1] As servant speakers, we offer our hearts, minds, and voices as God's tools for advocating justice in a broken world.

This chapter addresses our call to advocate for others in society. We should speak up for others as we would want to be supported if we were in our neighbors' situations. We need the knowledge, love, wisdom, and courage to speak up for victims of injustice, and against those who demean or even silence others.

Understand Biblical Justice

Scripture offers a view of justice linked to our love for neighbors because of their inherent worth as God's image bearers. Such biblical justice flows from our calling as stewards of God's world.

We speak up for others in need because they too are God's children and deserve to be served—just as we would want to be served. Our neighbors have the right to be treated fairly and loved as we would like to be loved. Such justice is grounded in the inherent worth that God gives every human being. We are the responsible species; we are the ones called under God to seek and promote justice as a fitting sign of our love for God and neighbor as self.

The Bible clearly calls us to seek justice for others as an expression of God's own heart. The prophet Amos declares, "But let justice roll on like a river, righteousness like a never-failing stream" (Amos 5:24). What could be more Christlike than to advocate for people in a way that does not benefit our self-interests? Jesus sacrificed his life so that we may be saved. If we are to be like Jesus, our actions need to be based on serving others rather than simply serving ourselves.

Part of loving our neighbors, then, is caring *for* (action) and *about* (attitude) them. Christian philosopher Nicholas Wolterstorff explains that "care combines seeking to enhance someone's flourishing with seeking to secure their just treatment."[2] If we genuinely love our neighbors, we desire to see them *flourish*—to grow in life-giving relationships. People cannot flourish when they are suffering injustice.

In cases where our neighbors are not treated rightly as human beings worthy of flourishing, we are called to *advocacy*—speaking up on their behalf. The root word *vocare* means "calling." We are called to care for neighbors in need partly by speaking up for them, just as God calls and sends the Holy Spirit as our advocate who caringly teaches us "all things" (John 14:26). When we advocate for others in a way that is motivated from a heart for justice, we are following God's example.

SERVANT SPEAKING TIP

Consider speaking about a volunteer experience that changed your life as well as served others. Advocate for those you served. Perhaps give a persuasive speech to recruit more volunteers.

Identify Communicative Injustice

This biblical view of care for and about others' flourishing is not just a big-picture concept. It includes our everyday relationships, including how we use language to build and destroy relationships. As servant speakers, we need to be especially mindful of *communicative injustice*—both demeaning others and excluding them from vital dialogue that affects their own flourishing.

Communicative justice can include how teachers verbally treat students and how world leaders speak to their fellow citizens. It can include relations between spouses, a congregation's relationship with its surrounding community, and a city mayor's relationship with citizens. Everywhere that people are being lied to, verbally abused, or excluded from conversations about their own futures, communicative injustice stifles human flourishing. We could become victims. Christian persecution, common

IN THE SPOTLIGHT

When to Speak Up in Society

- to advocate for religious freedom and for the freedom of religious expression (participative democracy)
- to empower the voiceless excluded from public discourse (communicative justice)
- to expose wrongdoing when direct confrontation has been insufficient (whistle-blowing)
- to repair others' reputations wrongly damaged by slander or libel (ethos restoration)

in parts of the world, includes condemning believers simply because of their religion and denying them voices in their own countries.

Gain Social Consciousness

Often we are not even aware of injustice. We are too busy working and caring for ourselves, family, and friends. When we have an opportunity to give a speech, we usually think within our own social circles and personal needs.

Old Testament scholar Walter Brueggemann challenges us to listen to broader social needs. He calls us, in tune with Scripture, to a "prophetic ministry" that seeks to "nurture, nourish, and evoke a consciousness and perception alternative to the consciousness and perception of the dominant culture around us."[3]

When we are part of the *dominant culture*—the everyday values and beliefs of most people in society—we easily ignore others' suffering and tend to be content in our own peaceful little world. We are not intentionally indifferent or uncaring; we are just unaware of others' suffering. We lack *social consciousness*—awareness of social issues beyond our personal experiences.

As we listen more attentively to others, we discover injustice both near and far. Missionaries, for instance, often report firsthand what life is like for others in distant parts of the world. Similarly, counselors and social workers from our own congregations can inform us about the needs of our communities.

Become Aware of Biblical Neighbors in Need

Scripture repeatedly addresses the needs of particular categories of people who tend to be treated unjustly in society. These categories point to justice-related speaking topics that might serve the poor, young, and oppressed.

Consider Speaking Up for the Poor

The apostle Paul and Barnabas met with Peter, James, and John to discuss their outreach to the gentiles and the circumcised. Paul said after the meeting that they agreed to "remember the poor" (Gal. 2:9–10). In Scripture the poor include the economically needy and the brokenhearted; they are frequently the same persons (Isa. 61:1).

When people lack basic resources to survive, they cannot flourish. If their primary concern is finding food, water, shelter, clothing, and basic health care, it is challenging to succeed in other areas. Often they do not have the means to tell their stories and advocate for potential social changes that might help them to flourish. And leaders on both the political right and left tend to use their plight to advance political agendas, without listening to those who are struggling.

As people who have been materially and spiritually blessed, we can help alleviate the suffering of the economically needy. Recognizing that it is nearly impossible for the needy to advocate for themselves while struggling to survive, we might be called to speak on their behalves, perhaps by persuading audiences to support the many local and global organizations committed to serving them.

SERVANT SPEAKING TIP

Search the internet for "local nonprofit ministries" to see which ones advocate for people in your community. Consider giving a speech about one of them.

Consider Speaking Up for Children

The Bible speaks abundantly about caring for children, who are a gift from the Lord (Ps. 127:3). Children are among society's vulnerable who depend on adults for all things. They need caring parents and other adults who will speak up for them, advocating for adoption, life-affirming policies, pregnancy counseling, foster homes, quality education, and the prevention of child neglect and abuse.

Christian attorney Bryan Stevenson, author of *Just Mercy: A Story of Justice and Redemption*, observes that in the United States alone over a quarter million children have been sent to adult prisons for long-term sentences. Moreover, some children are sentenced to life imprisonment without parole; nearly three thousand juveniles have been sentenced to die in prison.[4] How can that be? Might we study it and speak about it? Are there any ways we can serve children in our communities to help prevent it?

Consider Speaking Up for the Oppressed

The psalmist pleads with God's people to "defend the weak and the fatherless; uphold the cause of the poor and the oppressed" (Ps. 82:3). Who are the oppressors and oppressed—even today? James says *oppressors* are the ones who use their power to exercise harsh control over others (James 2:6).

Oppressors sometimes deny people basic human rights. They crush others' spirits through religious, ethnic, and racial prejudice. Most severely, they practice genocide, slavery, and violence against particular groups. Sex trafficking is an issue around the world today, often occurring invisibly in our own communities. In some parts of the world, Christians and members of other religious groups are silenced, discriminated against, and even killed for their faith.

The actual oppressors might be governments, fanatical religious movements, terrorists, or militarized groups seeking power. Authoritarian leaders demand obedience in many parts of the world. Wherever and whenever people are not free to speak up according to their consciences, oppressors are at work.

Just as we would not want to be physically or verbally enslaved, we speak in support of oppressed groups. Our voices might be essential in the court of public opinion for them to be heard.

Much of the church remained sympathetically silent if not apathetic during Hitler's reign in Germany. Dietrich Bonhoeffer, in contrast, spoke compassionately against the racial and political idolatry of that era, criticizing the "silent witnesses of evil deeds" and faulting the church for fighting "only for its self-preservation."[5] He was arrested, imprisoned, and executed toward the end of the war.

Long before the rise of democratic societies, the ancient Hebrews recognized God's mandate that people speak up for communicative justice.

God warned that people would be held responsible for failing to testify publicly about something they knew (Lev. 5:1).

Decide When and How to Advocate for Others

Speaking up for our neighbors in need is not simple. How do we know who is really in need? Who gives us the right to represent others? Can our own voice make a difference—or are we just wasting our time? There are important considerations.

Cultivate a Heart of Love for Neighbors

Are we rightly motivated? Rather than serving others to make us feel better about ourselves, we can engage in advocacy primarily to strengthen our neighbors' spirits and improve their circumstances. Selfless love, not pride or pity, can form our desire to see our neighbors flourish.

Understand Neighbors before Advocating

Before we advocate for neighbors, we must first be adequately informed about their circumstances and needs. Do we really know what we are talking about? Are we thinking merely in stereotypes? Is our interest in others superficial? Pity?

It is far too easy for us to think we can solve others' problems by telling them what to do. We do not like it when others tell us what to do. Something very deep and unexpected happens when we actually start listening to others.

We discover that God is already at work. We end up seeing and believing that God has spoken to others and things are happening. We find ourselves in communicative loops of grace. We thought we were going to help others, but by paying attention we realize that God is transforming us too. God does this partly by holding us back so we listen more and speak less. Before we know it, we are becoming advocates.

Know When to Speak Up

Sometimes the wisest action is to encourage people to speak for themselves. We must determine whether our voices are welcome by those for whom we would advocate. We are not called to tell the poor, young, or oppressed what to think and how to act. We are called to listen to them and speak only when appropriate.

Be Courageous

Christians and others often disagree about how to address social problems. Some wonder why any of us should speak up for those who supposedly do not help themselves. Are we willing to face criticism even from our own community if we address provocative topics and speak for demeaned groups? Do we have the courage?

This is especially true when we challenge common attitudes. Some Christians share society's implicit stereotypes, prejudices, and indifferences. They might wonder if we are just political pawns when we speak up for others.

A Christian speaker advocating for higher-education opportunities for prison inmates found that some believers disliked the idea. They felt it was wrong to provide educational services to convicted felons who, they argued, ought to be punished rather than rehabilitated.

Promote and Participate in Democratic Discourse

In addition to advocating for others, we can promote and participate in *democratic discourse*—respectful dialogue about shared interests. A government of the people works when citizens participate in the communication that will determine their own and their neighbors' futures.

We can participate in the public discourse about our neighbors' rights and responsibilities. This might include participating in town meetings, special lecture-discussions, government hearings, elected officials' public meetings, public debates, and many types of online audio and video discussions. YouTube has become a major platform for public discourse, even though some participants are uncivil.

Modern democracy is the exception rather than the rule around the world. As advocates for freedom and followers of Jesus Christ, we are called to participate in, foster, and protect civil democratic discourse. Human beings generally desire to shape their own futures by collaborating with their neighbors. We enjoy interacting with others in spite of the inevitable conflicts. As British statesman Winston Churchill put it, "Democracy is the worst form of government except for all the others that have been tried from time to time."[6]

We should not avoid democratic discourse because it is uncomfortable or inconvenient. Nor is it right for us to promote such discourse just so we can be heard in society. The world desperately needs civil, neighbor-serving, justice-promoting communicators. If we retreat into conflict avoidance and remain silent about injustice, we are not being responsible citizens and faithful followers of Jesus. When we advocate for democracy, we speak up for all who wish to participate; we champion the right even for those with whom we might disagree. This includes other religions.

Support Religion in the Public Square

Philosopher Richard Rorty has argued that people should never employ religious rhetoric in public life. He calls such language a "conversation stopper" that leaves no rhetorical room for political negotiation. If a believer says that abortion is murder, for instance, he supposedly eliminates rhetorical space for discussing other points of view.[7]

There is some merit to Rorty's concern. Even within churches, religious rhetoric can suffocate dialogue. Nevertheless, singling out religious rhetoric is unfair, since *any* deeply held conviction, religious or otherwise, can stifle public discourse. A secularist can be just as dogmatic as someone who believes in God. In fact, totalitarian leaders generally eliminate freedom of speech so they can silence all dissident voices. Moreover, a religious or nonreligious absolutist faces the same demands of public discourse as everyone else in a democratic society—making a credible, convincing case.

It appears that religious voices are being silenced in modern societies. Playwright Václav Havel, who was jailed for years under the Communists before becoming president of the liberated Czech Republic, says that the Western world is going through "a great departure from God which has no parallel in history." He warns that we are "living in the middle of the first atheistic civilization" and must rediscover a responsibility "higher" than human beings.[8] Havel is not speaking particularly as a Christian—and certainly not as an evangelical. He is addressing the modern tendency to cut off public discourse from the deeper, religious convictions and assumptions that can be found in many faiths.

We servant speakers need to recognize the rights of others to speak publicly in opposition to religion. But we can advocate for the right of people of all faiths to speak from their hearts and minds about public matters that potentially concern every citizen. To a large extent, religious faith provides the moral foundations for democracy, including respect for all persons and freedom of expression.

> **SERVANT SPEAKING TIP**
>
> Consider giving a speech about a Christian who, guided by faith and love, spoke for justice and made a positive difference locally or in the wider world.

Advocate with Others

When we feel called to speak against injustice, we can have greater impact by joining with like-minded people. Such partners likely share our faith.

We might even join with members of a socially marginalized group excluded from public discourse, helping them tell their stories. This kind of collaboration helps us understand others' circumstances, in their language. It teaches us humility and can deepen our love and respect for such neighbors.

When we partner with others to advocate for our neighbors, we form a social movement out of individual voices. We can be responsible participants in a choir of truth-seekers and truth-tellers. Two American examples are the abolitionist movement and the civil rights movement.

Historical Example 1: Speaking to Abolish Slavery

Slavery stains the history of many nations. Thankfully, democratic discourse and social movements rebuked and overthrew legal slavery in the United States.

While the voices of former slaves were essential for abolition, they were assisted by individuals who were not part of their group, such as Theodore Dwight Weld, Harriet Beecher Stowe, and William Lloyd Garrison.[9] They anchored antislavery rhetoric in biblical truth. Garrison proclaimed in an 1854 speech, "No Compromise with the Evil of Slavery,"

> If they are men; if they are to run the same career of immortality with ourselves; if the same law of God is over them as over all others; if they have souls to be saved or lost; if Jesus included them among those for whom he

Former Slave Frederick Douglass in 1852 on the Contradictions between Slavery and Christian Faith

You profess to believe "that, of one blood, God made all nations of men to dwell on the face of all the earth" [Acts 17:26], and hath commanded all men, everywhere, to love one another; yet you notoriously hate (and glory in your hatred) all men whose skins are not colored like your own. . . . The existence of slavery in this country brands your republicanism as a sham, your humanity as a base pretense, and your Christianity as a lie!

Frederick Douglass, addressing the Ladies' Anti-Slavery Society of Rochester, NY, July 4, 1882, quoted in Mark Noll, *A History of Christianity in the United States and Canada* (Grand Rapids: Eerdmans, 1992), 141.

laid down his life; if Christ is within many of them "the hope of glory"; then, when I claim for them all that we claim for ourselves, because we are created in the image of God, I am guilty of no extravagance, but am bound by every principle of honor, by all the claims of human nature, by obedience to Almighty God, to "remember them that are in bonds as bound with them," and to demand their immediate and unconditional emancipation.[10]

Garrison and Frederick Douglass together used biblical ethics to hold Christians accountable for their acts of slavery. Although Garrison was neither black nor a former slave, he sought justice for the flourishing of his African American neighbors. He challenged the dominant, slavery-supporting consciousness in much of the United States, including many churches.

Historical Example 2: Advocating for Civil Rights

While white churches in the 1960s were divided over equal rights for racial minorities, African American churches generally supported the growing civil rights movement, using the biblical cry for truth and justice to confront discrimination.

The Reverend Martin Luther King Jr. delivered one of the most impactful speeches in United States history. In his famous "I Have a Dream" address to 250,000 Americans gathered in 1963 at the Lincoln Memorial for the March on Washington for Freedom and Jobs, King declared it was "time to make justice reality for all of God's children." He concluded his commanding address, "When we allow freedom to ring—when we let it ring from every city and every hamlet, from every state and every city, we will be able to speed up that day when all of God's children, black men

---

**President John F. Kennedy Speaks
to the Nation about Civil Rights**

One hundred years of delay have passed since President Lincoln freed the slaves, yet their heirs, their grandsons, are not fully free. They are not yet freed from the bonds of injustice. They are not yet freed from social and economic oppression. And this Nation, for all its hopes and all its boasts, will not be fully free until all its citizens are free.

John F. Kennedy, addressing the nation in a televised speech from the White House on June 11, 1963, https:// americanrhetoric.com/speeches/jfkcivilrights.htm

and white men, Jews and Gentiles, Protestants and Catholics, will be able to join hands and sing in the words of the old Negro spiritual, 'Free at last, Free at last, Great God a-mighty, We are free at last.'"[11]

Conclusion

When the church speaker appealed to me and others to serve disadvantaged school children, I listened with my heart as well as my mind. I thought that God might be calling me to serve a young neighbor in need. Now I am grateful for the speaker who appealed to my heart and called me to action.

As a calling, servant speaking focuses our attention on the needs of our neighbors, including those who suffer injustices. The needs are all around us. We do not have to think big, as if we ourselves could solve world problems. As Jesus's followers, however, we cannot just observe and listen. We often must speak up.

FOR DISCUSSION

1. The words "justice" and "social justice" are frequently used in society today. What do people seem to mean by them? Do such meanings reflect a biblical understanding of justice as caring *for* (action) and caring *about* (attitude) human flourishing?

2. Micah 6:8 says, "And what does the LORD require of you? To act justly and to love mercy and to walk humbly with your God." How can we relate this verse to our servant speaking?

3. Can you identify any groups, organizations, or social institutions that you are part of that seem to prevent particular people from expressing themselves? Who does and does not get to determine the policies and programs? How might you speak up on behalf of the voiceless people?

4. How can we as Christians participate in public discourse in ways that do not alienate nonreligious citizens and truly do invite democratic discourse?

NINETEEN

Present in Groups

Heidi Petak

I attended a group presentation in which the leader had memorized every line spoken by the other presenters. He watched each speaker carefully and mouthed every word. I do not remember much of what the group said, but I can still picture him lip-synching.

Few of us truly enjoy group work, let alone group presentations. We dislike dealing with procrastinators, loafers, and disagreeable persons. We also resent having to waste time working in groups when we are already so busy.[1] And we dislike working with odd persons who do things like lip-synch other presenters.

Scripture often emphasizes individual speaking, but there are group presentations as well. Moses and Aaron attempted to persuade Pharaoh (Exod. 5:1–4). Two women presented their case to the wise King Solomon (1 Kings 3:16–28). Shadrach, Meshach, and Abednego stood together before Nebuchadnezzar (Dan. 3:13–18). Peter and the apostles appeared before the Sanhedrin (Acts 5:27–32).

This chapter explains how to use group presentations to serve audiences. Much of our dislike of group presentations stems from not knowing how to develop, plan, and conduct them well.

Consider Audience Views

While group work is typically divided up among participants, sometimes the whole group must deliver a written or oral report to an audience and then respond to questions. From the audience's perspective, such presentations reflect on the work of all members.

We implicitly compare and contrast ourselves with other team members. But audiences tend to evaluate overall group performances.

IN THE SPOTLIGHT

Common Group Presentation Contexts

- *Workplaces*—presentations to coworkers, clients, and shareholders
- *Communities*—neighborhood association and city council meetings
- *Churches*—worship planning, building projects, and event planning
- *Schools*—committee and board reports as well as classroom presentations

Follow Rhetorical Principles

The first thing to consider in adapting content to group presentations and audiences is the rhetorical purpose—to persuade, inform, or delight.[2] Then groups' presentations can follow the speech practices discussed in earlier chapters. For Christians, *group presentations* are shared callings to use the gift of communication cooperatively to serve particular audiences for specific purposes.

Adopt Servant Dynamics

Group presentations usually include multiple presenters. Rarely does one person speak for everyone in a group—unless the time available is very short and the presentation is just a brief summary. If nothing else, members might be called on to answer specific questions about their own part of the group work. Group members soon learn that they must depend on one another.[3]

The interpersonal dynamics among group members is vital, nurturing relational life or death. Some groups simply self-destruct; members become disrespectful toward one another and can no longer collaborate effectively.

As we prepare to serve an audience through teamwork, we must promise to serve one another individually and as a team throughout the research and planning. Such team-oriented servant-mindedness includes valuing all members, encouraging equal participation, and being mutually gracious.

Value All Members

Remembering that everyone has something to offer helps motivate us to ask helpful rather than accusatory questions and to listen in order to

Three Persons Speak as One "We"

Furious with rage, Nebuchadnezzar summoned Shadrach, Meshach and Abednego. So these men were brought before the king, and Nebuchadnezzar said to them, "Is it true, Shadrach, Meshach and Abednego, that you do not serve my gods or worship the image of gold I have set up? Now when you hear the sound of the horn, flute, zither, lyre, harp, pipe and all kinds of music, if you are ready to fall down and worship the image I made, very good. But if you do not worship it, you will be thrown immediately into a blazing furnace. Then what god will be able to rescue you from my hand?"

Shadrach, Meshach and Abednego replied to him, "King Nebuchadnezzar, we do not need to defend ourselves before you in this matter. If we are thrown into the blazing furnace, the God we serve is able to deliver us from it, and he will deliver us from Your Majesty's hand. But even if he does not, we want you to know, Your Majesty, that we will not serve your gods or worship the image of gold you have set up."

Daniel 3:13–18

discover each team member's knowledge and experience. We never know in advance how God has equipped individuals to contribute to the planning and content of group presentations. We might not like others' interpersonal communication style. We probably will stereotype others by their academics, appearances, or careers.

Moreover, all members have personal life stories. We might judge others unfairly, given everything else happening in their lives. Respectful listening and mutual encouragement are critically important from the start.

SERVANT SPEAKING TIP

At the first meeting, share some life stories. If members are reluctant to be transparent, begin yourself. One helpful question that everyone might be willing to answer is "What is something about you that others would never guess—such as a hobby, leisure activity, church connection, or travel interest?"

Foster Equal Participation

Group interactions can be plagued with inequality. Some members naturally speak up and tend to dominate. Others are reluctant. We need discussion processes that give everyone a chance to shape the presentation.

Taking turns speaking around a circle is usually the most inclusive way to begin and end meetings, with dynamic interactions in between. Individuals can just say "pass" if they have nothing to add. When someone asks a question or suggests something for the group to do, we can go around the loop so everyone has a chance to comment or pass.

Sometimes a quick group poll can be fun. When a member suggests something, and everyone has had a chance to speak about it, anyone can ask for a straw poll; then everyone immediately gives a thumbs up, a thumbs down, or a flat hand, which means "no opinion."

In work groups, the first round of planning involves agreeing on an agenda and then listening to any reports about work accomplished since the last meeting.

The last round involves making sure that the group agrees on what has been accomplished at the meeting, what needs to be done next, and who will carry out the necessary projects within specified deadlines.

Some members will not participate comfortably in team work until they feel that the relational environment is safe. They worry about whether others will like them. We need to nurture mutual respect for full and open participation by all members without any gossip or backbiting. Anything said about members beyond the group should be positive.

> **SERVANT SPEAKING TIP**
>
> When the group needs to make a *content*-related decision (what the presentation will include) or *process*-related decision (how the group will work together to plan the presentation) before members get to know one another, consider using a blind ballot with checkboxes to ensure that no one feels uncomfortable about expressing a personal opinion.

Be Mutually Gracious

We need to be gracious toward one another. We all irritate and offend others. We all can be dismissive or inattentive. We fail to prepare because of busyness or laziness. We fall short. Perfectionistic members of a team, who struggle with others who do not do things the "right" way, can benefit from practicing graciousness.

Even in the most seemingly secular contexts, graciousness is crucially important. We represent Jesus Christ even when team members do not know about our faith.

Delegate Group Work

Usually, group projects require members to delegate the research and writing (or just outlining) of each section. This makes it easier to decide later who should present sections.

> **SERVANT SPEAKING TIP**
>
> Consider that God has chosen you as a neighbor to this group, and the group members as neighbors to you. Ask yourself, "How can I best serve my team as I would like to be served?"

When possible, we can encourage group members to select, research, and outline main points about which they feel the most knowledgeable, interested, and passionate. This individual passion, used collectively across the group, will fuel energy for presentation planning and delivery.

Determine Presentation Roles

As a group delegates the research and writing of main points, it will also need to decide who will be presenting each section. Typically, members present the sections they researched and know the best.

But what if some group members are more skilled presenters? What if some fear public speaking? Does it make sense to go with presentational strengths rather than to equally distribute presentation sections?

Normally, each member verbally delivers part of the presentation. It is awkward for both the audience and the team when some members do not speak—especially if the silent members are introduced at the beginning or suddenly appear for Q&A.

One group member needs to oversee the creation of the multimedia elements, including PowerPoint presentations, videos, music, props, and posters, as well as to make sure that the technology is set up and operating before the presentation. Others may offer suggestions and even select, create, or bring to the presentation various media elements. Nevertheless, one person needs to develop the vision, get it approved by the group, and take the hands-on lead.

The group can ask if anyone is particularly skilled and would like to be the media leader. If not, it can randomly select a member.

Address Conflicts

Conflicts always arise in groups, especially when deadlines are nearing. Members get stressed out. Past conflicts reemerge. New ones escalate.

A common source of conflict is negative feelings toward members who did not do their share of the work. They might have missed meetings or failed to provide needed information. The rest of the group might even speak negatively about such persons when they are absent. Typically, a group disagrees about how to handle an underperforming member.

SERVANT SPEAKING TIP

When a team has significant differences of opinion, remember to look out for one another's interests (Phil. 2:3–4).

Communication scholar Stephen Lucas recommends keeping disagreements on a *task* level (group work) rather than a *personal* level (relationships). He says that personal dislike reduces group performance.[4] In other words, team members can nurture good relationships by discussing group work, not personalities.

Members can settle person-to-person conflicts outside the group whenever possible. When we become frustrated with a group member, we have an opportunity to practice the biblical principle of going to that person privately to address and resolve the situation (Matt. 18:15–17).

Sometimes conflicts about group presentations emerge from differences over personal taste rather than real substance. For instance, members might disagree over the fine points of presentational style, group attire, or Power-Point aesthetics. These kinds of elements might be critically important in some cases, but subjective viewpoints are always involved.

Often the best way to solve conflicts over nonessential elements is to discuss one central question: What will best serve the audience? Sometimes it helps to seek the advice of an objective group of friends, especially during the first presentation rehearsal. Assuming the outsiders represent the eventual audience, we can discuss their feedback after they leave.

Embrace Variety in Unity

Group presentations are created and delivered by individual members with personal communication styles. While this can be a challenge for presentational unity, it also can be a benefit. If everyone appears and sounds the same, presentations can get dull and seem contrived.

The key to nurturing variety in unity is to provide cohesion through the Main Idea, presentational methods, visuals, and overall presentational style. This way, different speaking styles can supplement one another for the greater good.[5] Just as artists use contrasting colors to create well-composed works, we can artfully unify the members' diversity.

A group can employ a unifying metaphor, repeated phrase, shared prop, or matching attire to create a sense of cohesion in the midst of rhetorically varied styles. These types of unifying symbols need to be handled carefully to avoid appearing tacky or exaggerated.

One of the major advantages of PowerPoint for groups is visual unity across different presenters. When the slides use the same visual elements—including text fonts, colors, and perhaps a group logo/name—audiences sense presentational cohesiveness.

Overall presentational style is best unified, especially regarding the seriousness of the topic. If the topic is less serious, such as "How to Dress for Business Casual" or "The Three Best Rides at Disneyland," then the style and look of the presentation can lean toward informality, with casual dress and lightheartedness. However, if the topic is serious, such as "Sexual Abuse in the Church," the presentation style and look can be more formal, with more polished appearance and serious delivery.

While embracing variety in unity, the group needs to ensure that none of the personal styles will be wildly different—such as comedic versus solemn. The presentational purpose and situation can shape the overall style.

Begin and End Well

As with all speeches, we begin group presentations with an engaging element, perhaps a statement, question, quotation, story, or statistic that introduces the topic. The introduction typically includes a preview of the outline points as well as a clear presentation of the Main Idea.

The conclusion is also similar to speeches. We review the main points (in the same order they were previewed in the introduction and explained in the body) and restate our Main Idea. We avoid offering any substantively new information in the conclusion. If appropriate, we tie our conclusion back to our introduction.

For example, suppose we began our presentation, "Four hundred and fifty years. That's the minimum amount of time it takes for one plastic bottle to decompose." We then might conclude, "By recycling one plastic bottle, we save our earth years of environmental energy; and not just one year, but at least 450 years."

The poet Henry Wadsworth Longfellow wrote, "Great is the art of the beginning, but greater is the art of ending."[6] The most effective conclusion clearly states what we want our audience to know, remember, or do—in tune with our presentational purpose. In a persuasive presentation, for instance, our conclusion can move the audience to adopt a thought or take an action.

Manage Time with Rehearsals

Just as in solo speeches, group presentations need to be concise and presenters need to time their sections strictly. Too many group presentations end up with the last person lacking adequate time because others took too long.

Group rehearsal is essential both to determine total timing and to practice speedy transitions from speaker to speaker. Group presentations always take longer than expected. If a group rehearsal is not possible, group members can practice their sections individually to be sure to stay well within the time limit. As a general rule, we might reserve 10 percent of the total presentation time for Q&A.

Introduce Members

Normally, we should identify our group participants to the audience. Our audience wants to know who everyone is and perhaps what they bring to the group—such as their area of expertise, position, or role. The situation is similar to a music concert, where the lead musician introduces other band members. There are no firm rules about when or how to make such introductions.

Some groups require presenters to wear legible name tags or, in the cases of table-based settings like panels, to display name cards in front of each presenter (in both cases, we ensure the names are written large enough with dark colors to be read from the rear of the room). One significant advantage of using large name tags or cards is that the audience can ask questions of particular presenters by name. When using PowerPoint, some groups insert the name of the presenter on the screen at the beginning of each section, and then project on the screen during the Q&A a list of all team members.

At a minimum, the presentation leader (or "moderator") who speaks first can introduce himself or herself and then manage the other introductions. One option is to have the members briefly introduce themselves at the beginning in order of presentation, or from the audience's perspective, from left to right across the front. Another option is to have presenters briefly introduce themselves when they begin their individual sections. A final option is for one member, presumably the leader who introduces himself or herself at the beginning, to introduce everyone at the end, just before the Q&A.

SERVANT SPEAKING TIP

Look at and speak to the audience, not to one another in the group. Help the audience feel included in the visual and verbal dynamics—not like outsiders merely watching the group present to itself.

Transition Smoothly

Transitions within a presentation are important. They are carefully crafted statements speakers make at the end of their segments that tie in with the next segment, and sometimes provide summaries of previous sections of the presentation as well. Transitions help the group presentation flow smoothly between outline points.

A common approach to transitions is like this: "And now Curt will address . . ." Sometimes a more audience-engaging approach is for each presenter to conclude with a logical question that the audience is likely thinking: "So what can we do about this problem? Curt will now address that question."

Attend to Self and Speaker

One of the most common problems in group presentations is individual members' inattentiveness when not presenting. All team members are essentially on stage even when they are not presenting. The audience will look occasionally at group members who are not currently presenting—often for facial reactions to their teammates. What the audience sees is important for the group overall. The presenter who lip-synched other presenters was a terrible distraction.

IN THE SPOTLIGHT

Group Presentations

- Delegate presentation roles.
- Appoint a technology leader-facilitator.
- Develop a unifying visual as well as verbal theme.
- Integrate the introduction and conclusion.
- Rehearse timing.
- Determine how to introduce presenters.
- Practice transitions between presenters with possible summaries of earlier sections.
- Determine how to facilitate Q&A.

First, every group member supports all other members by giving full nonverbal attention to the presenter. If a team member appears bored, or is not paying attention, the audience will tend to do likewise. Attentive group members encourage attentive audiences.

Second, team members need to remain relatively still when not presenting. One of the most distracting problems is fidgety team members who shuffle around, play with pens or remote controls, stretch necks and backs, crack knuckles, alternately stand up and sit down, and so forth. Inattentiveness and unnecessary bodily movement suggest to the audience that the team is bored and would prefer to be doing something else.

SERVANT SPEAKING TIP

When presenting, use "we" instead of "I" statements in order to express group unity and share work credit.

Facilitate Q&A

We can avoid confusion by delegating leadership of the Q&A long before the presentation. If it is an open Q&A, the leader might call on audience members who raise hands to ask questions. The leader can also direct a question to a particular presenter.

If the questions are written by audience members during the presentation and then collected by the group, the leader can gather the notecards, read the questions aloud, and direct the questions to particular group members to answer. While the next question is being asked, the leader can discretely distribute relevant question cards to team members to give them time to prepare answers.

Conclusion

Group work and group presentations are part of life. They remain widely disliked but also broadly used in nearly all organizations. Learning to participate in planning and presenting group work is essential today. A group that includes a member who lip-synchs other members is both funny and destructive. Each member's actions reflect on the others.

We servant speakers can view groups as similar to the church itself. Peter called for Jesus's followers to use every gift to be faithful stewards of God's grace in its many forms—including speaking (1 Pet. 4:10–11). In effect, a small group needs to function like a single body, parallel to the church as Jesus's body endowed with many different gifts to be used to the benefit of all (Rom. 12:3–8). Yet to accomplish this in church or society we have to serve one another as neighbors.

FOR DISCUSSION

1. What do you most dislike about working in groups to create group presentations? Why? How might a group leader minimize your dislikes?

2. If you were giving a speech on how to work effectively in a group, what advice would you share from your own good or bad experiences?

3. "One group member needs to oversee the creation of the multimedia elements." Explain why you agree or disagree.

4. What makes for an effective leader of group presentations? How would you describe the best leader you have worked with?

TWENTY

Stage with Technology

W hen I accept invitations to speak, my host usually asks, "What will you need?" What they really mean is "Will you need Power-Point?" Today, we equate public speaking technology with screen visuals.

As servant speakers, we need a broader view of technology. Our planning can be more like preparing for a staged theatrical performance—from properties (props) to lights, sound, and a slide or video screen. Unless presenting in a group, we can plan technology for a kind of solo performance.

This chapter explains how we can use technology appropriately and effectively to serve our audiences. It cautions against using unnecessary technology and addresses the range of visual and aural technologies to consider.

Perform for Stage

The ancient art of public speaking was associated with theatrical performance. Whether speaking indoors or outdoors, presenters treated their spaces as oratorical stages.

Today, we need to consider all older and newer *performance technologies*—everything that helps us communicate with a live audience. The most common speaking technologies are podiums (or lecterns), lighting (even just room lighting), sound systems, and screen imaging.

Reject Techno-Magic

We live in an age of technological optimism. We assume that there are technological solutions to just about all human needs, including communication. As a result, we tend to overuse technology.

For instance, sometimes we assume that developing a PowerPoint presentation is more important than crafting our message. That our technical glitz is more significant than our actual content. That what we show is more important than what we say.

For a sobering view of the overuse of PowerPoint, search the internet for "death by PowerPoint."[1] While presenters often think the technology is essential, audiences tend to be critical of how often and poorly Power-Point is used. Audiences come to hear the speaker, not to watch a screen presentation.

Advanced performance/presentation technologies never automatically improve communication. They might make our speech more engaging or entertaining. They might even impress our audience. But we might use them only when they will further our speech purpose. For instance, with a small audience, a whiteboard or flip chart might be more fitting and effective than PowerPoint—especially if we can write down key points in advance.

The key is using and adapting technology to best serve our audience. Sometimes we have to adapt technology to our speech, making sure the technology advances our speaking purpose and MAIN IDEA. Other times we have to adapt our speech purpose and MAIN IDEA to the available technology.

I spoke at a lecture series at a large church that urged all speakers to use the excellent projectors and audio system. The series was billed as "multimedia presentations." I wrote a presentation composed of an entertaining series of cartoon clips about technology. The clips demonstrated my MAIN IDEA: "Humanly created communication devices always create new communication problems."

My primary purpose was to delight the audience with satirical humor. My secondary purpose was to persuade attendees to reject the idea that we must have the latest communication technologies to be happy. I adapted my message and purpose to the technological venue as well as to my host's expectations. PowerPoint was essential. I could have delivered a speech with the same MAIN IDEA without using screen technology, but my speech would not have been as delightful or memorable.

SERVANT SPEAKING TIP

Never assume which technologies you will be able to use well without first visiting the venue. Try out existing technologies to see how well they actually work there—and how you might have to accommodate your speaking style, voice level, and content to the venue.

When I spoke in a meeting room to a group of about thirty corporate vice presidents about the importance of listening to employees, I used two small, stuffed toy birds—a chickadee and a Canada goose—that imitated their respective calls when squeezed. Chickadees are friendly and curious birds; they like to know what is going on around them. Canada geese are not; they tend to chase off interlopers. I asked attendees, "Which one are you?" I did not need a sound system, special lighting, or slides. My props communicated splendidly.

When we deliver highly informative presentations in a lecture style, we might want to use both screen technologies and printed handouts. For example, when I speak about writing effective résumés, I need to show examples on the screen and provide printed samples for the audience to make notes on and take home. I use a laser pointer to direct audience attention to specific spots on projected résumé pages.

Prepare a Menu

Once we know our audience size and location, we can create a menu of technological options to select from. Which ones will and will not work in the setting—both practically and functionally? If the location will not meet our needs, we might look for a different one.

The basic rule in selecting from our menu is to begin with lower-tech possibilities and gradually move to higher-tech options. If lower-tech options will work well, we probably can avoid complicating our preparation and presentation. For instance, what about using a prop or poster, depending on audience size? Are simple, less time-consuming, and less failure-prone options sufficient?

The more sophisticated and complicated the technology, the more planning and coordination required (such as possibly needing others to operate the lights, advance slides, or run the video or sound), and the greater likelihood of failure. Computers, projectors, remote controls, and

IN THE SPOTLIGHT

Technology Options

- *Podium/lectern*. Note floor or stage location options and any podiums, lecterns, and stands, including if they are movable, fixed, or desktop.
- *Props*. Note furniture, plants, and other movable items such as tables, chairs, and lamps, and where and how you would use any props that you bring along.
- *Banners*. Note possible locations, such as walls, ceiling grids (for hanging materials), and open areas for banner stands.
- *Blackboards/whiteboards*. Note size, location, visibility, and needed writing instruments.
- *Stands/tripods/flip boards/poster boards*. Note as needed for displaying posters and perhaps for writing during your speech and discussion.
- *Clock/timer*. Note location, movability, and readability if using a projector in a darkened room.
- *Natural lighting*. Note the speech time of day, extent of daylight, and functioning window coverings.
- *Artificial lighting*. Note room lighting and control, including zoned lighting (e.g., just front or back of room), dimmers, any delay after turning switches on or off, and any podium/lectern lighting for notes/reading.
- *Screen/projector*. Note location, movability, visibility, readability.
- *Pointers*. Note available laser pointers, sticks, or other means of directing the audience's attention to slides or other media.
- *Sound/audio*. Note room audio system with access to any microphone or computer-sound inputs, and available mics (wired and wireless with extra batteries).
- *Computer/tablet/phone*. Note type, location, and accessibility, as well as peripherals such as remote mouse/control, software, networking (Wi-Fi speed and access, and internet speed), cables, power outlets, and extension cords.

interconnecting devices fail regularly. Flip boards and banners do not. But maybe the audience and venue are so large that lower-tech media are not fitting options.

Finally, the more complex the technology, the more likely that small glitches will become significant interruptions. When we misspeak and correct ourselves, the audience is immediately forgiving. When we misspell a word on a whiteboard, no one really cares. A misspelled word on a PowerPoint slide looks careless and is distracting. When we have to fiddle with a remote control to get back to a missed slide on PowerPoint, the technology distracts.

Address Fear with Technology

One often-overlooked advantage of screen technologies like PowerPoint is that they can reduce speech apprehension. We can appropriately use the technology to divert the audience's visual attention away from us and toward the screen.

However, using screen technologies can also increase our anxiousness. We have to worry about producing and using screen images. Do we want the added stress?

Visualize for Memorability

We all tend to remember better when we can match words to images. We can use visuals to help our audience understand and then remember our main points both during and after our speech.

First, we can visualize text for our most important points. If we both speak and display key words, we enhance memorability.

Second, we can use visual graphics to reinforce what we are saying. When I speak about listening, I show photos of great listening postures—attentive, visually focused persons. If appropriate, I add satirical images of people ignoring others, such as texting while supposedly listening. Then the audience will better remember my comments about how to listen actively.

Third, we can use a *logo* (a graphic symbol) to reinforce our main point. If we are persuading our audience to exercise three times weekly, for instance, we might design a logo that combines a visual of someone exercising along with the number three; it could even be a simple caricature with a cleverly designed "3" as the face. We could display that logo prominently on our opening and concluding slides, and include a smaller version of it on every other slide. One life-size banner on stage displaying the same logo could also be effective.

Finally, we can follow the rule that less is actually more when it comes to visuals. The more we show, the less impact each visual has, and the less memorable they all become. By using only a stuffed chickadee and a goose, I was able to focus memorable, visual attention on the two props, with the bird calls reinforcing each one aurally.

SERVANT SPEAKING TIP

Use the power of just the right visual for just the right spoken message. One chart or graph, even a single photograph, can make an entire speech powerfully memorable. Sometimes just a prop, held up and lit well, can have the same impact.

Focus Lighting

Normally, we want to maximize light on us and minimize it on our audience. This focuses attention on us and lessens visual distractions for our audience.

When using a screen, however, we might need to reduce the room lighting at the screen location to improve image visibility for the audience. If the entire room lighting must be turned off just when we use the screen, we need a partner to run the lights for us. We can cue our partner with a quick glance of our eyes or similarly unobtrusive signal.

Direct the Audience's Gaze

Screen technologies create competing focal points. Attendees wonder if they should look at us or the screen—and when to do so. Telling the audience when to look at the screen is a poor solution: "Now please look at the screen." Such verbal directives take away from our speech content.

Implied directives are better: "Now I would like to show you an example" or "Here is a fine illustration of . . ."

When we project a new visual, the audience will automatically look at it. But if our spoken words do not seem to match the screen image, some members of the audience will look back at us while others will continue staring at the screen, waiting for a relevant visual.

We can also gesture toward the screen without verbal directives. The audience's gaze will move back to us when attendees feel they have adequately considered the screen content.

If we are not anchored at a lectern, we can direct the audience's gaze to and from the screen by walking toward and away from it. This is generally what I do in small rooms, including classrooms. When I want to direct the audience's attention to the screen, I walk toward it and then stand right next to it. When I want to move the audience's gaze back to me, I walk away from the screen while continuing to look at and speak to the audience. The audience naturally tracks me.

When I will not be using the screen for a while, I use the remote to "mute" the image. This turns the screen blank and reduces audience distraction.

Minimize Slide Design and Content

The biggest complaint I hear from audiences about screen technologies is speakers who put excessive text on slides and then read it all. That is "death by PowerPoint." A slide presentation never works as the speech manuscript. Audiences get bored and frustrated. They prefer that the screen be turned off.

Audiences secondarily complain about overly fancy slide designs with elaborate graphics, unnecessary object animations, and distracting visual transitions between slides. Such slides become visual noise. The way a slide is designed is inherently part of its message. Simplicity is best.

A helpful guide is to use a slide for each significant point on our outline. Then we can add one or two slides, as needed, to illustrate each point. Finally, we can include an introductory and a concluding slide along with slides for any key quotations or definitions. A ten-minute speech with three major points might include a deck of fifteen slides.

IN THE SPOTLIGHT

Rules for Using PowerPoint

- *Text.* Use text only to help the audience follow an outline, to present and emphasize key terms or definitions, to make outline point transitions, or to highlight important quotations with source citations.

- *Images.* Use only key images that support spoken ideas and examples/illustrations, or to provide visual transitions between sections of the speech.

- *Sound.* Play only essential audio, such as interview segments from sourced authorities.

- *Video.* Show moving-image video with sound for examples and illustrations that cannot be done well in person, or can be used solely in recorded format, such as video clips and interviews.

- *Slide design.* Maintain simple design unity across all slides and avoid fancy template designs, poor-quality images including much clip art, excessively small or large text, and text emphases (such as bold, italics, and underlines).

- *Laser pointer.* Hold it steady and use it sparingly; if you are too nervous to steady it, draw small circles around the area on the screen you wish to point out.

- *Blank screen (video mute).* Turn off the screen image when not using it.

Possible Handout Elements

- *Speech outline*—a brief version of the outline with the MAIN IDEA
- *Graphics/visuals*—important graphs, charts, models, and the like
- *Quotations*—with original sources
- *References/bibliography*—such as people, books, articles, organizations, and websites
- *Bio and contact info*—who you are and how people can get in touch with you
- *Additional credit*—any persons who helped you with any aspects of the speech/presentation (normally include this on the concluding PowerPoint slide as well)
- *Hyperlinks*—to any audio and video clips used, and perhaps to download the PowerPoint slide deck

Consider Print or Digital Handouts

Printed handouts can serve our audiences well. They can save us from near disaster when our screen technology fails. But they can also distract audiences and give away our upcoming aha moments. Even professional speakers disagree about when, if, and how to use printed handouts.

Some speakers believe that if they show their speech outline on a screen, slide by slide, they do not need to provide paper copies. Others always distribute printed outlines. Yet others use printed handouts only for lecture-like, information-rich topics.

Some speakers provide links to download digital copies of their screen slides after their presentations. They should announce this at the beginning so audience members do not feel like they have to take extensive notes.

Handing out extensive printed materials is risky. Unless we are dynamic speakers, some attendees might read the materials rather than pay attention to our speech, missing important explanations and background information.

Follow Copyright Law

In general, we do not have the right to present material that is *copyrighted*—owned by someone and not available for general public use. We ought to assume that just about everything online is copyrighted, unless the rights to use the material are explicitly stated.

Fortunately, there is a "fair use" doctrine that allows presenters to use some copyrighted material for educational purposes (such as an academic course) and critical purposes (such as a movie clip used in a movie review). Also, there are copyright-free websites designed specifically to provide usable materials in the *public domain*—available to the public as a whole and not subject to copyright.[2] Even when using such noncopyrighted material, we need to credit the source.

Amplify Voice

Why speak if others cannot hear us? This is a common problem in larger venues and smaller ones with poor acoustics.

> **SERVANT SPEAKING TIP**
>
> Always consider using props (properties) that are portable and the audience can see well. In the age of PowerPoint, we underestimate the visual power of one or two key props that symbolize our message.

Working with a voice amplification system is a special challenge because we cannot depend on what we hear as presenters in the front of the room with our ears toward the audience. We need help before and during our speech to ensure that audiences can hear us clearly. We need to arrive early and check the audio system with someone who will run it well, sit in the audience to make sure that everything is running smoothly, and quickly fix any problems that arise.

We should not wait to check the audio until we begin speaking; it is disruptive to begin a speech with the opening line "Can everyone hear me

---

From Flushing to Echoing:
An Audio Snafu Plagues an Hour-Long Speech

The craziest sound system snafu I ever witnessed involved a well-known Christian author speaking on a large platform in the front of a gymnasium filled with several thousand people. Just before he was going to be introduced, he rushed to the restroom. His lapel microphone was already turned on and everyone heard the flush.

By the time he returned to the stage area, his microphone had fallen off his lapel and was dangling in front of his belt.

Then he walked up to the podium and spoke for nearly an hour, producing vague noises that sounded like mumbling in an echo chamber. If we strained ourselves to make sense of the shadowy sounds, we could pick out a few words and phrases.

At first the audience was silent. But then attendees began giggling and even laughing because the sounds were so comical. The echoes and laughing continued for the duration of the speech. It was funny but disastrous.

No one—including me—had the courage to go up to the speaker to fix the problem. I still regret not doing it. But I was just too embarrassed for him and everyone else. The longer I waited, the more reluctant I was to help.

IN THE SPOTLIGHT

Tips for Voice Amplification

- *Voice projection*. Speak diaphragmatically (taking deep, diaphragmatic breaths, which singers call "belly breaths") to project your voice (there are many helpful YouTube videos on this), especially in larger venues lacking sound systems.
- *Wireless microphone*. If possible, use a wireless lavalier/lapel or headset microphone (hooked around an ear) to provide more freedom for gestures, greater opportunities to glance from side to side at the audience, and space to walk toward and away from a projection screen.

- *Handheld microphone*. Hold the mic steady at the same distance below your mouth (about 6 inches); avoid gesturing with the same arm; avoid switching hands with the mic.
- *Stand or podium microphone*. Speak across the top of the mic, not directly into it; direct your head toward the mic when speaking, and glance at the audience on the sides only when not speaking.
- *Popping*. If you hear popping sounds, note when they occur and adjust your speaking position to avoid them, including backing away from the mic or not speaking directly at the mic.

okay?" What if some people cannot hear us well? Will they speak up? If so, what will we do?

Conclusion

As servant speakers, we can consider using any technologies that will help us serve our audiences well. Adapting technology to our speech is essential. Like the ancient rhetoricians, we stage our presentations as compelling events using all appropriate means.

Modern technologies like PowerPoint are exceptionally useful if we learn when and how to employ them well. Otherwise, they prove that "fools with tools are still fools."[3]

FOR DISCUSSION

1. If a technology like PowerPoint is not always necessary or effective, does it ever make sense for organizations to require speakers to use it? Why would they do so?

2. When is screen technology a distraction rather than a communication aid?

3. What difference does it make technologically to think of our speech as part of a staged performance rather than just a speech?

4. Would you have had the courage to help the speaker whose wireless microphone was dangling? When, if ever, should an audience member step forward to assist with any kind of technological problem? Why not just let the assigned technical crew deal with it? What would we desire, if we were the speaker?

TWENTY-ONE

Speak through Video

KATHLEEN SINDORF

A flight attendant warmly welcomed and greeted me when I boarded a jet. I was pleased and impressed. But when he later used the on-board mic to deliver the standard departure information, he used a fake-sounding announcer voice to deliver his over-practiced message, discrediting his earlier authenticity.

Communication problems occur frequently when we do not know how to best use a medium. For instance, many of us will have to give live video interviews, speeches, and presentations. But we may lack understanding and skills to communicate well in these situations.

How is video different from speaking in person? How can we reduce additional fears caused by having to speak on camera?

I spent decades in television, cohosting and producing segments for a daily international Christian program, helping guests and hosts use the medium well. In this chapter I explain how to use video effectively as a servant speaker. Video has its own capacity for serving audiences, and it can be a powerful means to communicate with just one person or large groups.

Gain Biblical Perspective

Video is an inexpensive way of capturing, recording, and distributing moving images and sound. Even smartphones have cameras, editing software, and external microphone (mic) inputs.

Biblically speaking, video is part of the "opening up" of God's original creation. When we use video today, we are participating in the "things" that God has made available through Jesus Christ (John 1:3). We humans invent new technologies, but the source of all innovation is the God of all creation.

Video equips us to love our neighbor in new ways. It enables us to be more present to others in sound and image across geographic space and in record time—streaming in microseconds on the internet. When used well, video can help us get the job we always wanted, teach more effectively, participate in civic discourse, and spread the gospel.

Given our sinful natures, however, we misuse technology for personal gain and control over others. As the popularity of some YouTube channels shows, even previously unknown persons can build cult-like followings and promote anti-biblical ideas.

> **IN THE SPOTLIGHT**
>
> ## Common Uses for Video Speaking
>
> - vlogs (video blogs)
> - online meetings
> - televised and video-streamed news reporting
> - virtual conferences/webinars
> - job prescreenings and interviews
> - video résumés (recorded and uploaded)
> - lectures and other speeches
> - sales and new-product presentations
> - inspirational and motivational videos
> - educational videos for online and classroom use
> - sermon streaming and playback

Identify the Video Situations

Video speaking is complicated because of the many possible contexts and purposes. There are at least three types of video situations, each with its own image, audio, and presentational techniques: personal, meeting room, and stage.

Personal Video

When we prepare to be interviewed online for a job or to give a course or webinar presentation via the internet, we usually employ personal video. Using a single camera from a personal device such as a phone, tablet, or laptop, we present our face and voice to others, perhaps accompanied by some PowerPoint slides or video recordings that temporarily replace our face on the screen.

Personal video is intimate. It captures our face up close, typically from the mid-chest to just above the top of our head. By using an external mic, we can make it sound like we are in the room with our audience.

IN THE SPOTLIGHT

Personal Video

- Position yourself within the camera's frame with a close-up—just above your head to mid-chest.
- Maintain eye contact with the camera lens except when showing a slide or short video.
- Use an external mic and maintain a consistent voice level.
- Set up the camera to be level with your eyes, so you do not appear to be looking up or down. When using a laptop, phone, or tablet, place it on a stack of books or a box if not a tripod. Do not tilt the device to get your face on the screen because that creates an awkward visual angle and contorts your facial image.
- If possible, use natural light, such as from a window, coming from the side rather than in front or behind you.

Since we are speaking through video, we need to maintain strict eye contact with the tiny camera lens (not the device or screen) except when showing slides or video. Eye contact establishes our credibility and builds trust; when we avoid eye contact, it seems like we are unsure of ourselves, hiding something, or maybe even lying. Eye contact is probably more critical in personal video than any other form of public speaking.

We find video eye contact difficult because we naturally want to look at the other person's image on our device. We want to see if they are responding positively or negatively by reading their nonverbals. So if necessary, we need to minimize their image and avoid looking at it. We can even cover up their image on our screen. When there are multiple small images of people we are presenting to on our screen, we might have to cover up their images to avoid moving our eyes from person to person and not looking directly at our camera lens.

Meeting Video

In many organizations, presentational meetings are recorded and sometimes streamed live for remote locations and telecommuters. Videos focus on one individual or sometimes a panel of presenters at the front of a meeting room.

SERVANT SPEAKING TIP

In all types of video, use an external rather than internal microphone for good sound quality, and do not speak too loudly. A common video problem is speaking as if others cannot hear us—just as some people do on phones in public.

Although it is possible in these situations to use stage video techniques (see below) with multiple cameras, most meeting videos use one camera. The best ones require each speaker to stand at a lectern or a table rather than remain seated. The image can capture the presenter from about the waist up and at eye level—not at an up or down angle.

IN THE SPOTLIGHT

Meeting Video

- Bend your elbows so that your forearms are halfway up and relaxed, so you can make small, natural gestures.
- Maintain your position at the lectern/podium while using your upper body for expression. Avoid full-body movement, which will look exaggerated and be distracting.
- Keep eye contact with the room audience instead of looking at the camera.
- Use a wireless (preferably clip-on) mic connected directly to the camera, even if the meeting room is small or has its own audio-amplification system.
- Ask someone sitting near the door to keep seats open for latecomers; just before you begin, ask those who are leaving early to sit near the door as well—to avoid having people walk in front of the camera.

Stage Video

The popularity of TED Talks has sparked renewed interest in public lectures as important civic events. Many of these presentations are well made with multiple cameras, professional crews, excellent lighting, and superb sound. They set the standard for stage video. Part of their success has been finding engaging speakers, training them, and keeping speeches relatively short and on time.

IN THE SPOTLIGHT

Stage Video

- Consult with the producer or director about how and where on the stage you would like to present, but then listen to what the producer says is actually possible given lighting, camera placements, and the like.
- Maintain eye contact with the in-person audience, rarely looking at the cameras, unless you are instructed to briefly address the video audience.
- When using screen technology like PowerPoint, gesture toward the screen as you begin addressing content on it so that both the audience and producer know when to shift to the screen. Avoid telling the audience when to look at the screen and when to look at you, and avoid asking for the next slide.
- Stay in the same spot on the stage, changing only the direction of your head for eye contact across the audience—unless asked by the producer or director to move around within a designated space.
- Use your complete upper body for expression, especially arms, hands, and face.

IN THE SPOTLIGHT

Advantages of Video

- *Permanence*. Copies can be saved and reused as needed, even posted online.
- *Reviewing*. Recorded videos can be reviewed for self-assessment.
- *Editing*. Saved copies can be edited and reused.
- *Close-ups*. Close-up images can focus on items that are too small to see without the camera.
- *Viewing pace*. Viewers can speed up, slow down, and review sound and images for maximum comprehension.

Because such multiple-camera situations require professional producers, we must collaborate carefully with them. We are in their hands. They will make us look good or bad, depending on how well we understand what they are doing and how well we follow their directions.

The essential idea in stage video is to give video viewers a sense that they are part of the in-person audience—not that they are communicating with us one-on-one, as in personal video. We speak to the in-person audience and let the producers use the technology to engage remote viewers.

Consider Remote-Audience Challenges

Compared with in-person speaking, live or recorded video speaking is complicated by three challenges among remote audiences: distractions, multitasking, and expectations.

Unless a video viewer puts on headphones and sits in a darkened, distraction-free room, ambient sounds and visual distractions are likely (e.g., beeping phones, neighborhood or office noises, or unexpected visitors). It is like watching a movie at home rather than in the theater.

Remote viewers might be multitasking—such as texting, responding to email, or answering the door. We need to graciously give them the freedom to attend to their duties, even though it seems discourteous.

SERVANT SPEAKING TIP

Avoid recording in locations with ambient noise, such as from refrigerators and heating and air-conditioning systems. Record sample video without your voice and then listen to it with the volume turned up to assess room noise. Extraneous sounds can distract listeners and convey unprofessionalism.

Remote video audiences have expectations according to the type of video—personal, meeting, and stage. For instance, if we are speaking in a stage video, we will be compared with TED Talks and other popular examples. If we are giving a job interview, we will be compared with the quality of other interviewees' personal videos.

If our video communication is not fairly seamless, we will probably fail to meet expectations. We need to communicate without the technology interfering. The more technological hiccups, the worse our communication. In personal video, for instance, video audiences get frustrated with speakers who frequently go off screen, fail to maintain a consistent audio level, look away from the camera lens, and repeatedly adjust the camera or audio.

Record Self

One of the scariest parts of video is also a benefit—being able to prerecord a personal video. For example, organizations increasingly ask job interviewees to create and upload audio or video recordings, often answering specific questions. For most of us, this kind of *asynchronous interview*—recorded for later listening/viewing—is even more discomforting than *synchronous* (real-time) video. With a live interview, we can read the other party's feedback verbally and nonverbally, through facial expressions and perhaps gestures.

Sitting alone in front of a camera can be unnerving, but recording does give us a chance to practice, view ourselves, and improve our communication before submitting the official version. We can even ask knowledgeable friends or colleagues to critique our test performances.

In all public speaking contexts, recording and evaluating our own presentations is essential for growth as servant speakers. It is an intimidating but essential process.

Address Video Fears

For most of us, using a mic and facing a camera seem unnatural. They can even worsen our public speaking fears.

The vast majority of us do not like how we look and sound in recordings. Even many famous television and film actors refuse to watch recordings of their own shows and films. When we think about being on mic or on camera, we might start to feel the physical symptoms of fear and anxiety.

Some professionals who have done live television reporting and hosting for years still experience a rush of adrenaline when the camera is turned on. Their stomachs churn, their palms sweat, and their breathing accelerates. They need to remember to relax their faces and bodies, keep their voices from going high and their words from spilling out rapidly. One simple technique is to breathe slowly and deeply for fifteen seconds before speaking to the camera.

An On-Camera Exercise

Make a series of five one-minute personal videos. View each one before recording the next one.

1. Describe the physical symptoms you feel when the live camera is focused on you; try to express what you are afraid of when being recorded.

2. Close your eyes and talk your body through the process of relaxing, whether starting with the muscles in your face or those in your feet and toes; explain how you are unwinding, step by step.

3. Look closely at your tiny camera lens so you know exactly where it is. Wonder out loud how something so small can record your image. Start talking naturally to the lens as you focus on it. Tell it what you will be recording. Avoid looking at anything else.

4. Close your eyes on camera again and imagine grateful audience members; hear them in your head telling you how much your videos mean to them, how they look forward to the next one because they are so helpful and because you are so natural and real on camera.

5. Finally, look into the lens again, take a moment to relax in front of your audience, and then thank them for their encouragement and appreciation. Express your gratitude for the privilege of serving them.

6. Compare these five videos of yourself. What differences do you hear and see? Which one do you like best, and how can you project that image and sound when you next have the opportunity to be on camera?

Adapted from Linda Ugalow's meet-up exercise, World Domination Summit Conference, Portland, OR, June 27, 2018.

Be Natural

Why does a camera or mic make us feel like we need to perform rather than be our natural selves, like the flight attendant I mentioned earlier? For one thing, we think we need to impress others. For another, we have a concept in our minds about what a video professional sounds like; we think that we have to live up to such seemingly expert expectations. We then overcompensate and turn people off with an artificial style. It is similar to what happens when, during worship, a church member starts praying

SERVANT SPEAKING TIP

Be natural. Aim for authenticity and perhaps even vulnerability, not perfection. Imagine you are talking with a friend, but with slightly more emphasis and expressiveness.

out loud in an entirely different, unnatural voice.

Often with video communication we feel like we are not good enough, smart enough, or attractive enough. But trying to be something more or someone better will not help us connect with our audience. Viewers want to relate to a real person, imperfections and all. A few minor slipups can actually make a video speaker more likable and trustworthy.

Conclusion

We all need to learn how to be servant speakers through video, a complicated and sometimes intimidating medium. Video communication needs to be handled carefully because it amplifies our personal speaking strengths and weaknesses.

Moreover, paying attention to how we look and sound can help us become more aware of our good and bad mannerisms in all of our speaking, from job interviews to group presentations Viewing videos of ourselves can help us be more effective servant speakers.

IN THE SPOTLIGHT

Video Lighting

- Use a simple background, such as a wall, painting, and plants, preferably with some depth and angles behind you for a three-dimensional image.
- Shoot where the light is coming from one side, not from behind or in front of you.
- Capture natural light if possible, typically through a window, for the best color.
- Fill in the lighting of your facial image with an off-camera side lamp if needed.
- Make sure your eyeglasses are not reflecting light into the camera lens; try recording without glasses if you do not need to see notes.

IN THE SPOTLIGHT

Video Attire

- Dress in solid, jewel-tone colors.
- Do not wear white or black, which do not show up well on camera.
- Avoid showy or noisy jewelry.
- Avoid wearing anything with writing or logos that will be visually distracting or seem inappropriate.
- Wear nonseasonal clothing to look more professional and avoid appearing out of place across time zones and different parts of the world.

FOR DISCUSSION

1. What does it mean to suggest that video is part of the "opening up" of God's creation?

2. What does it mean to say that personal video is an intimate medium? Is it really?

3. How does it change your attitude about TED Talks to know that speakers

normally have to go through training to be allowed to participate? For instance, does that make such video speaking seem more or less authentic?

4. What most annoys you about how others act when you are doing video chat with them? Why? What do your own annoyances suggest about how we should use video professionally?

Afterword

CLIFFORD G. CHRISTIANS

Rarely do educational books meet all the relevant standards of excellence. *An Essential Guide to Public Speaking* is one of those rarities. It is innovative in theory, its scholarship is rigorous, its pedagogical purpose is impeccably designed and implemented, and as literature it is a masterpiece. Quentin Schultze refers in this book to his desire that students take their class notes home for ongoing use. His book fulfills that purpose in dramatic fashion. I expect this book will have a long shelf life, with readers returning to it frequently for inspiration and consultation when preparing speeches.

I am awestruck at the book's literary and intellectual precision. I fear that my best efforts at writing cannot meet the criteria for speaking that this book demands and illustrates. But its servant axis is captivating, and I will work without pretense from that perspective. The servant speaking mode requires concerted effort to give one's audience priority. Therefore, I choose to focus on the communications field I know—its students and teachers. From the perspective of rhetorical studies, I predict this book will become a classic. I aim to defend my assessment of its historic importance, explaining its gravity as an incentive for readers to take it seriously from cover to cover.

Rhetoric is a theoretically rich field, and influential scholarship in this tradition is dynamic with theory, understanding ideas from the inside and perceiving their relevance. This book matches that demanding standard.

For Professor Schultze, the philosophy of rhetorical studies establishes the framework for public speaking, and he engages that arena with impressive competence.

Theorist Schultze reminds us that language shapes reality and makes human relations possible. Therefore, servant speaking that sustains community is everyone's responsibility. Working rhetoric hard, Professor Schultze references wherever appropriate the Greco-Roman classics, including Aristotle's *Rhetoric* and Cicero's *On Oratory and Orators*. For contemporary scholarship, he enriches his research and conclusions with primary sources such as Kenneth Burke and important secondary sources such as David Cunningham. But this extraordinary field demands creative theorizing, not merely tedious explanations of the strengths and weaknesses of various theories. *An Essential Guide to Public Speaking* models that kind of scholarship. It presents a new rhetorical theory, one that accounts for theories but articulates its own.

With the overall context of rhetorical scholarship in view, this book centers on Augustine and does so astutely. Augustine is monumental in the history of ideas, but scholar Schultze does not permit the commonplace conclusion that rhetorician Augustine of Milan was converted from reasoned judgment to biblical theology as bishop of Hippo. Rather than retreating to dichotomies, Professor Schultze theorizes in parallel with Augustine and beyond him. In their composite view, human beings are the one species able to love, and the rhetorical process ought to be directed by love of God, one's neighbor, and oneself. This book compellingly makes the case that love's rise or fall is everyone's destiny.

One of the twentieth century's most influential thinkers, Hannah Arendt, wrote her PhD dissertation (published as *Love and Saint Augustine*) under the philosopher Karl Jaspers on Augustine's concept of love. For Augustine, as interpreted by Arendt, love for neighbors is fundamental because humans share a common origin and are therefore equals. The University of Chicago ethics scholar Martha Nussbaum, in her influential *Upheavals of Thought*, credits Augustine's love concept as a major philosophical achievement, unique and definitive in giving compassion and other emotions a central place in developing a distinctive concept of society.

Scholar Schultze recognizes in Augustine similar conclusions to his own about human relationships and so pursues him dialogically rather than hierarchically. Augustine is not simply explained at the beginning and then applied where relevant, but throughout he is Professor Schultze's collaborator. That collaboration identifies a treasury of important concepts for rhetorical studies, such as discernment, gratitude, walking in the Spirit, message integrity, affections, and testimony. A gifted educator is at work, demonstrating imaginatively how to teach and learn bedrock ideas.

In the rhetorical tradition, truth is fundamental. Without a sophisticated concept of truth, communication studies have an empty center. As a guru of rhetorical studies ought to do, Professor Schultze emphasizes knowledge and truth. Together, his chapters on research, on honestly using websites, books, essays, and interviews, and on evaluating sources and consulting experts represent rhetorical scholarship with integrity. For rhetoricians, truth is typically seen in elementary epistemological terms as accuracy and exact data. In servant speaking, being factual and avoiding lies is only the beginning. Truth-telling means respecting the audience as God's image bearers. When truth is articulated in biblical terms, servant speaking requires us to be true to God, the audience, and ourselves.

Truth-telling is an exemplar of this book's distinctive integration of faith and learning. In teaching us to think biblically, this book is a paradigm setter. It establishes a new approach in which rhetoric's major contribution does not culminate in truth but in wisdom. For Professor Schultze, the highest aim in biblical thinking is wisdom, sometimes referred to today as a biblical worldview. In servant speaking, wisdom means understanding biblical theology and applying it discerningly as the Holy Spirit directs. The Wisdom literature in the Old and New Testaments—Proverbs and James throughout, the books of Job and Ecclesiastes, and also Paul's Epistles when he speaks of the wisdom of God—integrates this book's biblical account.

An Essential Guide to Public Speaking is a model of Christian liberal arts education, advocating as it does the transformative idea of biblical wisdom and not merely critical thinking. It boldly demonstrates that a biblical foundation makes a distinctive difference in shaping our disciplines. It recognizes that if Christians and non-Christians draw the same conclusions on crucial issues, then the biblical worldview is unnecessary. Regarding issues that matter, if the orientation is the same for all, then Christianity may have been viable in the prescientific era, but it no longer can legitimately claim our allegiance. From this perspective, faith-based thinking has been placed outside science and therefore is extracurricular. In this book, such challenges are turned into hypotheticals. Consistent with J. de Waal Dryden's *A Hermeneutic of Wisdom*, this book shows that biblical wisdom establishes a new and distinctive standard for structuring knowledge.

In a graduate student seminar, one of my hard-nosed professors insisted that we read Jacques Ellul's *Propaganda*, while ridiculing this French thinker's Christianity. Ellul's scholarship was so impressive that all students were required to take him seriously. C. S. Lewis is in the canon of British literature for both Christians and non-Christians. Quentin Schultze can be considered in a similar way. *An Essential Guide to Public Speaking* is an academic leader in rhetoric, a difference maker for Christian higher education, and a work of profound interest to communication scholars at public and private universities who respect new theory in the Augustinian tradition.

Checklist for Preparing a Speech

____ I determined the audience's likely topical knowledge, attitudes, and expectations.

____ I narrowed down and focused my topic.

____ I established a clear purpose for serving my audience-neighbors (e.g., to inform, persuade, or delight).

____ If persuading my audience, I wrote a precise and possible goal for what I want my audience to believe or do.

____ I stated my MAIN IDEA in one clear, specific sentence.

____ I consulted credible primary and secondary sources on the topic.

____ I used credible sources ethically as representative of the views presented in my research (without fabrication or plagiarism).

____ I wrote and revised a sentence outline along with possible transition statements.

____ I organized the speech appropriately (e.g., using a topical, spatial, or problem-solution pattern).

____ I developed logical (*logos*) and/or emotional (*pathos*) appeals as appropriate.

____ I found illustrative stories that relate to my main points and will interest my audience; I practiced telling them extemporaneously to friends or coworkers.

____ I prepared appropriate technology, such as PowerPoint, audio, video, printed handouts, or posters.

____ I determined how to speak truthfully from a Christian perspective, taking Scripture into account as appropriate, and without fabrication and plagiarism.

____ I wrote a speech introduction that will gain audience interest, establish my servant ethos, present my purpose and MAIN IDEA, offer a preview, and transition to the body of the speech.

____ I practiced my entire speech with friends or classmates to become more verbally and nonverbally expressive (without hesitation and verbal fillers) and to hear positive and negative feedback for revision.

____ I anticipated three major audience questions and prepared answers.

APPENDIX B

Plan Speeches with the Holy Spirit

The Holy Spirit is a creative partner in our servant speaking. As we walk by the Spirit (Gal. 5:16), we discover ways to serve our neighbors.

This is a mystery. Somehow the Spirit speaks to us through our daily discourse and the meditations of our hearts (Ps. 19:14). We are most teachable when we are regularly involved in Bible study, worship, and fellowship.

I frequently use speech topics and MAIN IDEAS that just seem to grow within me as I think and converse under the guidance of the Spirit. Someone says something to me. I get an idea while listening to a sermon. A thought pops into my head while I am praying or listening to music. Whenever something seems to ring true, I assume that it might be worth exploring for my speech.

The Spirit blows as it pleases (John 3:8). Nevertheless, we need some practical ways of being open to the Spirit's direction.

First, keep thinking about your topic, beginning well in advance of the speech date. While planning a speech, we need reminders to stay engaged. Some speakers use phone apps. I post sticky notes.

My sticky notes display my speech topic, such as "stress and sleep." Posting them on my bathroom mirror reminds me to be attentive in the morning and at bedtime; I get some of my best ideas before drifting off to sleep. I even post a note on my car dashboard. The notes remind me to think about a topic, including to ask the Spirit to enlighten and direct me.

At church I write my upcoming speech topic on the bulletin to keep it in mind while listening to lyrics, Bible readings, the sermon, and the congregational prayer. This helps me take note of the connections between my faith and the speech.

Second, think prayerfully about your upcoming speech. Identify times and places that you personally practice prayer most effectively. Then, during such prayer time, listen to the creative work of the Holy Spirit in your speech planning. Think prayerfully about speech ideas, organization, and audiences.

I often plan speeches by going to a café, sitting in a quiet spot, and thinking. I begin by reflecting on God's blessings in my life, such as family, friends, work, health, and salvation.

Then I briefly recall and pray for my current life challenges, eventually focusing on an upcoming speech. I pray, "Lord, please keep your Spirit close to me as I submit to your wisdom for the sake of my audience-neighbors. I'm listening."

Prayer helps me stay attuned to the Spirit. It is different than simply petitioning God in prayer and then moving on to other life activities. I pray for my speech planning as I plan. Perhaps this is like what Paul had in mind when he encouraged "unceasing" prayer (1 Thess. 5:17).

I start writing down ideas. I draw pictures and list possible outline points. My visual process does not work for all speakers; we each must find our own effective method.

For me, speech-related reflection is like open prayer. Somehow, I listen to the Spirit and myself at the same time. I cannot explain it. I just do it, in faith. As Scripture comes to mind, I look it up on my phone app.

In the field of communication studies, *invitational rhetoric* is inviting others to dialogue *with* us rather than just speaking *to* them. We welcome others' thoughts and feelings as well as respectfully share ours.[1] Similarly, we can invite the Spirit into our speech planning. The Spirit will draw insights out of our hearts and into our minds. The writer of Proverbs says, "The purposes of a person's heart are deep waters, but one who has insight draws them out" (Prov. 20:5).

Third, stay spiritually alert while planning your speech. After asking his followers to stay alert, Jesus went to pray at Gethsemane. The disciples soon slept (Matt. 26:36–41). This is our spiritual condition today as well. We are distracted. We have trouble focusing on what is most important. We simply disobey God by not listening.

We need to stay alert as we journey with the Spirit while preparing speeches. Even when great ideas come to mind, we will tend to forget them.

Sometimes I make notes on receipts or napkins. US president Abraham Lincoln reportedly wrote his famous, two-minute Gettysburg Address on an envelope while traveling by train to the site of the historic civil war battle. Maybe the Spirit was with him as he wrote, "This nation, under God, shall have a new birth of freedom."

Form for Evaluating Speeches

Date: _____   **Length** (in minutes): _____

Title: _____

Speaker's Name and Position: _____

Occasion (Where and when was the speech?):

Purpose (How did the speaker intend to serve the audience or possibly other neighbors?):

Main Idea (What was the speaker's one-sentence MAIN IDEA?):

Introduction (Did the speaker quickly gain audience interest, establish a servant ethos, state a purpose, present a MAIN IDEA, offer a preview, and transition to the body of the speech?):

Conclusion (Did the speaker restate the MAIN IDEA, summarize main points, and, if it was a persuasive speech, call the audience to a specific belief or action?):

Sources (Did the speech and Q&A demonstrate that the speaker had adequately researched primary and secondary sources?):

Technology (Did the speaker use media/technologies appropriately, smoothly, and attractively?):

Organization (Did the speaker use an understandable organizational pattern—e.g., comparative advantages or problem-solution—along with transitions, summaries, and possibly memorable keyword acronyms, visual metaphors, or sequential numbering?):

Verbal Expressiveness (Was the speaker's vocal delivery aptly energetic, impassioned, and engaging without hesitancy, monotone, and verbal fillers?):

Nonverbal Expressiveness (Did the speaker dress appropriately, maintain eye contact, and use arms and body effectively in support of verbal expressiveness?):

Virtue (Did the speaker's ethos reflect good qualities of character, perhaps even relevant fruit of the Spirit?):

Storytelling (Did the speaker creatively tell fitting stories?):

The following served the audience well:

The following required additional attention:

APPENDIX D

Speaking from a Manuscript
Lessons from an Executive Speechwriter

Karl Payton

Note: This is adapted from a manuscript speech on how to develop and deliver manuscript speeches. Constraints of publication prevent us from displaying the text in the delivery format preferred by the author, but this speech includes detailed instructions for preparation of the physical manuscript. The formatted version is available on the publisher's textbook website or from the contributor (Karl Payton) or book author (Quentin Schultze).

Presenting a speech word for word from a prepared text is *not* the preferred method of delivery. Sometimes, though, we find ourselves in situations that require us to use a manuscript.

As servant speakers, we owe it to our audience to know how to do it well.

In an earlier career, I served as the executive speechwriter for the president of a major corporation. Since much of what he said was quoted by the press, he delivered almost every speech from a manuscript. My job involved putting his ideas on paper and helping him prepare for the presentations. In the process, I learned three major things that must be done properly in order to deliver an effective manuscript speech: (1) writing for the ear, (2) managing pages, and (3) reading aloud.

First, we have to write a manuscript for the ear, not for the printed page. Speaking from a manuscript means reading aloud, not reading silently. We need to pay attention to how the speech actually *sounds*, not how impressive it might look in print.

Our audience needs to be able to follow our thoughts as we read them aloud.

This means it is best to use simple words and short sentences. As an unknown writer put it, "Don't use a big word where a diminutive one will suffice." We might think that using fancy words will make us seem more credible. Sometimes it might, depending on the audience. But flowery language usually just gives the impression we are trying to show off. Never forget that we are there to communicate, and word choice is critical. As Sir Winston Churchill put it, "Broadly speaking, the short words are the best, and the old words best of all."[1]

Remember: simple words—short sentences.

That does not mean we have to write like Dr. Seuss in his children's books.

But neither do we want to sound like we're reciting the preamble to the US Constitution: "We the People of the United States, in Order to form a more Perfect Union, establish Justice, insure domestic Tranquility, provide for the common defense . . ."

And that is just the beginning of one long sentence. Imagine reading it out loud. By the time we have finished, our audience will have forgotten how the sentence began. The Constitution is fine writing, but it is hardly the model for a speech manuscript.

Second, we need to manage manuscript pages. When we look at our manuscript while reading, we need to be able to see words clearly, follow our language from line to line, remind ourselves how to express particular words and phrases, and attend to any "cues" we have written on the pages to help us express ourselves well. Here are some basic pointers:

1. *Use large type.* A 14-point type works much better than the usual 11- and 12-point sizes. Even readers with perfect eyesight find larger type easier to read aloud.
2. *Use serif-style font.* Fonts with serifs—the little squiggly marks at the tips of letters—work best. Times New Roman was, for many years, Microsoft's default font—for a very good reason. Studies show that

most people find serif-style fonts easier to read. The vast majority of books and periodicals still use serif-style fonts.

We can try sans-serif fonts—such as Calibri—but for words on the page, most readers prefer serif-style fonts. Since we have to be able to see and read our manuscript text as easily as possible, I recommend using serif-style fonts.

3. *Double-space text.* Double-spaced type is easier to see, and the vertical spacing gives us room to mark the text as needed, such as reminders, or "cues," about how we should speak when reading a word or sentence.

4. *Italicize words.* Italics remind us to *emphasize* some words when reading our manuscript. Italics make a word stand apart from the other words. Italics can remind us to give a word a different inflection, duration, or volume to draw appropriate attention to it.

5. *Use wide margins.* Wide margins mean narrow text columns, which reduce the total amount of space on the page that our eyes have to cover. Also, they provide room for notes—such as reminding ourselves to pause, speak more rapidly, or look up and smile.

6. *Keep pages short.* When reading aloud from a manuscript, we do not want words going all the way to the bottom of the page. When our eyes go that low, our audience sees the top of our head instead of our eyes. Even when reading, we need to maintain some eye contact. Keeping text high on the page helps us do that. I prefer at least a three-inch margin on the bottom of every page.

7. *Number pages obviously.* Numbering our pages with large and obvious numerals helps us see exactly where we are from page to page, and makes it easy to find our place if our pages get shuffled around. I print page numbers on all four corners of each page in bold, 18-point type.

8. *Use unconventional punctuation.* When we write an essay or memorandum, we rightly worry about using correct punctuation. When we write a manuscript to read aloud, we need to use whatever punctuation helps us read the speech more effectively. I have found that *dashes*—like these two em dashes—and *ellipses* (. . .) help regulate the flow of my reading. I also use double spaces after every period. Periods are there for a reason. They tell us to "*stop!*" The extra space reminds us to speak in distinct sentences and not to run them all together.

9. *Finish the thought.* For many speakers, just the process of getting from page to page becomes disruptive. Sometimes we stop in the

middle of sentences to pick up our continuing thought on the following page. We can keep that from happening by making sure a sentence never flows over to the following page.

Third, we need to read aloud well. Most of us do not. We think that all we have to do is get the words out of our mouths exactly as they are written on our manuscript. But then we sound like we are reading, not speaking. It is one thing for us to write down great thoughts. It is far more to express them orally to the delight and benefit of our audience.

Our goal should be to read so well that it does not sound like we are reading. We need to present our manuscript speech with the same easy, conversational flow that characterizes the best extemporaneous speeches. Then we really serve our audiences as our listening neighbors.

It does not come naturally to us. It takes practice, but the effort is well worth it.

Begin practicing the manuscript speech by making sure you can pronounce every word—effortlessly. Read the manuscript aloud and note any words or phrases that give you trouble. Some lines that look good in print just do not roll off the tongue as we would hope. If necessary, rewrite the awkward language. Sometimes we just need to split an idea into shorter sentences.

Then read the manuscript aloud again to make sure you are grouping the words together correctly. This includes paying attention to punctuation. *Pause* where we should. *Stop* where we should. We translate our writing into understandable speaking. We make our thoughts easy to understand by the way we speak them.

Now it is time to deliver the speech, and I have some final recommendations.

Never staple pages together or put them in a notebook, both of which require flipping pages. Keep your pages loose. Lay your manuscript on the right side of the lectern with all the pages in proper sequence. Before you begin, slide page one to the left. Your first two pages are then ready and waiting. When you finish page one, begin page two and discreetly slide it to the left as you continue reading. Page three will then be ready for you. Continue that process throughout the speech. Your next page will always be visible. There should never be a need to flip pages or pause in the middle of a thought, and the audience may never realize you are moving from page to page.

As I said, reading from a manuscript is *not* the best method of delivering a speech. But sometimes we need to do it. It might be a presentation at a formal occasion, a highly technical speech, an academic presentation, or maybe even prepared statements with legal ramifications.

I learned how to write and deliver an effective manuscript by authoring speeches for an executive—and coaching him along the way. I hope my experience helps us serve audiences even when we must speak from a prepared text.

Notes

Introduction

1. Carmine Gallo, "Billionaire Warren Buffett Says This 1 Skill Will Boost Your Career Value by 50 Percent," *Inc.*, January 5, 2017, https://www.inc.com/carmine-gallo/the-one-skill-warren-buffett-says-will-raise-your-value-by-50.html.

Chapter 1: Speak to Serve

1. Read about Rick and Barb Wise online at "A Hope Big Enough," Where Is God Ministries, https://whereisgod.net/a-spouses-love/a-hope-big-enough.

2. Read the story in Kevin Timpe, *Disability and Inclusive Communities* (Grand Rapids: Calvin College Press, 2018).

Chapter 2: Plan Neighbor-Serving Speeches

1. This is one of the major themes in Augustine's *On Christian Teaching* 4.2.3.

2. Augustine, *On Christian Teaching* 4.14.29, trans. R. P. H. Green (Oxford: Oxford University Press, 1997), 117 (italics added).

Chapter 3: Conquer Speaking Fears

1. Elie Wiesel, *And the Sea Is Never Full: Memoirs, 1969–*, trans. Marion Wiesel (New York: Knopf, 1999), 154.

2. Wiesel, *And the Sea Is Never Full*, 154.

Chapter 4: Compose an Outline

1. Statement modified from Katie Reilly, "Record Numbers of College Students Are Seeking Treatment for Depression and Anxiety—but Schools Can't Keep Up," *Time*, March 19, 2018, http://time.com/5190291/anxiety-depression-college-university-students.

Chapter 5: Speak Extemporaneously

1. Mark Twain, *Mark Twain Speaking*, ed. Paul Fatout (Iowa City: University of Iowa Press, 1976), 327.

Chapter 7: Think Biblically

1. See Quentin J. Schultze, *Communicating for Life: Christian Stewardship in Community and Media* (Grand Rapids: Baker Books, 2000), 131–34.

2. Frederick Buechner, *Wishful Thinking: A Seeker's ABC*, rev. ed. (San Francisco: HarperSanFrancisco, 1993), 90.

Chapter 9: Find and Evaluate Online Sources

1. Accessible at https://catalog.loc.gov.

2. Mark Galli, "Speak the Gospel: Use Deeds When Necessary," *Christianity Today*, May 21, 2009, https://www.christianitytoday.com/ct/2009/mayweb-only/120-42.0.html.

Chapter 10: Be Trustworthy (Ethos 1)

1. For an analysis of Augustine's strict prohibition of lying, see Roger D. Ray, "Christian Conscience and Pagan Rhetoric: Augustine's Treatises on Lying," in *Studia Patristica*, vol. 22, ed. Elizabeth A. Livingstone (Leuven: Peeters, 1989), 321–25; and Paul J. Griffiths, *Lying: An Augustinian Theology of Duplicity* (Grand Rapids: Brazos, 2004).

Chapter 11: Be Virtuous (Ethos 2)

1. Quintilian, *Institutes of Oratory* 12.1.1. The translations vary, but many rhetoricians use the snappy phrase that rhetoric is "a good man speaking well." In context, it is clear that Quintilian wanted to emphasize the quality of character of the speaker, including the speaker's motive, and not just the speaker's persuasive skills. See, e.g., Quintilian, *The Orator's Education*, Vol. 5: Books 11–12, ed. and trans. Donald A. Russel (Cambridge: Harvard University Press, 2002), 187.

2. James Houston, *In Pursuit of Happiness: Finding Genuine Fulfillment in Life* (Colorado Springs: NavPress, 1996), 14.

3. See David E. Fitch, *The Church of Us vs. Them: Freedom from a Faith That Feeds on Making Enemies* (Grand Rapids: Baker, 2019).

4. Aleksandr Solzhenitsyn, *A World Split Apart* (New York: Harper & Row, 1978), 27.

5. Søren Kierkegaard, *Provocations: Spiritual Writings of Kierkegaard*, ed. Charles E. Moore (Farmington, PA: Plough, 1999), 19, 350.

6. "St. Augustine of Hippo," Catholic Online, https://www.catholic.org/saints/saint.php?saint_id=418.

7. Eugene H. Peterson, *Christ Plays in Ten Thousand Places* (Winnipeg: CMBC Publications, 1999), 59.

8. Augustine, *On Christian Teaching* 3.2.1.

9. Rabbi Joseph Telushkin, *Words That Hurt, Words That Heal: How to Use Words Wisely and Well* (New York: Perennial Current, 1998), xx.

Chapter 12: Convey Ideas Passionately

1. Augustine, *On Christian Teaching* 4.2.3, trans. R. P. H. Green (Oxford: Oxford University Press, 1997), 101.

2. Monastic sign language is discussed in C. H. Lawrence, *Medieval Monasticism: Forms of Religious Life in Western Europe in the Middle Ages* (New York: Longman, 1984), 104.

3. Kenneth Burke, "Prologue in Heaven," in *The Rhetoric of Religion: Studies in Logology* (Berkeley: University of California Press, 1970), 288.

4. Augustine, *Expositions on the Book of Psalms*, ed. and trans. Philip Schaff (Grand Rapids: Eerdmans, 1956), 673.

5. Quoted in Duc De Broglie, *Saint Ambrose*, trans. Margaret Maitland (London: Duckworth, 1899), 45.

6. Cicero, *On Oratory and Orators* 3.59, ed. and trans. John Shelby Watson (Carbondale: Southern Illinois University Press, 1970), 258.

Chapter 13: Speak to Inform Dramatically

1. "Neil Simon, The Art of Theater No. 10," interview by James Lipton, *Paris Review* 125 (Winter 1992), https://www.theparisreview.org/interviews/1994/neil-simon-the-art-of-theater-no-10-neil-simon.

Chapter 14: Tell Stories (Mythos)

1. See James Hutton, *Aristotle's Poetics* (New York: Norton, 1982), 54.

2. James M. Houston, *I Believe in the Creator* (Grand Rapids: Eerdmans, 1980), 63.

3. Wendell Berry, *Standing by Words* (Berkeley: Counterpoint, 1983), 62.

4. See Terry Lindvall, *God Mocks: A History of Religious Satire from the Hebrew Prophets to Stephen Colbert* (New York: NYU Press, 2015).

5. For a wonderful overview of indirect communication, see Benson P. Fraser, *Hide and Seek: The Sacred Art of Indirect Communication* (Eugene, OR: Cascade, 2019).

6. Wendell Berry, *What Are People For?* (New York: North Point, 1990), 157.

7. Frederick Buechner, *Telling the Truth: The Gospel as Tragedy, Comedy, and Fairy Tale* (San Francisco: HarperSanFrancisco, 1977).

Chapter 15: Speak to Persuade Logically (Logos)

1. Chrysostom's views on the importance of rhetorical education for Christians are addressed in Lauri Thurén, "John Chrysostom as a Rhetorical Critic: The Hermeneutics of an Early Father," *Biblical Interpretation* 9, no. 2 (2001): 183.

2. Augustine, *On Christian Teaching* 4.2.3, trans. R. P. H. Green (Oxford: Oxford University Press, 1997), 101.

3. The history of Christian rhetoricians' competition with other rhetoricians is discussed in David S. Cunningham, *Faithful Persuasion: In Aid of a Rhetoric of Christian Theology* (Notre Dame, IN: University of Notre Dame Press, 1991), xiv. The critical importance of rhetoric for the early church is addressed in Averil Cameron, *Christianity and the Rhetoric of Empire: The Development of Christian Discourse* (Berkeley: University of California Press, 1991). For a short history of Christian rhetoric, see George A. Kennedy, *Classical Rhetoric and Its Christian and Secular Tradition from Ancient to Modern Times*, 2nd ed. (Chapel Hill: University of North Carolina Press, 1999).

Chapter 16: Speak to Persuade Emotionally (Pathos)

1. See David G. Benner, *Human Being and Becoming: Living the Adventure of Life and Love* (Grand Rapids: Brazos, 2016), 12.

Chapter 17: Share Special Moments

1. Frederick Buechner, *Wishful Thinking: A Seeker's ABC*, rev. ed. (San Francisco: HarperSanFrancisco, 1993), 27.

2. Eugene H. Peterson, *Subversive Spirituality* (Grand Rapids: Eerdmans, 1997), 148.

3. Quoted in Garry Wills, *Saint Augustine* (New York: Viking, 1999), 71.

4. See "Hebrew Word Puns," *The Culture of the Bible*, December 20, 2012, https://biblicalculture.wordpress.com/2012/12/20/hebrew-word-puns/.

5. Quoted in Peterson, *Subversive Spirituality*, 151.

Chapter 18: Advocate for All Neighbors

1. Augustine, *Confessions* 3.9.17.

2. Nicholas Wolterstorff, *Justice in Love* (Grand Rapids: Eerdmans, 2011), 101.

3. Walter Brueggemann, *The Prophetic Imagination*, 2nd ed. (Minneapolis: Fortress, 2001), 3.

4. Bryan Stevenson, *Just Mercy: A Story of Justice and Redemption* (New York: Random House, 2014), 15.

5. Dietrich Bonhoeffer, *Letters and Papers from Prison*, rev. ed., ed. Eberhard Bethge (New York: Macmillan, 1967), 17.

6. See R. R. James, ed., *Winston S. Churchill: His Complete Speeches, 1897–1963* (New York: Chelsea House, 1974), 7:7566.

7. Richard Rorty, "Religion as a Conversation-Stopper," in *Philosophy and Social Hope* (New York: Penguin, 2000), 168–74. Christian philosopher Nicholas Wolterstorff responded to Rorty in "An Engagement with Rorty," *Journal of Religious Ethics* 31, no. 1 (Spring 2003): 129–39.

8. Václav Havel, *Disturbing the Peace: A Conversation with Karel Hvížďala*, trans. Paul Wilson (New York: Vintage, 1990), 11.

9. Mark Noll, *A History of Christianity in the United States and Canada* (Grand Rapids: Eerdmans, 1992), 314.

10. William Lloyd Garrison, "No Compromise with the Evil of Slavery" (speech, 1854), Lit2Go, https://etc.usf.edu/lit2go/185/civil-rights-and-conflict-in-the-united-states-selected-speeches/5061/no-compromise-with-the-evil-of-slavery-speech-1854/.

11. Martin Luther King Jr., "I Have a Dream" (speech delivered in 1963), National Archives, https://www.archives.gov/files/press/exhibits/dream-speech.pdf.

Chapter 19: Present in Groups

1. See, e.g., Sarah Hooker, "5 Reasons Why I Hate Group Projects," Thought Catalog, April 15, 2014, https://thoughtcatalog.com/sarah-hooker/2014/04/5-reasons-i-hate-group-projects; and Maryellen Weimer, "My Students Don't Like Group Work," The Teaching Professor, July 12, 2017, https://www.facultyfocus.com/articles/teaching-professor-blog/my-students-dont-like-group-work.

2. Cicero discusses these three purposes in *De Optimo Genere Oratorum* (*On the Best Style of Orators*) 1.3; *Orator* 69; and *De Oratore* (*On Oratory*) 2.28.

3. Ronald Adler and Jeanne Marquardt Elmhorst, *Communicating at Work: Principles and Practices for Business and the Professions*, 9th ed. (New York: McGraw-Hill, 2008), 256.

4. Stephen E. Lucas, *The Art of Public Speaking*, 11th ed. (New York: McGraw-Hill, 2012), 371. See also Dianne Hofner Saphiere, Barbara Kappler Mikk, and Basma Ibrahim DeVries, *Communication Highwire: Leveraging the Power of Diverse Communication Styles* (Yarmouth, ME: Intercultural Press, 2005), 31.

5. Lucas, *Art of Public Speaking*, 371.

6. Henry Wadsworth Longfellow, "Elegiac Verse" (1882), Maine Historical Society, https://www.hwlongfellow.org/poems_poem.php?pid=310.

Chapter 20: Stage with Technology

1. See David J. P. Phillips, "How to Avoid Death by PowerPoint," April 14, 2014, https://www.youtube.com/watch?v=Iwpi1Lm6dFo, for a TED Talk with helpful advice about pitfalls to avoid.

2. For instance, Wikimedia Commons (https://commons.wikimedia.org) maintains a collection of over fifty million freely usable media files that anyone can contribute to.

3. Charles J. Chaput, "Fools with Tools Are Still Fools," *Nuntium*, June 1998, available at http://www.evangelizationstation.com/htm_html/Biographies/Chaput/fools_with_tools _are_still_fools.htm.

Appendix B: Plan Speeches with the Holy Spirit

1. Sonja K. Foss and Cindy L. Griffin, "Beyond Persuasion: A Proposal for an Invitational Rhetoric," *Communication Monographs* 62 (March 1995): 2–18.

Appendix D: Speaking from a Manuscript

1. From remarks in London, November 2, 1949. "Wit and Wisdom," *Finest Hour* 128 (Autumn 2005), https://winstonchurchill.org/publications/finest-hour/finest-hour-128/wit -and-wisdom-6.